# CYCLING IN THE FRENCH ALPS

## About the Author

Paul Henderson was born in Durham in 1963. Despite a lifetime's passion for outdoor sports, he was a relative latecomer to cycling, buying his first bike at the age of 32. It was his wife, Alice, who talked him into this rash expenditure when they moved to Chambéry and he had to give up his company car. Since then, he has cycled tens of thousands of kilometres and enjoyed numerous cycle touring trips around the French Alps and Provence.

This guidebook is the result of his wish to share with others his enthusiasm for cycling and for the wonderful area in which he is fortunate enough to live.

He earns his living as a freelance translator.

# CYCLING IN THE FRENCH ALPS

By
**Paul Henderson**

2 POLICE SQUARE, MILNTHORPE, CUMBRIA LA7 7PY
www.cicerone.co.uk

Second edition 2008
ISBN-13 978-185284-551-3

First edition 2005
ISBN-10 1-85284-445-0
ISBN-13 978-1-85284-445-5

A catalogue record for this book is available from the British Library.
All photographs, maps and route profiles by the author

## Preface to the Second Edition

First published in November 2005, *Cycling in the French Alps* has been extensively revised and updated to ensure the information it contains is as accurate and up to date as possible. The new edition also includes an additional chapter describing the Southern pre-Alps and Mont Ventoux, thereby completing the guide's coverage of the Alpine massifs of southeast France.

The updates in this second edition include changes to route access information, modifications to the itineraries (e.g. due to the completion of work that was on-going when the first edition was being prepared), and revisions to tourist office and accommodation information. Due to a prolonged road closure, the original route for the Tour of the Southern Alps is likely to remain impracticable for some time; therefore alternative routes have been suggested for both road cyclists and mountain bikers.

The new Tour of the Southern pre-Alps describes an area of the French Alps that, due to time constraints, was omitted from the first edition. This tour takes in some of the most spectacular roads in France, through the gorges of the Vercors and below the towering peaks of the Dévoluy, as well as cycling's greatest summit, the magnificent Mont Ventoux.

*Paul Henderson, 2007*

## Acknowledgements

This book would not have been possible without the support and enthusiasm of my wife, Alice.

Thank you to Claude, Marie-Christine, Simon, Richard, Jo and all my other friends who accompanied me on exploratory bike trips, stopping whenever asked so that I could set up photos and take notes. I would also like to thank Jacques Leleu, journalist with the *Dauphiné Libéré*, for his help in checking facts and anecdotes in the newspaper archives.

A special mention must go to Tom Payne for his advice and proofreading skills, which have made this a better book than it otherwise would have been. Sandrine Rutigliano's research on the facilities available around Vinadio was also invaluable.

Finally, I would like to thank Pierre Lortet for his encouragement and for all the work he has done for cyclists in Savoie and around France.

*Front cover:* Cycling up the Col de la Croix de Fer (Tour of the Ecrins and Grands Rousses)

# CONTENTS

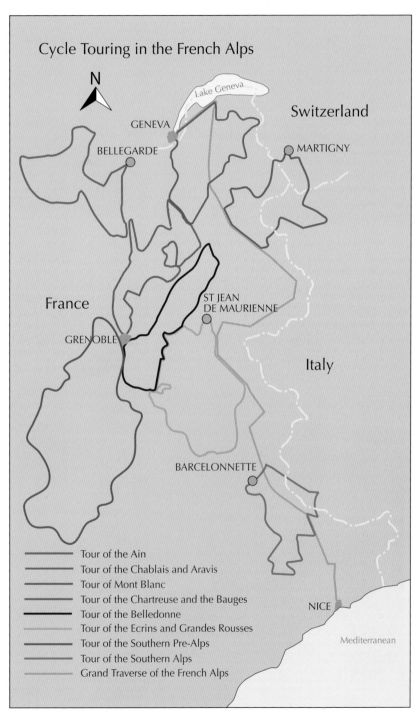

# Cycle Touring in the French Alps

N

Lake Geneva

Switzerland

GENEVA

MARTIGNY

BELLEGARDE

France

ST JEAN
DE MAURIENNE

GRENOBLE

Italy

BARCELONNETTE

NICE

Mediterranean

Tour of the Ain
Tour of the Chablais and Aravis
Tour of Mont Blanc
Tour of the Chartreuse and the Bauges
Tour of the Belledonne
Tour of the Ecrins and Grandes Rousses
Tour of the Southern Pre-Alps
Tour of the Southern Alps
Grand Traverse of the French Alps

# INTRODUCTION

For most cyclists the French Alps conjure up images of the great champions of the Tour de France racing up legendary passes such as the Galibier, Izoard or Madeleine. Many dream of following in their tracks, but most are realistic enough to know that if they do so it will be at much more modest speeds. No matter how long the ascent takes, cycling over the summit of a mountain pass is a marvellous experience that never pales. The feeling of achievement is immense and there is a wonderful sensation of being both alive and at peace. As though this were not compensation enough for all the hard work of getting to the top, most high passes also offer outstanding views and an exhilarating descent as a final reward.

Of course, mountains do not have to be snow-capped giants to provide worthwhile cycling. Many lower areas are criss-crossed by quiet roads that meander through varied landscapes of open pastures, dark forests, deep gorges and unspoilt villages. The scenery is often just as beautiful as in the high mountains, but this beauty tends to be gentler and less ostentatious.

*Cycling in the French Alps* describes nine cycling routes through south-east France, between Lake Geneva and the Mediterranean. Eight of the routes are circular tours that start and finish at the same place; the final route is the Grand Traverse of the Alps from Geneva to Nice. As well as exploring the 'true' Alps, the routes cover the pre-Alps and the southern tip of the Jura. With the exception of the Tour of the Ain, which would be a good introduction to cycle touring in the mountains, all of the routes are difficult and aimed at fit and experienced cyclists.

When cycling in the mountains, the amount of vertical height gain is a much better indication of the difficulty of a route than the distance covered. The circuits were planned with this in mind and most stages include an average of between 1000 metres and 1500 metres of height gain, with an absolute maximum of 2000 metres for any single day (the stage from Bourg St Maurice to Bessans in Route 9 is the one exception to this rule). Most of the stages are between 50km and 80km

*River Rhone, Lac du Lit du Roi (Route 1, day 1)*

*Entremont-le-Vieux and Mont Granier (Route 4, day 6)*

long. Of course, some people will want to do longer stages than others. With this in mind, the facilities chart for each day (see below) shows all of the places along the route where accommodation can be found.

Anyone with basic map-reading skills can plan a cycling trip, so why would they need a guidebook? The answer is very simple: there are a lot of things that a map will not tell you – where you will find accommodation, shops, water and banks; what there is to see along the way; where the quietest roads are (the colour-coding systems used by maps for major and minor roads do not always tell the whole story); the best ways to cycle through larger towns and cities; the ins and outs of using public transport in a foreign country, and so on. This book provides all of this information and more in order to help you get the most from a cycling holiday in the French Alps.

The routes were chosen to include the areas I have most enjoyed cycling around during the thirteen years that I have lived in the Alps. In some areas, the choice of itinerary was easy as there are only a very small number of options. In other areas, the choice was more difficult and some wonderful places and spectacular passes had to be omitted. Even my adopted home (Chambéry) has not made it into the guide, despite being a beautiful city and superbly situated for cycling. With the

exception of the Grand Traverse, which will take most cyclists two weeks, the routes were designed so they can be completed within one week. If you would like to do a longer tour, why not combine two of the routes. The two combinations I would recommend the most highly would be the Tour of the Ain plus the Chartreuse-Bauges and the Tour of the Ecrins and Grandes Rousses plus the Tour of the Southern Alps (linked via the Col de Vars and the Col de Pontis).

## HOW TO GET THERE

### By car

The distances and approximate driving times from the ferry terminal at Calais to the start/finish point of the tours are given in the introduction to each tour. These distances are based on RAC or AA recommended routes, avoiding Paris, which adds about 20 to 25km to your journey, but reduces the risk of getting caught up in heavy traffic. French motorways are toll roads and are quite expensive, but it is rare for them to be congested, with the notable exception being roads to the south of France on Saturdays during the summer holidays. Useful route planning information can be obtained from **www.theaa.com** and **www.rac.co.uk**.

## By rail and coach

> It is always easier to use public transport if your bike is stowed in a bike-box or bike bag. Most hotels and B&Bs will look after bike-boxes/bags if you stay with them for at least one night at the beginning and one night at the end of the tour, however you should check this when you book.

France has an excellent train service (when it is not on strike!), but there is no national coach network.

There are regular coach and rail services from Britain to most of the start points, but, with the advent of low-cost airlines, overland travel is not always the cheapest option. Bicycles will only be allowed on long-distance coaches and most high-speed trains if they are packed in a bike-box/bag. Coaches often have very strict limits on the amount of luggage they will accept. Check with the coach operator before leaving. There is no luggage limit on trains.

Timetable and pricing information can be found on the International Coach Services website: **www.eurolines.com**; and Eurostar train services: **www.eurostar.com** or **www.sncf.com**.

## By air

Generally the quickest way to arrive at your destination when using public transport is to fly to a nearby airport, generally Geneva or Lyon, and then use local train or bus services. There are also regular flights from many airports in the UK and Eire to Grenoble and Chambéry. However, in 2007 the only all-year-round services to Grenoble were from London Stansted and Dublin, with other cities being served only during the ski season.

If you are thinking of flying to France and then renting a car, it is better to organise the

> The **Tour of the Chablais–Aravis** starts and finishes at Geneva airport. **The Grand Traverse of the Alps** starts at Geneva airport and finishes at Nice airport.

rental before leaving home. Car rental in France is expensive and many companies impose a mileage rate as well as the daily rental charge.

**Lyon St Exupéry Airport** The only trains that stop at Lyon St Exupéry are high-speed TGVs; therefore tickets must be booked in advance. Some TGVs will now carry bikes that are not in a bike bag, and there are plans to provide bike space on all TGV trains within the next

*Naves-Parmelan and the Dents de Lanfon (route 2, day 7)*

*Looking down towards Lullin from below the Col du Feu (Route 2, day 2)*

few years. Go to **www.voyages-sncf.com** for more details. There are regular shuttle bus services to most of the major towns around the airport (Lyon, Grenoble, Annecy, Chambéry, etc). These buses will accept bikes that are not in bike-boxes or bags 'if there is room' and the decision is left to the driver's discretion. If your bike is in a box or bag, there should be no problem putting it on the bus. If the shuttle bus will not take your bike, and there is no convenient TGV service to your destination, the only alternative is to cycle to a railway station and take a regional train.

It is much easier to cycle to one of the stations outside Lyon than to go into the city centre. Depending on your final destination, you can either cycle to Meximieux (for destinations north and north-east of Lyon) or La Verpillière (for destinations south or south-east of Lyon). For destinations that are more or less due east of Lyon, such as St Jean-de-Maurienne (**Tour of the Ecrins and Grandes Rousses**), the best station to cycle to will depend on the times of the trains to your final destination. Details of how to cycle from the airport to these stations are given in Appendix 1. **The Tour of the Ain** can be started directly from Lyon airport by cycling to Meximieux.

For more information about Lyon airport shuttle buses, go to **www.satobus.com** or **www.lyon.aeroport.fr.**

For more information about train services, go to **www.sncf.com.**

**Geneva–Cointrin Airport** Geneva airport has its own railway station with regular services to Bellegarde (**Tour of the Ain**) and to Martigny (**Tour of Mont Blanc**). Rail services from Geneva to Grenoble and to St Jean-de-Maurienne (**Tours of the Chartreuse–Bauges, Belledonne** and **Ecrins and Grandes Rousses**) are limited so check that there is a suitable connection before booking your flight. It is theoretically possible to travel by public transport from Geneva to Barcelonnette (**Tour of the Southern Alps**), but the journey Geneva–Grenoble–Gap, by train, and then Gap–Barcelonnette, by bus, will take at least a day!

For the **Tour of the Chablais–Aravis** and the **Grand Traverse of the Alps** directions from and to the airport are given in Appendix 1.

For more information about Geneva airport, go to **www.gva.ch**. For more information about train services, go to **www.sncf.com** or **www.cff.ch**.

**Grenoble – St Geoirs Airport** There are now regular year-round services to Grenoble airport from London–Stansted and Dublin. Grenoble airport is ideally situated for starting the Tours of the Chartreuse-Bauges, the Belledonne and the Southern pre-Alps. The route between the airport and Grenoble city centre (a distance of 48km) is described in Appendix 1. It is a very pleasant ride along quiet roads and the excellent cycleway beside the River Isère.

For the Tour of the Chartreuse-Bauges, I would recommend cycling straight from the airport to Lake Aiguebelette, via Le Grand-Lemps, Chirens and St Geoire-en-Valdaine, a distance of approximately 60km. If you don't have time to get all the way to Lake Aiguebelette, there is a full range of accommodation in Charavines (4km west of Chirens, on the shores of Lake Paladru).

If you would prefer to take the train into the centre of Grenoble, go to the railway station at Rives (14km from the airport – the nearest railway station is actually at Le Grand-Lemps, but there are far fewer services from here). There is at least one train every hour and the journey takes approximately 30 minutes.

*The spectacular view of Entrevaux from below the Col des Félines (Route 8, day 4)*

**Chambéry Airport** There are flights to Chambéry from several UK airports from mid-December until early April. It is possible to start the Tour of the Ain and Tour of the Chartreuse-Bauges directly from Chambéry airport, and there is an excellent rail service from Chambéry to Grenoble (Tour of the Belledonne, Tour of the Southern pre-Alps). The railway station is in Chambéry city centre, 10km south of the airport. See Appendix 1 for airport access details.

### GETTING AROUND BY TRAIN

**French railways (SNCF)** French trains are usually quite reliable, but the French railway company, SNCF, has a reputation for not being particularly accommodating to cyclists. However, in all the years I have transported my bike around France (at least half a dozen journeys per year), I have never had any problems. The following pointers should help you avoid major problems when using the trains.

### TIPS FOR TAKING BIKES ON FRENCH TRAINS

**1**. Many high speed (TGV) and long-distance express (Corail) trains will only carry bikes if they are packed in a bike-box/bag; however, SNCF are fitting all new and refurbished TGV trains with space for bikes. (NB: seats on TGV trains must be booked in advance.)

**2**. All regional trains (TER) in the Rhone–Alps Region (Routes 1–5, plus the northern parts of Routes 6, 7 and 9) accept bikes. All TER trains in the Provence–Alps–Cote d'Azur Region (Route 8, plus the southern parts of Routes 6, 7 and 9) accept bikes except for services between 7am and 9am. Bikes are carried free of charge.

**3**. Passengers are responsible for loading their own bikes onto the train.

**4**. Bikes should be put in the goods wagon, if the train has one. These generally have hooks to hang bikes from and are usually the first or last carriage of the train.

**5**. Modern 'commuter' trains have one or two cars with hooks for bikes. There is a bike symbol on the door of these carriages.

**6**. If the train does not have a goods wagon or any specific place to put bikes, you will usually be allowed to put your bike in the spaces at the end of each carriage.

**7**. SNCF's website gives timetable and ticket price information in several languages, including English. A bicycle symbol is used to indicate which trains accept bikes, but the absence of the symbol does not necessarily mean that bikes are not accepted!

**NB** On most trains there is a limited amount of space for bikes, and you may not be the only cyclists on the train. Many trains only have space for up to six bikes. (This is not always the case; a ticket inspector once told me about a group of German cyclists that had taken the train from Chambéry to Bourg St Maurice – there were 18 of them! Fortunately, the train had a goods wagon).

For timetable and ticket price information, including connections to Switzerland, go to **www.sncf.com**.

**Swiss railways (CFF)** As you would expect, Swiss trains are extremely punctual. Most, but not all, will accept bicycles, although advance booking is obligatory on some trains and there is a supplement for bikes. Details, in English, French and German, are given on the Swiss railways website. For timetable and ticket price information, including connections to France, go to **www.cff.ch**.

### WHEN TO GO

The cycling season in the Alps runs from the middle of April to the middle of October for areas below 1500 metres, and from the middle of May to the end of September for higher areas. The winter months, from November to March, are usually too cold for enjoyable cycling in the mountains.

## Access to mountain passes

Many mountain passes are closed during the winter. As a general rule, passes that are lower than 2000 metres are closed from November to April/May, passes at altitudes of between 2000 metres and 2500 metres are closed from late October to late May/early June, and passes above 2500 metres are closed from mid October to early/mid June. Actual closure dates vary according to the height of the pass and the harshness of the winter. Information about which passes are open and which are closed can be obtained at **www.bison-fute.equipement.gouv.fr** in the section 'accés aux cols'. The following websites provide more detailed information.

**Savoie:**
   **www.savoieroute.com/savoie_
   route_carte_de_la_circulation-1.html**
**Isère:**
   **www.isere.equipement.gouv.fr/
   infostrafic/routes38.htm**
**Hautes-Alpes:**
   **www.cg05.fr/dyn/routes05/index2.php**
**Alpes-de-Haute Provence:**
   **www.cg04.fr/proximite/etat_cols.php**

   If you need more precise information, contact the tourist office nearest to the pass you are interested in.

## Weather

Another major consideration when planning a cycling trip is the weather. Though mountain weather is very variable, both from day to day and from year to year, it is still possible to make a few general comments.

   a) In most areas, the driest months of the year are July and August.

   b) Rainfall during the summer is often in the form of violent but short-lived afternoon storms. A typical summer day starts with clear blue skies, but cloud starts to build up towards the end of the morning. Generally, the weather does not become too threatening until the middle of the afternoon. Storms usually do not break until at least 3pm and only last a few hours.

   c) September is often an excellent month for cycling, although the temperatures are a little cooler, especially at altitude.

   d) Changes in the weather can be very sudden and quite brusque. Temperature variations of up to 10°C from one day to the next are not uncommon.

   Average temperature and rainfall statistics for five towns at different latitudes and altitudes are given in Appendix 2.

   The average adiabatic lapse rate is 6.5°C per 1000 metres, so for every 1000 metres increase in altitude, the temperature falls by 6.5°C. The lapse rate is often greater than this and there can be a much bigger difference in temperature between the valleys and the high passes than expected. For example, if it is 30°C in the shade at Bourg St Maurice (800 metres), it might only be 10°C at the Col de

*Arriving at the Col de Larche (Route 8, day 1)*

*Mount Obiou as seen from the Col de l'Holme (Route 6, day 5)*

l'Iseran (2770 metres), not the 17°C you would expect. If there is a breeze, wind chill will also add to the feeling of cold. Above 2000 metres snow is not uncommon, even in July and August, although it generally won't last for long. Be prepared.

**Weather forecasts** There are numerous websites that give weather forecasts for the Alps. Sites that I have used include: **www.meteo.fr**, **www.meteoconsult.com** and **www.met-office.gov.uk**. Many tourist office websites also give weather forecasts. The Chamonix site gives a particularly good mountain forecast: **www.chamonix.com**. When you are in France, weather forecasts can be obtained from most tourist offices.

**Traffic**
When planning your trip, another factor to consider is traffic. The Alps are a very popular holiday destination and the busiest time of year is from the beginning of the second week in July to the end of the third week in August. Although the tours avoid busy roads wherever possible, there is always a certain amount of traffic on the roads up to the highest and most famous passes. The best time to do the tours of the Chablais–Aravis, Mont Blanc, Ecrins and Grandes Rousses and the Grand Traverse is before the middle of July or after the middle of

August. In the less touristy areas, such as the Ain and the Chartreuse–Bauges, you are unlikely to encounter heavy traffic even in the middle of the summer holidays.

## CYCLING IN FRANCE

**Language**
Most hotels, restaurants and shops in resort towns will have staff who speak at least a little English. In quieter areas, there is no guarantee that this will be the case. Wherever you are, people will always appreciate it if you try to speak French, even if you are limited to a few simple words and feel as if you are massacring the language. A common complaint from shop staff is that many English visitors do not even say *bonjour* when they enter a shop. Being able to use a few basic French sentences in bakeries, cafés and hotels can radically change the degree of friendliness with which you are welcomed.

A short glossary of French cycling terms and some useful French phrases for getting your bike repaired are given in Appendix 3.

**Local government**
As when visiting any foreign country, you will notice that things are done differently in France compared to your home country. The sometimes perplexing place names or the way the French road-numbering system works,

may seem confusing and frustrating. However, once it is understood that many of these things are related to the country's complex system of local government, you may find them easier to tolerate.

There are three basic levels of government in France: the *region*, the *département* and the *commune*. The regional council is responsible for, amongst other things, large-scale infrastructure, such as major roads and new railway lines. *Départemental* councils are responsible for the secondary road network and for the development of tourism within the *département*. The tours in this guide go through two regions (Rhone-Alps and Provence-Alps-Cote d'Azur – usually abbrevi-

ated to PACA) and nine *départements* (Ain, Haute-Savoie, Savoie, Isère, Drôme, Hautes-Alpes, Vaucluse, Alpes-de-Haute-Provence and Alpes-Maritimes). Each *département* is sub-divided into a number of district councils or *communes*, which are responsible for very minor roads (C-roads) and local tourism development. Each level of government jealously guards its own prerogatives and responsibilities, and there is often quite a lot of competition between neighbouring authorities, whether it be on the regional, *départementale* or *communale* level.

The main practical repercussions of this for the cycle-tourist (or tourist in general) are as given in the box below.

### TIPS FOR CYCLING IN FRANCE

1. If a road number changes without any apparent reason, you have probably crossed the border between two *départements*.

2. A *commune* may include several villages and cover several square kilometres. The sign at the entrance to each of these villages will give the name of the *commune* first, with the name of the village below. The *Chef-lieu* is the main town/village in the *commune*. Addresses on internet sites and in brochures will sometimes give the name of the *commune*, but not the exact location. Be careful when booking accommodation as you may find yourself several kilometres away from where you wanted to be.

3. Occasionally, the boundary between two *départements* will go through the middle of what appears to be one village. Sometimes the two villages will have the same name and sometimes they will have different names. For example, during the Tour of the Chartreuse–Bauges you will go through St Pierre d'Entremont (Savoie) and St Pierre d'Entremont (Isère). Later the same day you will get to Entre-Deux-Guiers (Isère) which is contiguous with Les Echelles (Savoie).

4. Most local tourist offices are run by the *commune* and will only have information about that commune and its immediate surroundings. Fortunately, many *communes* are starting to work together to provide tourist services for wider areas. Tourist offices in larger towns will usually have some information for other parts of the *département*, but very rarely for neighbouring *départements*, however close the border may be.

### Public Holidays

France has several public holidays during the spring and summer, although the government is trying to reduce the number. With the exception of Easter Monday and Ascension, the holidays are on a fixed date regardless of which day of the week they fall.

**French public holidays in spring and summer are**: Easter Monday (NB Good Friday is not a holiday), 1st May, 8th May, Ascension, 14th July (not called Bastille Day in France) and 15th August.

**Swiss public holidays are**: Good Friday, Easter Monday, 1st May, Ascension, Pentecost and 1st August.

**Italian public holidays are**: Easter Monday, 25th April, 1st May, 2nd June and 15th August.

### Money

The cost of living in France is generally considered to be about 20% less than in the UK, but whether or not life appears to be cheaper depends on the exchange rate. Since the

St Hugues and the
Grand Som
(Route 4, day 7)

introduction of the Euro on 1st January 2002 the exchange rate has varied between 1.3 and 1.6 Euros to the pound.

If you are on a tight budget it is possible to live for as little as 25 Euros per day, by camping and cooking for yourself, but this won't include very many luxuries. A more reasonable budget would be around 35 to 40 Euros per day.

There are a lot of quite cheap but pleasant hotels and *gîtes d'étapes* in France, so it is possible to travel light at a reasonable cost, especially if there are two of you to share a room. Two people travelling together should expect to spend a minimum of around 50 Euros per person per day. Of course, the amount you spend will depend on the quality of the hotels you choose and how much you spend on meals.

Most restaurants offer a choice of set-price menus, which are usually very good value for money. Expect to pay between 15 and 25 Euros per person, not including drinks. If a set menu costs more than 25 Euros, the quality should be exceptional. Naturally, eating *à la carte* will be more expensive.

### Cycling on French roads

As well as the difficulty (for British cyclists) of cycling on the right-hand side of the road,

there are a number of other particularities of the French Highway Code and French driving habits that should be noted.

**1**. Where there is no give-way sign or line, vehicles approaching from your right have right of way, even when they are on a minor road that joins a major one. When they know they have right of way, many drivers don't even look to see if another vehicle is coming as they expect oncoming traffic to give way to them. When you don't know the roads, it is not always easy to see if there is a give-way sign, so be careful whenever a road joins from the right. A white diamond-shaped road sign with a yellow diamond in the middle indicates a stretch of road where you have right of way over vehicles coming from the right. A similar sign with a black line through the yellow diamond indicates the end of this section of road.

**2**. At roundabouts, traffic should give way to vehicles that are already on the roundabout. The rule is simple, but drivers often try to force their way onto the roundabout and will not even slow down unless a collision is imminent. Cyclists are not always considered an 'obstacle' worth braking for! Some people, especially older drivers, will stop to let another car join the roundabout – be careful not to run into the back of somebody who brakes unexpectedly.

3. Very few drivers indicate at round-abouts and lane discipline is a completely alien concept. Just because a vehicle is in the right-hand lane does not mean that it will be turning right, or even going straight on.

4. Most drivers will move over a reasonable distance when overtaking cyclists, although not many respect the legal minima of 1 metre in towns and 1.5 metres elsewhere. On average, 250 cyclists are killed on French roads every year.

5. Drivers often cut corners on winding mountain roads, even if they can't see what is coming towards them! Be extremely careful, especially when speeding downhill.

6. Road numbers change surprisingly frequently and the numbers that you see on maps do not always correspond to the numbers on road signs.

7. Other changes to the road system can occur through urban development or natural events such as landslides. Temporary road closures due to landslides or rock fall are quite common: for example, in 2003 the main trunk road from Ugine to Megève was closed for a total of 212 days because of a succession of landslides. Road works may also lead to road closures.

8. Specific rules for cyclists include:

a) Bicycles must be fitted with a bell (a law that is never enforced).

b) The use of cycle lanes or cycleways is not mandatory.

c) Lights are mandatory at night, but not during the day or in tunnels. However, it is a good idea to have a light on your bike as many mountain roads go through unlit or poorly lit tunnels.

d) Wearing a helmet is not mandatory, but it is highly recommended.

*Le Mourre Froid from Siguret (Route 6, day 3)*

## Cycling in the mountains

When cycling in the mountains, your average speed will be much lower than on the flat as the time 'gained' during the descents will not compensate for the time 'lost' going uphill. Hills can be very long so the golden rule is to start gently, find a comfortable speed, and then relax and enjoy the scenery. Remember, the only imperative is to get to a place where you can eat and sleep before nightfall.

Few Alpine roads are as steep as those in the English Pennines or Lake District, but the climbs are very much longer. Maximum gradients rarely exceed 10% and average gradients tend to be around 6 to 7%. To gain 1000 metres of altitude at a gradient of 6% means covering a distance of 17km. To be able to cycle uphill for such long distances, without exhausting muscles or damaging tendons, it is essential to have a bike with suitable gear ratios (see the 'What to take: Bikes and luggage' section below).

## WHAT TO TAKE

### Insurance, health, accidents and emergencies

Visitors to France from the European Union should have a completed E111 form (available from post offices in the UK). Any health care you need should be free, but it is a good idea to take out some general travel insurance in case there are incidental expenses, such as repatriation, to be covered.

According to the World Health Organisation, France has the best health service in the world. It is not perfect, but the treatment you get is both good and quick. If you have a specific medical condition, it is a good idea to carry a letter from your doctor, translated into French, giving details. If you need to carry any medicines with you, keep the prescription with them, especially if the medicine is in the form of pills packaged loose in a jar. I once spent a very uncomfortable few hours with French customs accused of drug smuggling because the ibuprofen I had with me tested positive for amphetamines!

All major UK mobile phone services work in France and coverage in the mountains is now very good, although there are some areas were there is still no service. Even if you cannot make a standard call, you should be able to contact the emergency services. **In case of an accident call 112** (the number for the emergency services in any country within the EU). You should be connected with an operator who speaks your language. French emergency services (sapeurs-pompiers) can be contacted by calling 18. The police can be contacted by calling 17.

Should you be stranded due to a mechanical failure and you have booked your accommodation in advance, you can call your next port of call and ask them to organise a taxi for you. Numbers for taxi firms can also be obtained from any directory enquiries service (eg. 118 000, 118 218 and 118 711).

### Bikes and luggage

This is not the place for a detailed review of different types of cycle-touring gear. Every cyclist will have his/her own preferences and ideas about what to take and how much they are prepared to carry. However, I would like to make a few comments that are specifically related to cycling in mountain areas.

Weight is a much more important factor when cycling in the mountains than on the flat. As a rule of thumb, for every 1kg increase in the weight of the bike, you will use 1% more energy. A heavy bike is also less manoeuvrable and will have a much greater braking distance. How much weight there is on the bike will depend on whether you are camping or using hotels, but when packing 'keep it light' should be the constant watchword.

A road bike or standard cycle-touring bike is perfectly adequate for all of the tours. Only two of the circuits (Chablais–Aravis and Ecrins and Grandes Rousses tours) involve off road sections (4km and 2km respectively) and both of these sections are at least 75% cycle-able with a road bike. There is no advantage to be gained from using a mountain bike apart from the very low gear ratios such a bike offers.

Having the right gear ratios is extremely important when cycling in the mountains. On long hills, even if the gradient is not extreme, it is much more comfortable to maintain a

*Rustic kilometre post on the way up to the Col de l'Iseran (Route 9, day 5)*

relatively high cadence with a short develop-ment than a low cadence with a long development. (The development is the dis-tance the bike moves forward for each rotation of the pedals, calculated by multiplying the diameter of the wheel by the ratio of the num-ber of teeth on the chain-ring and the number of teeth on the sprocket). Most of the cyclists I know in the Alps use a triple chain-ring (30/42/52 or 30/40/50) and a nine or ten-speed sprocket (12–23 or 13–26).

Given the scarcity of bike shops, it is a good idea to carry a full repair kit, including spare inner tubes, tyre levers, puncture repair kit, spanner(s), screwdriver(s) chain tool, spoke tool and spare brake/derailleur cable. In nine years of cycling in the Alps, I have never had to do more than repair a chain or unbuckle a wheel. The most frustrating incident was having to push my bike for 11km in 35°C heat after multiple punctures irreparably destroyed three inner tubes. Of course, the most important thing is to make sure that your bike is in excel-lent condition before setting off.

A bike lock is essential, even if many hotels, B&Bs and *gîtes* have garages where you can leave your bike. In one hotel, we had to leave our bikes in the bar – no one minded, but it was reassuring to be able to lock the bikes to the water pipes.

## Tents

Storms in the Alps can be violent, so, as well as being lightweight and compact, any tent used for cycle touring must be sturdy and com-pletely waterproof.

## Clothing

Most of the time while cycling, a light T-shirt or cycling jersey, combined with a windproof jacket for long descents, is sufficient. However, in the high mountains you need to be prepared for very variable conditions: tem-peratures can reach 40°C in the valleys or fall to zero at the top of the high passes. A layered system, consisting of a light base layer, warm middle layer and waterproof outer layer, should be sufficient to cope with all eventuali-ties. Leggings may be very welcome early or late in the season. It is highly advisable to wear a helmet, especially during descents.

Most evenings will be spent at relatively low altitude, but it can still get chilly enough to require long trousers and a light sweater or fleece jacket. During the summer months, any clothes that you wash at the end of the day will usually dry over night, so you do not have to take too many clothes.

## Food and drink

Always carry at least one or two cereal/energy bars and 1 litre of water (2 litres is a good idea if it is hot), as shops and water fountains can be few and far between. Remember, the human body loses moisture more quickly at altitude than at sea level. Dehydration can become a major problem if you don't drink regularly: aim for a minimum of 1 litre per hour. While you are cycling it is almost impossible to drink enough to replace all the water your body is losing, so try and re-hydrate at the end of the day (preferably before ordering that long anticipated cold beer).

## Maps

The route descriptions have been designed to give all necessary navigational information and can be followed without recourse to a map. However, I would not advise anyone to set off on a cycle-tour without the relevant map(s) as you may need to change your itinerary due to unforeseen circumstances – accident, bad weather, road closures, etc.

I use a combination of Michelin and French Geographical Survey (IGN) maps. The new series of 1:150,000 Michelin 'Local' maps are ideal for cycle-touring and usually only one map is needed for each circuit. The Michelin 1:200,000 'Regional' maps give a good overview of an area and are generally detailed enough for day-to-day navigation. The revised IGN 'TOP 100' series of 1:100,000 scale maps give more detail than the Michelin maps but you will usually require at least two or three sheets for each tour. There is also a series of 1:250,000 scale maps ('TOP 250'), but they do not always give enough detail, especially around towns.

I have given the reference numbers of the relevant Michelin 1:150,000 and 1:200,000 and IGN 1:100,000 scale maps in the intro-ductory section of each tour.

*The vineyards of Jongieux, home to some of Savoie's best white wines (Route 4, day 2)*

## HOW TO USE THIS GUIDE

Each chapter begins with a chart showing the distance covered and height gained on each day, followed by an outline map and description of the route. These travelogues give an overview of the area through which you will be cycling, pointing out places to visit, things to see, local traditions and interesting snippets of history. This is followed by detailed navigational information, in the form of a route card, a facilities chart and a route profile. A list of accommodation for the recommended overnight stops and the telephone numbers and internet addresses of local tourist offices are given at the end of each chapter. The spellings of place names can vary in France; here they conform to those on the Michelin maps except in cases where a sign post is being quoted when the exact spelling used on the sign is given.

### Route cards

The route descriptions are presented in the form of daily route cards, which contain all necessary navigational information. It would be impossible to note every junction along the route, so directions are only given for when a decision needs to be made. If no directions are given, continue straight on.

Local authorities seem to enjoy building new roundabouts, so do not be surprised if a junction marked on the route card has metamorphosed into a roundabout.

The summits of passes are also shown on the route cards, as are the lengths and AVERAGE gradients of all the significant climbs. To be regarded as significant, an uphill section must be at least 2km long and/or involve at least 100 metres of height gain. Note that uphill sections do not always neatly start and finish at junctions or significant landmarks (nor are passes always the highest point of the road) so the distance given in conjunction with a gradient does not necessarily correspond to the distance between two points on the route card.

Distances were measured with a computer on a bike and are quoted to the nearest 100m. Even assuming that the computer is perfectly calibrated, it is very difficult to measure distances with pinpoint accuracy. Errors can be caused by differences in tyre pressure, stopping and starting and not cycling in a straight line, for instance. Comparisons with other bike computers, road signs and distances marked on maps indicate that the distances quoted are accurate to within 2%.

Each stage starts and finishes at an easily recognisable and easy to find point in the town or village. This is usually the tourist

## ABBREVIATIONS USED

So that the information can be presented in a precise and easy to read form, the following abbreviations have been used:

L = left
R = right
jtn = junction (either a crossroads or a T-junction)
(Grenoble) = follow road signs for Grenoble
[Grenoble] = follow cycling or pedestrian signs for Grenoble
TO = tourist office
station = railway station
D911/D912 = junction between D911 and D912
D201–D154 = road number changes other than at a junction, for example, at the border between *départements*.
Turn L – D81 (Albanne) = Turn left onto the D81 and follow signs to Albanne

office, railway station or *mairie/hôtel de ville* (town hall). The description for the start of each stage is given assuming that you are coming out of this building.

### Route profile

More information about the nature of the terrain is given in the form of a route profile. There is one profile for each day of the tour. The same vertical and horizontal scales have been used throughout the guide so that individual stages can be compared at a glance.

### Facilities chart

A facilities chart is provided for each stage, showing where essential/useful services can be found along the route. These services are:

**Water:** unless marked with a sign reading *eau non-potable*, the water from fountains is drinkable. As drinking water has to be regularly tested by the local council, more and more fountains are marked *eau non-contrôlée* (not tested) or are being turned into flowerbeds! You drink *eau non-contrôlée* at your own risk. All the water points marked in the facilities chart provide tested drinking water. The list does not contain cemeteries; by law, all cemeteries in France must have a source of drinking water.

**Shops:** at least a *boulangerie* or an *épicerie* where you can buy food. Opening hours tend to be 9am to 12 noon and 2pm to 7pm. Bakeries open at 7 or 7.30am. The lunchtime break will sometimes start at 12.30

(especially for bakeries) and may last longer than two hours. Most food shops are open from Monday to Saturday. Bakeries and shops in resorts may be open on Sundays. Many shops in small villages are closed on Mondays.

**Cafés:** includes cafés, bars and restaurants.

**Campsites:** the chart shows all of the campsites along the route, but some are only open in July and August.

**B&Bs:** this list includes standard bed-and-breakfast style accommodation (*chambres d'hôtes*), as well as youth hostels (*auberges de jeunesse*) and *gîtes d'étapes*. Bed and breakfast accommodation is becoming very popular in France and the number of establishments is growing rapidly. The price range for this type of accommodation is enormous: from 25 to 100 Euros per person. *Auberges de jeunesse* are very similar to UK youth hostels. *Gîtes d'étapes* provide excellent value for money; most are small, family run hostels with a combination of individual rooms and small dormitories that sleep four to eight people. You will need to have your own towels and toiletries. Blankets or duvets are supplied but some *gîtes* require you to use a sheet sleeping bag or hire a sheet for the night. Half-board rates are usually between 30 and 40 Euros per night and this often includes wine with the evening meal. They are designed for 'outdoor' people, so the breakfasts are generally copious. Many have accommodation-only rates (from 10 to 15 Euros per person) and provide cooking facilities for people who want to go self-catering. *Gîtes d'étape* should not be confused with *gîtes rural*, which are holiday cottages.

**Hotels:** Hotels in France are much cheaper than in Britain. Room rates for two people sharing in a two-star hotel are between 30 Euros and 60 Euros a night. Room rates for three-star hotels are around 40 to 75 Euros per night. Breakfast is not included. Half-board rates are sometimes available, but they can be limited to guests who stay for two or more nights, especially during the summer holidays. Outside the main holiday season, some hotels close for one night of the week, often the Monday night. Outside the main towns and major resorts there are surprisingly few three-star hotels and virtually no four-star establishments. Many good hotels in rural areas have a relatively low star rating simply because they lack a specific facility, such as televisions in the rooms. Other hotels have simply opted out of the star-rating system, preferring to be classified as *hôtels du charme*, although this label gives no more than a very general indication of the quality of the establishment.

**Banks** (and post offices with ATMs): banks are open from Tuesday to Friday from 8.30am to 12 noon, and from 2pm to 6 or 7pm. They are also open on Saturdays from 8.30am to 12 noon. Banks in small villages may only be open one or two days per week. Most ATMs accept Visa and Mastercard, but not all accept American Express. Most shops and hotels will accept credit cards, but you may need your passport to prove your identity.

**Bike shops:** outside the main towns, true bike shops are few and far between. Many of the bike shops in resorts deal mostly with mountain bikes and only have a very limited range of spare parts for road bikes. If there is no bike shop at one of the recommended

*Bonneval-en-Tarentaise (Route 5, day 3)*

Kilometre post, Col de la Cayolle (Route 8, day 5)

overnight stops, I have shown where the most easily accessible bike shop is. In some areas, especially in the Southern Alps, the nearest bike shop can be more than 60km away.

## Accommodation list

The accommodation list gives the names and telephone numbers of the campsites, B&Bs/hostels and hotels at all of the recommended overnight stops. For campsites, the opening dates are also given. Other than during the main summer holiday period, or where there is only a very limited choice of accommodation, it is not usually necessary to book in advance. In a book of this size, it would be impossible to list all the options in the larger towns/resorts (there are more than 100 hotels in Geneva alone), so where there are more than six campsites, B&Bs or hotels, the reader is referred to the local tourist office. Phone numbers and internet addresses for both *départementale* and local tourist offices are given at the end of the accommodation section.

# ROUTE ONE

# TOUR OF THE AIN

| Day | Route | Distance | Height Gain |
|---|---|---|---|
| 1 | Bellegarde to Yenne | 63.4km | 898m |
| 2 | Yenne to St Rambert-en-Bugey | 64.3km | 912m |
| 3 | St Rambert-en-Bugey to Chatillon-sur-Chalaronne | 77.2km | 500m |
| 4 | Chatillon-sur-Chalaronne to Thoirette | 74.4km | 615m |
| 5 | Thoirette to Hauteville-Lompnes | 66.9km | 1197m |
| 6 | Hauteville-Lompnes to Bellegarde | 46.1km | 535m |
| | **Totals** | **392.3km** | **4657m** |

The Tour of the Ain explores a very accessible but poorly known *département* of south-east France. Despite its proximity to both Lyon and Geneva, the Ain has remained relatively unspoilt: an authentic corner of *La France profonde*, dotted with sleepy villages, rambling farms and dense forests. The geography of the area is dominated by three large rivers: the Saone, which marks the *département's* western border; the Rhone, which marks its eastern and southern borders; and the Ain, which runs through the middle. The countryside to the west of the River Ain is almost completely flat and dotted with hundreds of lakes and marshes, whereas to the east the landscape is much more rugged: this is the southern end of the Jura Mountains. The area's unspoilt countryside and picturesque villages, combined with a very well developed network of virtually traffic-free roads, make it a fabulous place for cyclists. One of the reasons why the roads are so quiet, even during the summer holidays, is that the Ain is very much a tourist backwater. Consequently, most towns and villages have very few hotels and restaurants and the overnight-stops noted here had to be chosen as much for the range of facilities they offer as for their historical, cultural or scenic interest.

This circuit focuses on the southern part of the *département*, and takes you through the mountains of the Haut-Bugey and the wetlands of the Dombes. Although the route includes some quite long climbs, the Tour of the Ain is the least mountainous circuit in this guide and therefore provides an ideal introduction to cycle touring in the mountains. The tour can easily be extended by combining it with the Tour of the Chartreuse-Bauges, or by incorporating one or more of the 25 signposted circuits described in a cycling guide published by the Ain Tourist Board (available from **www.ain-tourisme.com**).

Bellegarde-sur-Valserine, a small town on the banks of the Rhone, was chosen as the start and finish point for the tour because it is within easy reach of Geneva airport. There is a regular train service from Geneva and the journey takes around 25 mins. Despite being only 40km from Geneva, cycling to Bellegarde is not recommended, as it is impossible to avoid the very busy and dangerous main roads. If you are flying into Lyon, it would be better to start at Meximieux.

Bellegarde offers little to retain even the most open-minded visitor – perhaps its greatest claim to fame is that it was the first town in France to install electric streetlights, in 1883. However, the town is quickly left behind as you head south-east into the Bugey, via the Col de Richemont. Although long (around 15km), the climb is never too steep and you will soon be at the top with the satisfaction of having the hardest part of the day's cycling behind you. Once over the Col de Richemont, the road emerges from the forest to give spectacular views of the idyllic Séran Valley and

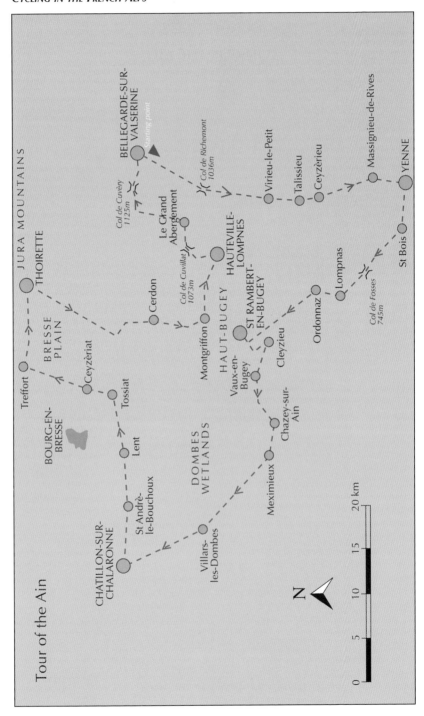

Tour of the Ain

*Virieu-le-Petit: a typical French village scene*

the rolling hills of the Haut-Bugey. The next 20km wind gently downhill, across the western flanks of the Grand Colombier, to the village of Talissieu. If you found the climb to the Col de Richemont easy, you may like to make a detour over the Grand Colombier. There are several roads to the top of this mountain; the steepest starts in Virieu-le-Petit and rises 865 metres in a little under 9km with gradients of up to 19%. As you would expect from the highest mountain in the area, the views from the top are superb. The standard route from Talissieu to Ceyzérieu crosses the northern edge of the Lavours Marsh, one of the last remaining, large continental marshes in western Europe and now a nature reserve. It is also one of the few places in France where you can see highland cattle! The reserve's visitor centre, a very pleasant café and the start of a 2.4km long nature trail are in Aignoz, 1.5km east of Ceyzérieu. The countryside to the south, with its unspoilt villages and vineyards, set against a backdrop of spectacular mountains, is picture-postcard France at its very best. The area also has its little surprises, such as the sculptures at the Lac de Barterand, the largest of which depicts a local legend of the giant Gargantua breaking open the mountainside to free the mermaid of the vines who had been trapped inside (no one seems to know why she had been imprisoned). From the lake, a short descent takes you back down into the Rhone Valley at a point where there are two branches to the river. The first branch is quickly crossed, but you won't cross the second until you reach the small market town of Yenne, 9km further along the road.

From Yenne, the route heads due west along the *route nationale*, through the Gorges de la Balme. After about 5km, in the village of Virignin, you leave the traffic behind, and the rest of the day follows quiet country lanes through forests, fields and open moorland. This is perfect cycling country where other vehicles are rarely seen – you can consider yourself unlucky if you are passed by more than a handful of cars in the 50km that separate Virignin from St Rambert. However, there are also very few opportunities to buy any sort of refreshments so, unless you want to rely on one of the cafés in Lompnas or Ordonnaz being open, take a packed lunch with you. The wooded banks of Lake Ambléon, just before the Col de Fosses, provide an ideal picnic site. Other than the superb scenery, there are few tourist attractions along the route (one being the Palaeoecology Museum in Cerin). St Rambert is the only village in a 20km radius to have hotels (both 1.5km east of the village), a B&B (in Serrières, 1km west of the village) and a campsite (1km east of the village). It is a former industrial village that is now making strenuous efforts to raise its tourist profile, having recently opened both a local heritage museum and an art gallery.

The third leg of the tour starts with a final incursion into the Bugey, past the village of Cleyzieu to Vaux-en-Bugey, before turning its back on the hills to cross the floodplain of the River Ain. Of all the picturesque villages in the Ain, the most spectacular is undoubtedly the mediaeval citadel of Pérouges. The village was probably founded in Roman times, but most of the buildings that you can see today date from the 15th century. Wandering through the cobbled streets is like walking back through time, an impression that is enhanced by little details, such as the bakery that leaves its bread to rise in the sun of an open window. Pérouges is also the gateway to the wetlands of the Dombes, a huge expanse of lakes and marshes that boasts extremely rich flora and fauna. Although most of these lakes (there are more than a thousand of them) have existed for centuries, they are nearly all man-made – fish farming is not a recent development. They provide an excellent habitat for many species of sedentary and migratory birds, including kestrels, grey herons and storks. An even greater variety of birds, from all around the world, can be seen at the Villars-les-Dombes Bird Garden, 20km northwest of Pérouges.

The day ends at Chatillon-sur-Chalaronne, a very pretty town of half-timbered houses that prides itself on its gastronomy. There is no better place to try frog's legs, a local speciality, followed by local freshwater fish or wildfowl. For the inquisitive visitor there are also several interesting museums and historical buildings to visit, including the castle ruins and the 17th-century market hall, which still houses the local market every Saturday morning.

Day 4 picks up where day three left off, crossing the northern part of the Dombes and skirting round Bourg-en-Bresse, the capital of the Ain. Cycling through such peaceful countryside is always enjoyable, but the pleasure is even greater early in the morning when the air smells freshest and the mist still hovers above the lakes. Once across the wetlands, the itinerary turns north and follows the eastern edge of the Bresse Plain to Treffort. This is an excellent place for a short break before leaving the flat plains behind and heading back into the mountains. The cafés are in the main square at the bottom of the hill, however the prettiest corner of the village, with its 14th-century church and castle, is at the top of the very steep Rue Ferrachat. The view across the Bresse Plain to the hills west of Macon is well worth the climb. From Treffort the route runs more or less due east across the foothills of the Jura to Thoirette on the banks of the Ain. Thoirette has little to offer the cultural tourist, but its superb riverside location and very welcoming hotels and campsite make it an ideal stopping-off point.

On leaving Thoirette, the route turns right to follow the banks of the Ain southwards for about 20km. The strenuous cycling starts just before the village of Merpuis, where a steep, but short climb leads through Challes, over an unnamed pass and down to Cerdon. Cerdon has three claims to fame: its show caves, its working coppersmith's and an eponymous sparkling rosé wine. Unfortunately, getting to the show caves involves a detour of about 6km (turn right from D85A onto D11, then D11H and N84), but the coppersmith's and wine museum are in the village itself. Many local wineries are also open to the public: a map in the village gives details. Once past Cerdon, the road rises again to go over the Col de Montratier and onto the central plateau of the Haut-Bugey. From here it is possible to head straight to Hauteville-Lompnes, but the most picturesque route branches off the main road at Châtillon-sur-Corneille to explore the hidden valleys to the south. This is deepest rural France and certainly not the sort of place you would expect to find an Australian restaurant (in the tiny hamlet of Pezières – 18km from Cerdon). Hauteville-Lompnes, the next port of call, is the capital of the Haut-Bugey. For a small town of less than 4000 inhabitants it can be quite a lively place with music, dance and arts festivals all through the summer.

The final leg of the tour is quite short, although there are several ways in which it could be extended (eg. via Brénod, Col de Belleroche, Le Poizat and Col de Bérentin). The most direct route takes you over the Col de Cuvillat and through Les Abergements to

Lac de Barterand:
Gargantua freeing the mermaid of the vines

*Chatillon-sur-Chalaronne*
*(Day 3)*

the Plateau de Retord, home to one of the area's largest cross-country skiing centres. The journey truly ends on a high, as the pass that marks the eastern edge of the plateau, the Col de Cuvéry, is the highest point on the circuit and the14km descent back to Bellegarde is great fun. If you are not in a rush, why not celebrate the end of the tour with lunch at the excellent Auberge de la Fontaine in Ochiaz, just outside Bellegarde?

**Via Chambéry:** If you fly into Chambéry, you can join the tour at Yenne (end of Day 1). Directions from the airport to Yenne are given in Appendix 1. A better option for the final day of the tour would then be to follow Day 6 as described to Le Grand Abergement. From here take the D39 to Hotonnes, and then follow the D9 for about 4.5km to join Day 1 of the standard route at the D9/D30 junction, just below the Col de Richemont.

## GETTING THERE

### By car
Bellegarde-sur-Valserine is 775km from Calais.

### By plane
**Via Geneva:** Take the train from the airport to Geneva central station (Cornavin). The number of trains from Geneva–Cornavin to Bellegarde varies from one train every two hours to three trains per hour, depending on the time of day. The journey takes around 25 mins.

**Via Lyon:** If you fly into Lyon St Exupéry, you can start the tour by cycling from the airport to Meximieux. Directions are given in Appendix 1.

## WHEN TO GO

Due to its modest altitude, this tour is feasible from April to October. The roads are always quiet, even during the peak holiday months of July and August. Given the limited number of hotels and campsites, it is advisable to book accommodation in advance.

## MAPS

**Michelin:** Local – Sheet 328, Ain, Haute-Savoie

**Michelin:** Regional – Sheet 244, Rhône-Alpes

**IGN:** Top 100 – Sheet 44: Lyon, Genève and Sheet 51: Lyon, Grenoble

*The River Rhone near Yenne (Day 1)*

# Day 1 – Bellegarde-sur-Valserine to Yenne

Large sections of a projected cycleway along the Rhone Valley from Lake Geneva to the Mediterranean have now been completed. At the end of 2007, the north-ernmost part of the cycleway ran from Chancy (about 15km southwest of Geneva airport) to Clarafond (about 10km southeast of Bellegarde). From Clarafond, pleasant minor roads can be followed to join the main route at the foot of the Col de Richemont. For more details and maps of the completed sections go to **www.dulemanalamer.com**.

| Distance | Location | Directions |
|---|---|---|
| 0.0 | Bellegarde station | Come out of the station and turn R onto Rue Joseph Bertola (Centre Ville) |
| 0.1 | Traffic lights | Turn R – Rue Lafayette |
| 0.6 | Jtn | Turn R (Genève) and go under railway line |
| 1.0 | Roundabout | Turn L 3rd exit D25 (Billiat) |
| 7.7 | Billiat: D25/D991 | Turn R – D991 (Génissiat) |
| 9.1 | D991/D30 | Turn L – D30 (Injoux): 9.7km at 6% |
| 18.8 | Col de Richemont | Go straight on |
| 22.6 | D30/D9 | Turn L – D30 (Brénaz) |
| 28.0 | Brénaz: D30/D69 | Turn L – D69 (Virieu-le-Petit). Go through Virieu-le-Petit to Munet |
| 34.8 | Munet: D69/D105 | Turn L – D105 (Talissieu) |
| 37.0 | Jtn | Turn R (Artemare) |
| 37.5 | Jtn | Turn L (Talissieu) |
| 40.3 | Talissieu: D105/D904 | Turn L – D904 |
| 41.1 | D904/D105 | Turn R – D105 (Ceyzérieu) |
| 43.8 | D105/D37 | Turn R – D37 |
| 44.9 | Ceyzérieu: D105/D37 | Go straight on along D37 and go through Vongnes |
| 50.4 | D37/D37A | Turn L onto D37A (Cressin) |
| 52.8 | Jtn | Turn R (Belley) |
| 53.9 | D37A/D992 | Turn R – D992 (Belley) |
| 54.6 | D992/D37 | Turn L – D37 (Massignieu) |
| 56.8 | D37/D37A | Turn R – D37 (Yenne) |
| 62.9 | D37/N504 | Turn L – N504 (Yenne), and then immediately R to go into the village |
| 63.4 | Yenne: *mairie* | The *mairie* is on the L |

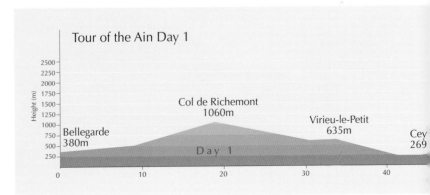

*Wheat fields and the Rhone Valley near Cressin*

## FACILITIES AND SERVICES

| Location | Distance (km) | Water | Shops | Café | Campsite | B&B | Hotel | Bank | Bike Shop |
|---|---|---|---|---|---|---|---|---|---|
| Bellegarde | 0.0 | x | x | x | x | — | x | x | x |
| Billiat | 7.7 | x | x | x | — | — | — | — | — |
| Brénaz | 28.0 | x | — | — | — | — | — | — | — |
| Virieu-le-Petit | 33.3 | x | — | — | — | — | — | — | — |
| Ceyzérieu | 44.9 | x | x | x | — | x | — | — | — |
| Massignieu | 56.8 | x | x | x | x | — | — | — | — |
| Yenne | 63.4 | x | x | x | x | x | x | x | (1) |

(1) Nearest bike shop is in Belley, 12km northwest of Yenne

| iver Rhone 233m | Yenne 230m | St Bois 300m | Ambléon 400m | Col des Fosses 745m |
|---|---|---|---|---|

Day 2

60        70        80        90        100

ance (km)

In 2003, France was hit by the worst heatwave in living memory. At least 15,000 people died as temperatures peaked at more than 40°C after three long months of exceptional heat and drought. Forest fires ravaged the countryside, coming uncomfortably close to many towns and villages. To give just one small example, the blackened stumps of trees around St Bois (still visible in 2005) show how close the village came to being destroyed. Water levels in major rivers, such as the Rhone and the Ain, fell to record lows and many power stations had to be run at reduced capacity because the water was too hot to cool them. Fish stocks in the rivers were devastated and even the water that emerged from underground springs was warm.

| Distance | Location | Directions |
|----------|----------|------------|
| 0.0 | Yenne *mairie* | Turn R in front of the *marie* and go to N504 |
| 0.5 | N504 | Turn L – N504 (Lyon) |
| 2.6 | N504/N516 | Turn R – N504 (Belley) |
| 4.5 | Virignin: N504/D31A | Turn L – D31A (Peyrieu) and cross the Rhone Canal: road turns sharp L and becomes D31B |
| 6.2 | D31B/D24A | Turn R along D31B (Champtel) |
| 8.0 | D31B/D992 | Turn R – D992 (Belley) |
| 9.6 | D992/D10 | Turn L – D10 and go through (Peyzieu) |
| 12.8 | D10/D24 | Turn R – D24 (St Bois) |
| 22.7 | D24/D41 | Turn L – D41 (Innimont): 6.3km at 5.5% |
| 29.0 | Col des Fosses | Go straight on |
| 30.3 | D41/D87 | Turn R – D87 (Lompnaz) |
| 32.0 | D87/D87D | Turn R along D87 and go through Cerin |
| 37.4 | Lompnas: D87/D94 | Turn R – D94 (Ordonnaz): 3.6km at 6.5% |
| 43.5 | Ordonnaz: D94/D32 | Turn L – D32 (Col de Portes) |
| 47.4 | D32/D99 | Turn R – D99 (Col de Portes) |
| 48.0 | D99/D73 | Turn R – D73 (St Rambert-en-Bugey) |
| 60.0 | D73/D104 | Go straight on along D73 |
| 63.1 | Roundabout: D73/N504 | Turn R – N504 (St Rambert-en-Bugey) |
| 64.3 | St Rambert-en-Bugey | TO is on the R |

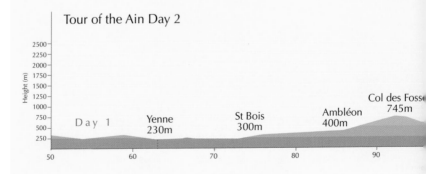

*Ordonnaz: fountain decorated for Tour de France 2003*

## FACILITIES AND SERVICES

| Location | Distance (km) | Water | Shops | Café | Campsite | B&B | Hotel | Bank | Bike Shop |
|---|---|---|---|---|---|---|---|---|---|
| Yenne | 0.0 | x | x | x | x | x | x | x | (1) |
| Virignin | 4.5 | — | x | — | — | — | — | — | — |
| Ambléon | 20.9 | x | — | — | — | — | — | — | — |
| Cerin | 32.4 | x | — | x | — | — | — | — | — |
| Lompnas | 37.4 | — | — | x | — | — | — | — | — |
| Ordonnaz | 43.5 | — | — | x | — | x | — | — | — |
| Conand | 56.4 | x | — | — | — | — | — | — | — |
| St Rambert | 64.3 | x | x | x | x | x | x | x | (2) |

(1) Nearest bike shop is in Belley, 12km northwest of Yenne

(2) Nearest bike shop is in Ambérieu-en-Bugey, 10km west of St Rambert

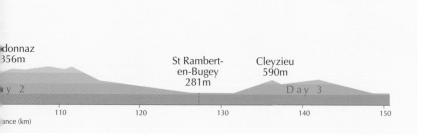

Ordonnaz 856m

St Rambert-en-Bugey 281m

Cleyzieu 590m

Day 2     Day 3

ance (km)

Periodically, the fish-producing lakes of the Dombes are drained and planted with wheat, oats or maize. After the harvest, the lakes are re-filled and re-stocked with fish.

| Distance | Location | Directions |
|---|---|---|
| 0.0 | St Rambert-en-Bugey TO | Come out of TO and turn L – N504 |
| 1.2 | Roundabout: N504/D73 | Turn R – D73 (Le Chauchay) |
| 3.2 | Le Chauchay | Turn L – D60 and cross N504 (Cleyzieu) |
| 8.5 | Cleyzieu | Bear R past fountain (Vaux-en-Bugey) |
| 14.2 | D60/D60A | Turn R – D60A (Vaux-en-Bugey) |
| 20.2 | Vaux-en-Bugey | Go straight on – D77A (Leyment) |
| 25.4 | Leyment: D77B/D77 | Turn L – D77 (Ste Julie) |
| 27.4 | D77/D77C | Turn R – D77C (Chazey-sur-Ain) |
| 30.1 | Chazey-sur-Ain | Turn R onto Grande Rue (D40) |
| 31.7 | D40/N84 | Turn L – N84 (Meximieux) |
| 35.2 | 2nd roundabout | Turn R (Meximieux) |
| 35.4 | Meximieux: jtn | Turn L and follow railway line past station |
| 36.2 | Roundabout | Turn L (Pérouges) |
| 36.5 | Jtn | Turn R onto D4 (Pérouges) |
| 42.3 | Roundabout: D4/D22 | Go straight on along D4 (Le Montellier) |
| 42.6 | Jtn | Turn R (Joyeux) |
| 47.7 | Jtn | Turn R onto D61 and go through Joyeux |
| 50.0 | D61/D904 | Turn L onto D904 (Villars-les-Dombes) |
| 55.6 | Villars-les-Dombes: lights | Go straight on – D904 (Chatillon-sur-Ch.) |
| 56.5 | D904/D70 | Turn R – D70 (Ste Olive) |
| 64.2 | Ste Olive: D70/D82 | Turn R – D82 (Chatillon-sur-Ch.) Follow D82 to Chatillon |
| 75.8 | Chatillon-sur-Chalaronne | Turn R onto Boulevard de la Resistance. Go into village and follow one way system to jtn with D2 |
| 76.7 | Jtn | Turn L – D2 (Bourg-en-Bresse) |
| 76.9 | Roundabout | Go straight on (Centre Ville) |
| 77.2 | Main Square | Mairie is on the L (set back from the road) |

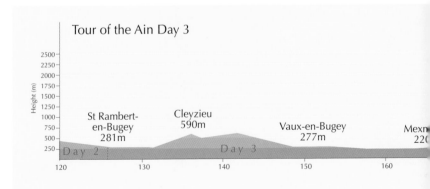

*Pérouges: a superbly well-preserved mediaeval village*

## FACILITIES AND SERVICES

| Location | Distance (km) | Water | Shops | Café | Campsite | B&B | Hotel | Bank | Bike Shop |
|---|---|---|---|---|---|---|---|---|---|
| St Rambert | 0.0 | x | x | x | x | x | x | x | (1) |
| Cléyzieu | 8.5 | x | — | — | — | — | — | — | — |
| Vaux-en-Bugey | 20.2 | x | x | x | — | — | — | — | — |
| Leyment | 25.4 | — | x | x | — | — | — | — | — |
| Chazey-sur-Ain | 30.1 | — | x | x | — | — | x | — | — |
| Meximieux/Pérouges | 36.2 | x | x | x | x | — | x | x | x |
| Joyeux | 42.5 | — | — | x | — | x | — | — | — |
| Villars-les-Dombes | 55.6 | x | x | x | x | x | x | x | — |
| Ste Olive | 64.2 | — | — | x | — | — | x | — | — |
| Chatillon-sur-Chalaronne | 77.2 | x | x | x | x | x | x | x | x |

(1) Nearest bike shop is in Ambérieu-en-Bugey – 10km west of St Rambert

Villars-les-Dombes
282m

Chatillon-sur-
Chalaronne
240m

Day 4

| 180 | 190 | 200 | 210 | 220 |

1ce (km)

## Day 4 – Chantillon-sur-Chalaronne to Thoirette

| Distance | Location | Directions |
|----------|----------|------------|
| 0.0 | Chatillon *mairie* | Come out of the *mairie*, turn R then R again |
| 0.3 | Roundabout | Turn L – D7 (Chalamont) |
| 1.5 | Jtn | Turn L (Montaplan) |
| 2.1 | Jtn | Turn R (no sign) |
| 3.9 | Jtn | Turn R – hiking sign (St Georges-sur-Renon) |
| 6.7 | St Georges-sur-Renon | Go straight on – D67 (St André-le-Bouchoux) |
| 10.7 | D67/D26 | Turn L – D26 into St André-le-Bouchoux |
| 10.9 | D26/D17 | Turn R – D17 – then L – D67 (St André/Vieux Jonc) |
| 15.1 | Jtn | Turn R (no sign) onto minor road. The jtn is just after a lake on L of road and before a house on R |
| 16.3 | Le Buttoir: jtn | Go straight on |
| 18.6 | Jtn | Turn R – D64 and go through Servas to (Lent) |
| 21.5 | Lent D64/D22 | Turn R – D22 (Meximieux) |
| 21.9 | D22/D23 | Turn L – D23 (Certines) |
| 22.5 | D23/D64 | Turn R – D64 (Certines) then (Tossiat) |
| 32.4 | Tossiat: D64/D52 | Turn R – D52 (Ceyzériat) |
| 37.3 | Ceyzériat | Turn R (Centre Village) |
| 37.5 | Jtn | Turn L (Observatoire) |
| 37.8 | Jtn | Turn R – D52 (Treffort) |
| 41.7 | Jasseron: D52/D936 | Turn R – D936 and then L – D52 (Treffort) |
| 49.1 | Jtn | Turn R to go into Treffort |
| 49.4 | Treffort | Turn R – D3 (Corveissiat): 2.7km at 6.5% |
| 54.0 | D3/D936 | Turn L – D936 (Corveissiat) |
| 56.3 | D936/D3 | Turn L – D3 (Chavannes-sur-Suran) |
| 58.0 | Chavannes: D3/D42 | Turn L – D42 then R – D3 (Arnans): 5.2km at 5% |
| 63.9 | Arnans | Go straight on (Aromas) |
| 67.0 | C7/D86 | Go straight on (Ceffia) |
| 68.8 | D59/D200 | Go straight on – D59 (Thoirette) |
| 73.6 | D59/D936 | Turn L – D936 (Thoirette) |
| 74.4 | Thoirette campsite | Campsite entrance is on the R |

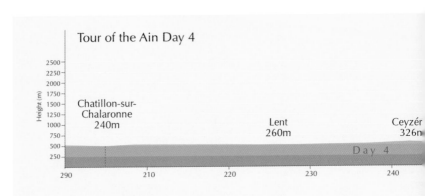

*Church near St Georges-sur-Renon*

## FACILITIES AND SERVICES

| Location | Distance (km) | Water | Shops | Café | Campsite | B&B | Hotel | Bank | Bike Shop |
|---|---|---|---|---|---|---|---|---|---|
| Chatillon-sur-Chalaronne | 0 | x | x | x | x | x | x | x | x |
| St André-le-Bouchoux | 10.7 | — | — | x | — | — | — | — | — |
| Lent | 21.5 | — | x | x | — | — | x | — | — |
| Certines | 28.7 | — | x | x | — | — | — | — | — |
| Ceyzériat | 37.3 | x | x | x | x | — | — | x | — |
| Treffort | 49.4 | x | x | x | x | x | x | x | — |
| Chavannes-sur-Suran | 58.0 | — | x | x | x | — | — | — | — |
| Arnans | 63.9 | x | — | — | — | — | — | — | — |
| Thoirette | 74.4 | x | x | x | x | x | x | x | (1) |

(1) Nearest bike shop is in Oyonnax, 16km east of Thoirette

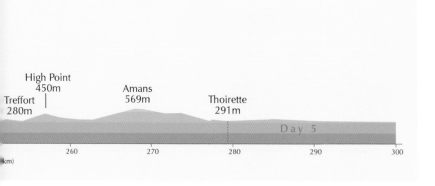

High Point
450m
Treffort
280m
Amans
569m
Thoirette
291m

Day 5

260    270    280    290    300

km)

# Day 5 – Thoirette to Hauteville-Lompnes

On the left-hand side of the road just before entering Hauteville, you cannot fail to notice a rather modest-looking quarry. This is the home of Hauteville marble, an orangey-yellow limestone that has been used in the construction of some of the world's most famous buildings, including the White House, the elevator halls of the Empire State Building and the plinth supporting the Statue of Liberty.

| Distance | Location | Directions |
|---|---|---|
| 0.0 | Thoirette campsite: D936 | Turn R – D936. Go through village and over river. |
| 0.6 | D936/D91 | Turn R – D91 (Granges) |
| 11.6 | D91/D91A | Bear R – D91 (Poncin) |
| 22.7 | Jtn | Turn L (just before Merpuis) (Route du Bugey): 2.5km at 7% |
| 26.5 | Jtn | Turn R and go into Challes la Montagne |
| 26.8 | Challes | Turn L (Route du Bugey): 1.9km at 5.5% |
| 30.0 | C1/D85A | Turn L (no sign) |
| 30.6 | D85A/D11 | Turn R – D11 (Cerdon) |
| 35.3 | D11/N84 | Go straight on – D11 (Corlier): 6.1km at 4.5% |
| 39.3 | D11/D11J | Turn L – D11 (Hauteville-Lompnes) |
| 40.1 | D11/D12 | Turn L – D12 (Hauteville-Lompnes) |
| 41.4 | D12/D12C | Turn R – D12C (Boyeux-St Jérôme) |
| 43.5 | Boyeux: D12/D12C | Turn L – D12C (St Jérôme) |
| 43.6 | Jtn | Turn L (Montgriffon): 2km at 11% |
| 46.6 | D12B/D11 | Turn R – D11 (Montgriffon) |
| 48.3 | Montgriffon: D11/D63A | Turn L – D63A (Resinand): 2.8km descent then 6.7km at 5% |
| 52.4 | Resinand: D63A/D34 | Turn L – D34 (Aranc) |
| 55.9 | Aranc: D34/D102 | Turn L onto D102 and then R back onto D34 (Rougemeont) |
| 59.9 | D34/D8 | Turn R – D8 (Hauteville-Lompnes) |
| 64.7 | Roundabout | Go straight on (Hauteville-Lompnes) |
| 66.5 | Roundabout | Go straight on (Centre Ville) |
| 66.7 | Hauteville-Lompnes | Bear R onto Rue Jean Miguet |
| 66.9 | Centre of Hauteville | Stop in front of Bistrot de la Fontaine |

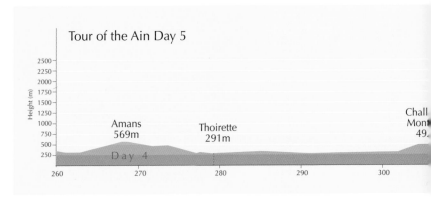

Tour of the Ain Day 5

*Early morning mist over the River Ain at Thoirette*

## FACILITIES AND SERVICES

| Location | Distance (km) | Water | Shops | Café | Campsite | B&B | Hotel | Bank | Bike Shop |
|---|---|---|---|---|---|---|---|---|---|
| Thoirette | 0.0 | x | x | x | x | x | x | x | (1) |
| Granges | 5.9 | x | — | — | — | — | — | — | — |
| Cerdon | 33.8 | x | x | x | — | x | x | — | — |
| Montgriffon | 48.3 | x | — | — | — | — | — | — | — |
| Pezières/Resinand | 52.0 | x | — | x | — | — | — | — | — |
| Hauteville-Lompnes | 66.9 | x | x | x | x | x | x | x | x |

(1) Nearest bike shop is in Oyonnax, 16km east of Thoirette

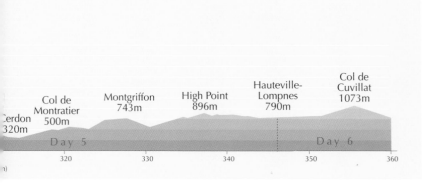

41

Extra day: At Thoirette, you already have one foot in the Jura, so why not explore the *département* a little further? The village of Orgelet, reached via Arinthod, provides a picturesque objective for a day trip. The return leg takes you past the Lac de Vouglans, a lake on the River Ain formed by a hydroelectricity dam, and then through Cernon and Condes. There are no big hills along the route, but cycling through such rolling countryside can be just as tiring as going over a high pass.

| Distance | Location | Directions |
|---|---|---|
| 0.0 | Hauteville-Lompnes: Bistrot de la Fontaine | Go past the public toilets and up to a T-jtn in front of MMA Assurances |
| 0.1 | Jtn | Turn L |
| 0.5 | Roundabout | Turn R – D21 (Champdor) |
| 5.5 | Champdor: D21/D57A | Turn R – D57A (Le Petit Abergement): 4.6km at 5.5% |
| 9.4 | Col de Cuvillat | Go straight on |
| 13.8 | D57A/D31 | Turn R – D31 (Le Petit Abergement) |
| 14.3 | Le Petit Abergement: D31/D39C | Turn L – D39C (Le Grand Abergement): short descent then 11.2km at 3.5% |
| 15.9 | Le Grand Abergement: D39C/D39 | Turn L – D39 (Les Plans d'Hotonnes) |
| 18.2 | D39/D39A | Go straight on – D39 (Le Poizat) |
| 19.5 | D39/D55 | Turn R – D55 (Bellegarde) |
| 26.0 | D55/D101 | Turn R – D101 (Bellegarde) |
| 30.4 | Col de Cuvéry | Go straight on |
| 39.7 | D101/D101B | Turn R – D101B (Ochiaz) |
| 40.5 | Ochiaz: D101B/D991 | Turn L – D991 then first R onto Route de Mussel. Keep going downhill to jtn with D25 |
| 44.0 | Jtn | Turn L – D25 – Rue de l'Avenir |
| 44.9 | Roundabout | Turn R – filter lane (Annecy) |
| 45.2 | Traffic lights | Turn L (Centre Ville) |
| 45.8 | Jtn | Turn L onto Rue Joseph Bertola – next to the *hôtel de ville* |
| 46.1 | Bellegarde station | |

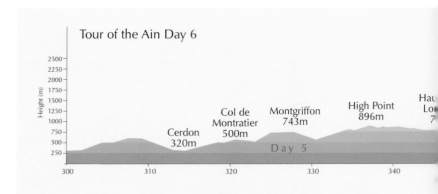

*Snow in late May on the Retord Plateau*

## FACILITIES AND SERVICES

| Location | Distance (km) | Water | Shops | Café | Campsite | B&B | Hotel | Bank | Bike Shop |
|---|---|---|---|---|---|---|---|---|---|
| Hauteville-Lompnes | 0.0 | x | x | x | x | x | x | x | x |
| Champdor | 5.5 | x | x | x | — | — | — | — | — |
| Les Abergements | 15.0 | x | — | x | — | — | x | — | — |
| Col de Cuvéry | 30.4 | — | — | x | — | — | — | — | — |
| Ochiaz | 40.5 | x | — | x | — | x | x | — | — |
| Bellegarde | 46.1 | x | x | x | x | — | x | x | x |

Col de
Cuvillat
1073m
Le Petit
Abergement
770m
Col de
Cuvéry
1125m
Bellegarde-sur-
Valserine
380m

Day 6

360    370    380    390    400

(km)

# ACCOMMODATION

## Bellegarde-sur-Valserine

**Campsites**

Le Crêt d'Eau (all year), Tel. 04 50 56 60 81

**Bed & Breakfast**

There are no bed & breakfasts in Bellegarde

**Hotels**

La Belle Epoque (***), Tel. 04 50 48 14 46

La Colonne (**), Tel. 04 50 48 10 45

Hotel Gril Adria (**), Tel. 04 50 48 14 10

Touring Hôtel (**), Tel. 04 50 56 08 08

Hotel 1ere Classe, Tel. 04 50 56 62 53

## Yenne

**Campsites**

Camping du Flon (mid-June to end August), Tel. 04 79 36 82 70

Les Soudans (early May to end September), Tel. 06 86 32 56 89

**Bed & Breakfast**

Au Tote Sayon (in Nattages, 4km north of Yenne), Tel. 04 79 44 40 69

**Hotels**

Le Fer à Cheval (**), Tel. 04 79 36 70 33

## St Rambert-en-Bugey

**Campsites**

L'Ermitage, Tel. 04 74 36 32 97

**Bed & Breakfast**

L'Albarande, Tel. 06 33 30 53 77

**Hotels**

Le Calypso, Tel. 04 74 36 36 80

Auberge de l'Adret, Tel. 04 74 36 30 76

Le Refuge de l'Ermite, Tel. 04 74 36 20 20

## Villars-les-Dombes

**Campsites**

Les Autières (early April to end Sept), Tel. 04 74 98 00 21

**Bed & Breakfast**

Mr and Mrs George, Tel. 04 74 98 05 44

**Hotels**

Ribotel Le Parc, Tel. 04 74 98 08 03

## Thoirette

**Campsites**

Camping Municipal (dates not known), Tel. 04 74 76 88 43

**Bed & Breakfast**

There are no bed & breakfasts in Thoirette

**Hotels**

L'Auberge du Pont, Tel. 04 74 76 80 46

L'Auberge de Thoire, Tel. 04 74 49 22 05

## Hauteville-Lompnes

**Campsites**

Camping Municipal (all year), Tel. 04 74 35 36 73

**Bed & Breakfast**

La Praille, Tel. 04 74 35 29 81

Résidence Bernard, Tel. 04 74 35 17 45

Mme Decrenisse, Tel. 04 74 35 25 16

Mme Jandard, Tel. 06 09 02 49 02

**Hotels**

Brasserie des Tilleuls, Tel. 04 74 35 30 25

Le Provençal (**), Tel. 04 74 35 30 43

## TOURIST INFORMATION

### Regional Information

|  | Telephone | Website |
| --- | --- | --- |
| Ain | 04 74 32 31 30 | **www.ain-tourisme.com** |

### Tourist Information Offices

| Location | Telephone | Website |
| --- | --- | --- |
| Bellegarde | 04 50 48 48 68 | **www.pays-de-gex.org** |
| Yenne | 04 79 36 71 54 | **www.avant-pays-savoyard.com** |
| Ordonnaz | 04 74 39 80 92 | **http://perso.wanadoo.fr/pierre.bonny** |
| St Rambert-en-Bugey | 04 74 36 32 86 | **www.tourisme-albarine.com** |
| Villars-les-Dombes | 04 74 98 06 29 | **www.villars-les-dombes.com** |
| Thoirette (Oyonnax) | 04 74 77 94 46 | **www.tourisme-oyonnax.com** |
| Hauteville-Lompnes | 04 74 35 39 73 | **www.plateau-hauteville.com** |

*Half-timbered house in Chatillon-sur-Chalaronne (Day 3)*

# ROUTE TWO

# TOUR OF THE CHABLAIS–ARAVIS

| Day | Route | Distance | Height Gain |
|---|---|---|---|
| 1 | Geneva to Thonon-les-Bains | 51.1km | 200m |
| 2 | Thonon-les-Bains to Chatel | 61.6km | 1390m |
| 3 | Chatel to Samoëns | 52.8km | 1480m |
| 4 | Samoëns to La Clusaz | 56.4km | 1390m |
| 5 | La Clusaz to Annecy | 61.3km | 680m |
| 6 | Annecy to Geneva | 74.9km | 1300m |
| | **Totals** | **358.3km** | **6440m** |

Chablais is a name that everyone in the *département* of Haute-Savoie uses to describe the northernmost part of the pre-Alps, but no two people seem to agree on exactly where the boundaries of this region lie. Here, I have used the broadest possible definition of the term to encompass the whole area between Lake Geneva and the Arve Valley. On the other hand, the Aravis Range is much easier to define, as it is a single chain of mountains that runs south-east from the Arve Valley to the town of Faverges, just south of Lake Annecy. The tour of the Chablais–Aravis also includes the out-lying mass of Mont Salève, generally considered to be Geneva's own mountain.

Quite understandably, the French are extremely proud of their country's culinary reputation and if you talk to any French person for long enough, the conversation will inevitably turn to food and, more particularly, to local gastronomy. Every region of the country has its own specialities and the Chablais and the Aravis are no exceptions. Being so close to Lakes Geneva and Annecy, it is not surprising that many restaurants in the area specialise in locally caught fish. At higher altitudes, lush alpine pastures provide ideal grazing for the dairy cows which produce the milk used to make the area's cheeses, three of which – Abondance from the Chablais, and Reblochon and Chevrotin from the Aravis – have been awarded Appellation d'Origine Contrôlée (AOC) status. Many local dishes

(raclette, tartiflette, reblochonade, etc) are simple variations on the theme of meat, potatoes and cheese, the only differences between them being the type of cheese and the way they are cooked. These are good, hearty farmhouse dishes – just what you need after a long day's cycling, especially if the evenings are cool.

Geneva was chosen as the start point for the tour as it is both easy to get to by public transport and easy to cycle through. Geneva City Council has made strenuous efforts to promote cycling, developing an extensive network of cycleways and cycle lanes, providing free bicycle hire and producing a free map of cycle routes around the city. (To obtain this map, contact Mr Claude Morel at Geneva City Council: **claude.morel@ville-ge.ch**).

Despite its long and colourful past, Geneva is a thoroughly modern and forward-looking city, best known as the home of international organisations such as the United Nations and the Red Cross. More interestingly for the visiting tourist, Geneva also boasts a wide range of excellent museums that deal with subjects as diverse as art, archaeology and automobiles. The Swiss are famous for their common sense and pragmatism, so it is perhaps unsurprising that Geneva's most famous landmark, the water jet of 140m, was originally created as a simple pressure relief valve for the city's water pumps. The first jet, created in 1886, was only a few metres high; it wasn't until 1891 that it was moved to

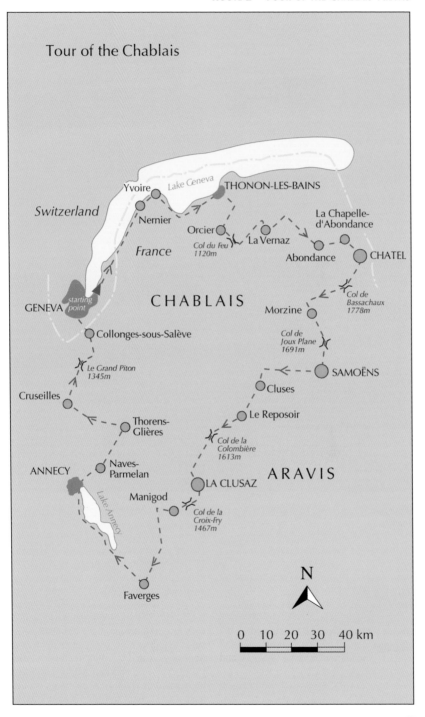

Tour of the Chablais

Lac de Montriond from the Col de Bassachaux

its present position and turned into a decorative fountain.

As Thonon-les-Bains is only 51km from Geneva, it may be possible to do this first leg of the tour the day you arrive, although it would be a shame to be in too much of a rush to make the minor detours necessary to visit the lakeside villages of Nernier and/or Yvoire. Nernier, the smaller and quieter of the two ports, is a charming hamlet of stone-built houses on the edge of the lake. Yvoire's beautifully preserved mediaeval streets and castle have made it one of the most popular tourist attractions on the southern shore of Lake Geneva. The village is renowned for its flowers and gardens and is

regularly awarded the highest distinctions by the Conseil National des Villes et Villages Fleuris (France in Bloom) organisation. A more peaceful side to Yvoire can be seen in the early morning or late evening, when the daytime hustle and bustle gives way to a much more contemplative atmosphere.

From Yvoire, the route turns south to briefly join the main RN5, and then heads back to the lakeshore near Séchex. The road into Thonon is very easy to follow, as it is part of the well signposted Tour de Bas Chablais cycling itinerary. This is just one of 90 one-day cycling tours set up by Haute-Savoie and Savoie and described in a guide that can be downloaded, free of charge, from **www.savoie-mont-blanc.com** (brochures page).

Although Thonon's pedestrianised town centre is quite pleasant, most visitors make a beeline for the lakefront and the fisherman's harbour. Over 50 fishermen still make a living from the lake, supplying fresh fish to local restaurants. The most popular fish is perch, but other local specialities include *fera* (lake white-fish), *lotte* (burbot) and *omble-chevalier* (char). One of the best views of the harbour is from the gardens surrounding the Chateau de Sonnaz (home to the Chablais Museum), from where a steep path leads down to the shore. From the harbour it is a very pleasant stroll to the 15th-century Chateau de Ripaille, a luxurious castle built by Marie of Burgundy, wife of Amadeus VIII, the First Duke of Savoie. When Marie died Amadeus retreated into a more spiritual exis-tence and founded the Order of Saint Maurice. He later became Pope taking the name Felix V.

From Thonon the route heads into the foothills of the Chablais and up to the first pass of the tour, the Col du Feu. The last 6km below the col are quite steep, but the panorama of the lake and the Jura Mountains beyond provides ample reward for your hard work. A short, but steep descent leads to Lullin and then to Vailly, where the route turns right to reach the junction of the Gorges de la Dranse and the Abondance Valley. The village of Abondance, with its traditional wooden houses and magnificent 11th-century abbey, is one of the most beautiful in the Chablais. Its two main attractions, other than the simple pleasure of ambling through such a lovely place, are the abbey cloisters, which house some exceptional 15th-century frescoes, and the Maison du Val d'Abondance, a local her-itage museum, where pride of place is given to the valley's eponymous cheese.

Chatel was chosen as the overnight stop-ping point at the end of this first stage of the tour because of the range of accommodation it offers and because it is conveniently situated at the foot of the Col de Bassachaux. The village is pleasant and has some magnificent alpine chalets, but it does not have the same charm as Abondance. Chatel is first and foremost an out-door-sports resort and one of its more unusual summer attractions is the 'Fantasticable', a giant zip-wire ride that will quicken the pulse of even the most hardened 'adrenaline junky'. During the 3km 'flight', you swoosh across the valley at 100kph, suspended from a cable up to 240 metres above the ground. At 34 Euros, the thrills do not come cheap, but it is an unforgettable experience.

At 1783m, the Col de Bassachaux is one of the highest road passes in the Chablais. Despite being a challenging climb up a very quiet road, it is much less well known to cyclists than the neighbouring Col de Joux Plane: probably because the paved road ends at the summit and to traverse the pass to Morzine you have to cycle along a forest track for about 4km. Even with slick tyres, it is pos-sible to cycle at least 75% of this off-road section and the beauty of the surroundings, especially the view down onto the Lac de Montriond, more than compensates for having to push your bike for a few minutes.

Where the forest track rejoins the paved road you can either turn left to go over the Col de Joux Verte, or turn right, as described here, to go down the Montriond Valley. If the café at the Col de Bassachaux was not open and you are looking for refreshments, there are plenty of cafés and restaurants at Les Lindarets, the first village you pass on the descent to Montriond and Morzine. Les Lindarets is also known as the 'village of the goats' for reasons that will quickly become clear as you near the first houses – be careful, goats never look before crossing the road!

Morzine, like Chatel, is primarily a ski resort and part of the Portes du Soleil ski area, although for cyclists it is better known as a regular host town for both the Tour de France and the Critérium de Dauphiné Libéré. The most famous pass accessible from Morzine is the Col de Joux Plane, but to get to it you first have to go over the Col de Ranfolly: an 8km climb at an average gradient of 8.5%. Fortunately, the last 2.5km from the Ranfolly to the Joux Plane are easy so you can relax and soak up the magnificent views of Mont Blanc before enjoying the sinuous and technical descent to Samoëns.

Samoëns is the only outdoor-sports resort in France to be listed as an historic monument by the National Historic Monuments Commission. The village square, with its ancient lime tree and 12th-century gothic church, is surrounded by delightful streets of wood and stone-built houses. In 1906, Marie-Louise Cognacq-Jaÿ created a botanical garden amongst the streams and waterfalls that tumble down the slopes on the northern edge of the village. These gardens, which now contain more than 8000 species of plant from all over the world, are undoubtedly the jewel in Samoëns' crown.

Day 4 starts peacefully beside the River Giffre, but after around 11km the route is forced to join the busy road that goes over the Col de Chatillon and down to Cluses. Cluses is the biggest town in the Arve Valley, Haute-Savoie's industrial heartland and a major centre for precision engineering. Fortunately, the valley is soon left behind as the road climbs into the Aravis Mountains over the Col de la Colombière. The first part of the ascent, to Le Reposoir, is a mere warm-up for the serious work ahead: over the last 8km to the summit the average gradient is almost 9%! The descent to Le Grand Bornand is one of the most enjoyable in the area: a 'mere' 12km, but the road surface is excellent and there are few tight bends. From here, another 5km, most of which is gently uphill, takes you through St Jean-de-Sixt to La Clusaz.

La Clusaz, surrounded by lush pastures and encircled by precipitous limestone peaks, lies at the heart of the Aravis Mountains. As well as being the perfect gradient for skiing in winter, the surrounding slopes provide excellent grazing land in summer and the valley produces several different cheeses. The most famous is Reblochon, an AOC cheese that is one of the main ingredients of tartiflette, the traditional Savoie dish par excellence. Other cheeses, such as Tomme Blanche, Chevrotin and Persillée des Aravis, are produced in smaller quantities and are worth looking out for.

When travelling south from La Clusaz, most cyclists head for the famous Col des Aravis (see Route 9), but the route described here goes over the less well known Col de la Croix-Fry (pronounced 'croix-free') in order to avoid the main road between Flumet and Ugine. It cannot be said that the Croix-Fry is a difficult pass to cycle over, but the road is steep in places, especially at the beginning. The last part of the climb is through dense forest and it is not until you get over the pass that the view opens out to reveal the picturesque Fier Valley and the imposing mass of the Tournette. After a winding descent through a traditional landscape of pastures, chalets and craggy peaks, the route turns left towards the Col du Marais. During

*Le Reposoir and the Aravis Mountains*

this second climb of the day, the gradient is never too severe and you are soon on your way down to St Ferréol and the Annecy Basin. If you are looking for a stiffer challenge, turn right at Vesonne and cycle up to the Col de la Forclaz above the eastern shore of Lake Annecy. The climb is hard, averaging 9% for 8km, but the view of the lake from the top is stunning.

Annecy is not only one of the most beautiful cities in the Alps, it is also one of the oldest: recent archaeological work has uncovered the remains of a village that dates back to at least 3100BC. The site was also occupied from Roman times through the Dark Ages, although very few buildings from that period have survived. The Annecy we know today first came to prominence in the 12th century when it became the seat of the Counts of Geneva, who had been forced out of their home city in a dispute with local bishops. Ironically, four centuries later, the Bishop of Geneva himself fled to Annecy to escape the turmoil of the Protestant Reformation. By this time, the Dukes of Savoie had succeeded the Counts of Geneva as lords of Annecy, and it was Amadeus VIII who rebuilt the city after it had been devastated by a series of fires in the middle of the 15th century. Of all the historic buildings to visit in Annecy, pride of place must go to the castle, perched on a low hill overlooking the old town. Even if you don't have the time or inclination to visit any of the city's many monuments, Annecy's old town is a fabulous place to explore.

The final leg of the tour follows the northwest edge of the Aravis to Thorens-Glières, and then heads west to Cruseilles and the foot of Mont Salève. The road to the top of the Salève climbs steadily through dense forest, which blocks the view but provides welcome shade on hot days. Near the first of the mountain's two summits the forest thins revealing the surrounding countryside, but the best views are from the second summit, 2.5km north of La Croisette. As the Salève stands apart from the neighbouring massifs, isolated

between the Jura and the Aravis, the panorama from the top is truly exceptional. As usual, the mighty summit of Mont Blanc draws the eye, but even the highest summit in Europe cannot eclipse the spectacular view of Lake Annecy and the Tournette.

After a final café-break at La Croisette, it is time to head back to the big city bustle of Geneva. The first part of the descent is exceptionally steep, with gradients of up to 15%, so check your brakes before setting off. All too soon you are back at the Franco–Swiss border and at the end of this great circuit.

## GETTING THERE

### By car
Geneva is 760km from Calais.

### By plane
**Via Geneva:** the tour starts directly from Geneva airport.

## WHEN TO GO

The best months to do this tour are May and June, or September and early October.

The roads over the Col de Bassachaux, Col de Joux Plane and Col de la Colombière are closed from late November to early May (although at the beginning of May it is usually possible to get through on a bike even if the roads are officially still closed). Being so close to Geneva, Annecy and Mont Blanc, the Chablais and Aravis can be extremely busy during the summer holidays.

## MAPS

**Michelin:** Local – Sheet 328, Ain, Haute-Savoie

**Michelin:** Regional – Sheet 244, Rhône-Alpes.

**IGN:** Top 100 – Sheet 45: Annecy, Lausanne; Sheet 53: Grenoble, Mont Blanc is also needed for the area to the south of Lake Annecy (Day 6)

Switzerland has a well-deserved reputation for being a very expensive country and Geneva is no exception: there cannot be many cities in the world with more four- and five-star hotels than one- and two-star establishments. If you are travelling on a tight budget, I would recommend Geneva City Hostel (listed as a one-star hotel, tel. (022) 901 1500). It is only a few minutes from the central railway station and offers accommodation for as little as 18 Euros per night. However limited your resources, the magnificent view of Mont Blanc, the lake and the Jura from the top of the towers of St Peter's Cathedral is well worth the 2 Euro entrance fee. Of course, many of the city's landmarks, such as the floral clock and the Reformation Wall, can be visited for free.

| Distance | Location | Directions |
|---|---|---|
| 0.0 | Geneva airport | For directions from airport to Franco–Swiss border see Appendix 1 |
| 22.5 | Hermance: Franco–Swiss border | Go straight on – D25 |
| 24.7 | Chens-sur-Léman: D25/D20 | Turn L – D25 (Thonon). Follow D25 through Messery, Yvoire and Excenevex to Sciez |
| 39.5 | Sciez: D25/N5 | Turn L – N5 (Thonon) |
| 41.0 | N5/D325 | Turn L – D325/Route du Port (Port de Sciez-Plage) |
| 41.6 | Roundabout | Turn R (Le Chatelet) |
| 43.2 | Roundabout | Turn R (Thonon) |
| 43.6 | Jtn | Turn R – D35/Route du Port de Sciez |
| 43.9 | Séchex: Jtn | Turn L – Rue Centrale/D35 |
| 45.8 | Anthy-sur-Léman | Turn L in centre of village [Tour du Bas Chablais]. Follow these blue cycling signs to Thonon |
| 50.5 | Thonon: roundabout | Go straight on (Office de Tourisme) |
| 50.7 | Jtn | Turn R onto Rue Vallon (Centre Ville–Rue Pietonnée). Follow road around to L and turn immediately R into square with large fountain. Go across square and then straight on along Rue St Sebastien |
| 51.0 | Jtn | Turn R onto Place du Marché |
| 51.1 | Thonon TO | TO is on the L |

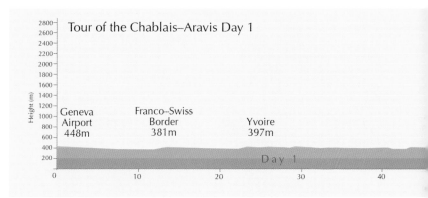

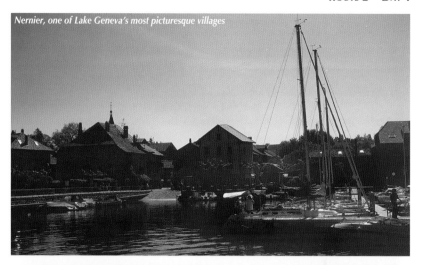
*Nernier, one of Lake Geneva's most picturesque villages*

## FACILITIES AND SERVICES

| Location | Distance (km) | Water | Shops | Café | Campsite | B&B | Hotel | Bank | Bike Shop |
|---|---|---|---|---|---|---|---|---|---|
| Geneva | 0.0 | — | x | x | x | x | x | x | x |
| Vésenaz | 13.7 | — | x | x | — | — | x | x | x |
| Hermance | 21.9 | — | x | x | — | — | x | — | — |
| Chens-sur-Léman | 25.7 | x | x | x | x | — | x | — | — |
| Yvoire | 32.2 | x | x | x | x | — | x | — | — |
| Excenevex | 35.5 | — | x | x | x | x | x | — | — |
| Sciez (1) | 39.2 | — | x | x | x | x | x | x | (2) |
| Séchex | 43.6 | x | — | x | x | — | — | — | — |
| Thonon-les-Bains | 50.8 | x | x | x | x | — | x | x | x |

(1) There are campsites, hotels and restaurants in several places between Sciez and Thonon
(2) The bike shop is actually in Bonnatrait, 1km from Sciez

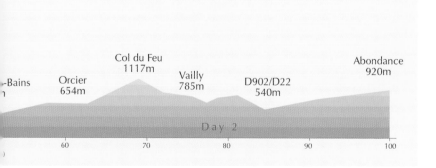

It was whilst cycling up the Abondance Valley that I was first introduced to the world of Brévets. A 'Brévet' is a cycling challenge in which the objective is to cycle a set course within a fixed time. In theory, it is not a race and, as long as you arrive within the deadline, your exact time is unimportant. This approach ensures that the day is almost as much a social event as a sporting occasion and many of the participants are happy to chat to other cyclists to take their mind off how far their aching legs still have to go. In this way, I was able to glean a great deal of information about the most beautiful and quietest roads in the area. I also found out that, as friendly as the organisation is, the refreshment stands at strategic points along the route are only for registered participants!

| Distance | Location | Directions |
|---|---|---|
| 0.0 | Thonon TO | Come out of the TO and turn R. After about 50 metres turn L onto Rue des Granges |
| 0.1 | Roundabout | Go straight on (Chatel) and go over the level crossing |
| 0.9 | Roundabout: D902/D26 | Take first exit – D26 (Armoy) 5.6km at 3.5% |
| 6.9 | Armoy: D26/D35 | Turn R – D35 (Orcier) |
| 11.9 | Orcier D35/D36 | Turn L – D36 (Col du Feu) 6.2km at 7.5% |
| 13.3 | D36/D36A | Turn R – D36A (Col du Feu) |
| 14.1 | D36A/D36 | Go straight on – D36 (Lullin) |
| 18.1 | Col du Feu | Go straight on – D36 (Lullin) |
| 21.1 | Lullin: D36/D22 | Turn L – D22 (Vailly) |
| 23.9 | Sous la Côte: D22/D26 | Turn L – D26 (Vailly) |
| 24.7 | Vailly: D26/D22 | Turn R – D22 (Chatel). Short descent, then 1.4km at 7% |
| 30.3 | La Vernaz: D22/D22A | Turn L – D22A (Thonon) |
| 33.5 | D22A/D902 | Turn L – D902 (Thonon) |
| 33.9 | Roundabout: D902/D22 | Turn R – D22 (Chatel). Follow D22 to Chatel |
| 61.6 | Chatel TO* | TO is on the L |

* If you are camping, about 2km after La Chapelle d'Abondance turn R onto the D230. After 4.5km, turn L onto D228, and immediately L again just after the bridge. The campsite is about 300 metres on the L.

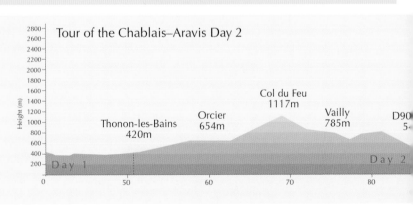

Tour of the Chablais–Aravis Day 2

54

*La Vailly: looking towards the Dent d'Oche*

## FACILITIES AND SERVICES

| Location | Distance (km) | Water | Shops | Café | Campsite | B&B | Hotel | Bank | Bike Shop |
|---|---|---|---|---|---|---|---|---|---|
| Thonon-les-Bains | 0.0 | x | x | x | x | — | x | x | x |
| Armoy | 6.9 | — | x | x | — | — | x | — | — |
| Orcier | 11.9 | x | — | x | — | — | — | — | — |
| Col du Feu | 18.1 | — | — | x | — | — | — | — | — |
| Lullin | 21.1 | x | x | x | — | — | x | — | — |
| Vailly | 24.7 | x | — | x | — | x | — | — | — |
| Abondance | 49.9 | x | x | x | x | x | x | x | — |
| Chatel | 61.6 | x | x | x | x | x | x | x | x |

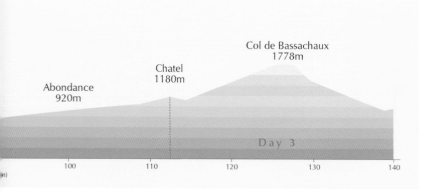

## Day 3 – Chatel to Samoëns

Although a recent addition to the Tour de France (first included in 1978), the Col de Joux-Plane has already featured in the race ten times. It is a pass that has frequently smiled on French riders, with six out of the ten winners of this stage being French, the most recent of whom was Richard Virenque in 2000. Other prestigious winners of Joux-Plane stages include Lance Armstrong in the 2002 Critérium du Dauphiné Libéré.

| Distance | Location | Directions |
|---|---|---|
| 0.0 | Chatel TO | Come out of TO and turn R – D228 (Col de Bassachaux)* 9km at 7% |
| 12.7 | Col de Bassachaux | From end of tarmac, follow the track on the L, slightly uphill at first [Les Lindarets] – red and white waymarkers |
| 14.5 | Chairlift | Go under chairlift [Lac Vert] |
| 14.9 | Jtn | Turn R and follow mountain bike signs [Les Gets] (short sections of the path are not suitable for road bikes). |
| 15.1 | Jtn | Keep following the wide track downhill |
| 17.1 | Jtn with paved road | Turn R and follow D228 to Montriond |
| 26.1 | Montriond: roundabout | Turn L (Morzine) |
| 26.3 | D228/D229 | Turn L – D229 (Morzine) |
| 28.6 | Morzine: jtn | Go straight on (Office de Tourisme) |
| 28.7 | 'Semi' roundabout | Go straight on (Avoriaz) |
| 29.1 | Roundabout | Turn R (Cluses) |
| 29.4 | Roundabout | Turn R (Col de Joux Plane) |
| 29.5 | Jtn | Turn R – D354 (Col de Joux Plane) 8.1km at 8.5% |
| 37.6 | Col de Ranfolly | Go straight on |
| 40.2 | Col de Joux Plane | Go straight on |
| 47.0 | Jtn | Turn R (Poids Lourds et Bus) |
| 52.5 | Samoëns | Turn R |
| 52.6 | Jtn | Turn L (Centre Ville) |
| 52.7 | Roundabout | Turn L (Toutes Directions) |
| 52.8 | Samoëns TO | TO is on the L |

* If you do not want to do any off-road cycling, go back through Abondance and over the Col du Corbier to follow the D902 back to Montriond

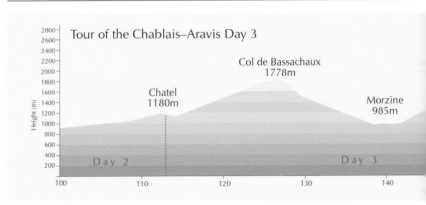

Tour of the Chablais–Aravis Day 3

*Les Lindarets*

## FACILITIES AND SERVICES

| Location | Distance (km) | Water | Shops | Café | Campsite | B&B | Hotel | Bank | Bike Shop |
|---|---|---|---|---|---|---|---|---|---|
| Chatel | 0.0 | x | x | x | x | x | x | x | x |
| Les Lindarets | 17.5 | x | — | x | — | — | — | — | — |
| Montriond | 26.1 | x | x | x | x | — | x | — | — |
| Morzine | 28.6 | x | x | x | — | x | x | x | x |
| Col de Joux Plane | 40.2 | — | x | — | — | — | — | — | — |
| Samoëns | 52.8 | x | x | x | x | x | x | x | (1) |

(1) Nearest bike shop: Cluses, approx 18km south-west of Samoëns

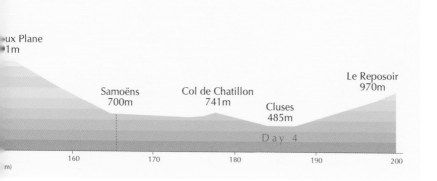

If you have some energy to spare when you get to Samoëns, I strongly recommend the 25km round-trip to visit the Cirque du Fer à Cheval. The cycling is easy and the destination is one of the most spectacular corners of the Alps. Take a bike lock with you so you can stroll up the valley from the road head to get the best views of the spectacular cliffs, rock towers and waterfalls that make the cirque 'Un Grand Site de France'. For those who find even a small resort such as Samoëns too busy, there is a campsite at the entrance to the cirque and *gites d'étape* and hotels in the village of Sixt-Fer-à-Cheval. Go to **www.sixtferacheval.com** for details.

| Distance | Location | Directions |
|---|---|---|
| 0.0 | Samoëns TO | Come out of the TO and turn L |
| 0.1 | Roundabout | Turn R – D4 (Cluses) |
| 0.8 | Roundabout | Turn R – D4 and follow (Cluses) through Morillon |
| 10.9 | D4/D902 | Turn L – D902 (Cluses) 1.5km at 5% |
| 12.4 | Col du Chatillon | Go straight on |
| 17.8 | Cluses: roundabout | Go straight on (Centre Ville) |
| 18.2 | Traffic lights | Turn L (Centre Ville) and go through Cluses town centre |
| 19.3 | Roundabout | Turn R – N205 (Bonneville) |
| 20.0 | Roundabout | Turn L (Col de la Colombière) |
| 21.1 | Roundabout | Turn L – D4 (Col de la Colombière) 17.7km at 6.5% |
| 38.8 | Col de la Colombière | Go straight on |
| 50.4 | Jtn | Turn R (Annecy) |
| 50.9 | Le Grand Bornand: roundabout | Turn R (Annecy) and follow D4/D12 to St Jean de Sixt |
| 53.4 | St Jean de Sixt*: roundabout: D12/D909 | Turn L – D909 (La Clusaz) |
| 56.1 | La Clusaz: roundabout | Turn L and then take the first R (Centre village) |
| 56.4 | La Clusaz TO | TO is on the R |

\* If you are camping, you may want to spend the night at the campsite in Saint Jean de Sixt; the campsite at La Clusaz is 2km east of the village and 150 metres higher!

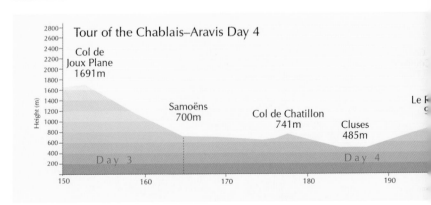

Tour of the Chablais–Aravis Day 4

Col de la Colombière

## FACILITIES AND SERVICES

| Location | Distance (km) | Water | Shops | Café | Campsite | B&B | Hotel | Bank | Bike Shop |
|---|---|---|---|---|---|---|---|---|---|
| Samoëns | 0.0 | x | x | x | x | x | x | x | (1) |
| Morillon | 4.5 | x | x | x | x | x | x | — | — |
| Cluses | 17.8 | — | x | x | x | — | x | x | x |
| Le Reposoir | 31.1 | x | x | x | x | — | — | — | — |
| Le Chinaillon | 43.2 | — | x | x | — | — | x | — | — |
| Col de la Colombière | 38.8 | — | — | x | — | — | — | — | — |
| Le Grand Bornand | 50.9 | x | x | x | x | x | x | x | x |
| St Jean de Sixt | 53.4 | x | x | x | x | — | x | — | x |
| La Clusaz | 56.4 | x | x | x | x | x | x | x | x |

(1) Nearest bike shop: Cluses, approx 18km south-west of Samoëns

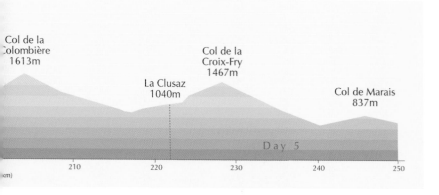

Col de la Colombière 1613m

Col de la Croix-Fry 1467m

La Clusaz 1040m

Col de Marais 837m

Day 5

210    220    230    240    250

(km)

59

# Day 5 – La Clusaz to Annecy

If you would like to have a rest day in La Clusaz or Annecy, why not get a bird's-eye view of the Alps? The most luxurious way to fly is in a hot-air balloon, but this is also a very expensive option, with flights costing 250 Euros per person. For details of flights from Le Grand-Bornand go to **www.bapteme-montgolfiere.com**. A tandem flight in a paraglider is more reasonably priced at 80 to 120 Euros, but you will only be in the air for between 20 minutes and 1 hour. Several companies offer introductory flights at similar rates, for example **www.lespassagersduvent.com** and **www.aeroslide.com**. Pleasure flights in light aircraft provide the best value for money (around 200 Euros for a 1hr flight for three people), but the nearest airport to propose such excursions is Chambéry.

| Distance | Location | Directions |
|---|---|---|
| 0.0 | La Clusaz TO | Come out of TO and turn R to go past police station |
| 0.1 | Jtn | Turn R onto Route de l'Etale and go past cinema |
| 1.7 | Jtn | Bear L onto Route de Sence (just after tiny chapel on R) |
| 2.6 | Jtn | Turn R – D16 (no sign) |
| 6.6 | Col de la Croix-Fry | Go straight on and follow D16 through Manigod to D12 |
| 18.5 | D16/D12 | Turn L – D12 (Faverges) |
| 24.0 | Col du Marais | Go straight on |
| 34.3 | St Ferréol: roundabout | Turn R – D12 (Faverges) |
| 36.0 | Roundabout | Turn R (Viuz)* |
| 36.7 | Roundabout | Turn R [Tour de la Tournette] |
| 37.0 | Jtn | Go straight on (Rocher d'escalade). Continue through Vesonne to Jtn with D42 |
| 39.6 | Jtn | Turn L – D42 (no sign) |
| 40.0 | D42/N508 | Go straight across N508 to join Annecy cycleway |
| 58.5 | End of cycleway | Turn R – N508 |
| 60.7 | Roundabout | Go straight on (Centre Ville) |
| 61.3 | Annecy *hôtel de ville* | *Hôtel de ville* is on the R |

* The Annecy cycleway has now been extended through Faverges to Ugine, although the very quiet road through Vesonne remains the more picturesque option. If you would prefer to follow the cycleway, head towards the centre of Faverges and turn right when you come to the cycleway.

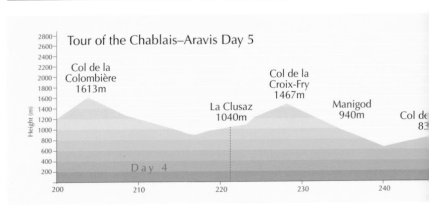

*La Tournette from below the Col de la Croix-Fry*

## FACILITIES AND SERVICES

| Location | Distance (km) | Water | Shops | Café | Campsite | B&B | Hotel | Bank | Bike Shop |
|---|---|---|---|---|---|---|---|---|---|
| La Clusaz | 0.0 | x | x | x | x | x | x | x | x |
| Col de la Croix-Fry | 6.6 | — | — | x | — | — | — | — | — |
| Manigod | 13.8 | x | x | x | — | — | x | — | — |
| Serraval | 26.7 | x | x | x | x | — | — | — | — |
| St Férreol | 34.3 | — | x | x | x | — | x | — | — |
| Faverges (1) | 36.7 | x | x | x | — | x | x | x | x |
| Doussard | 42.3 | — | x | — | x | x | x | x | — |
| Annecy | 61.3 | x | x | x | x | x | x | x | x |

(1) The route goes around the edge of Faverges; all the facilities are in the town centre

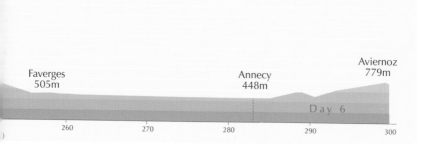

Faverges
505m

Annecy
448m

Day 6

Aviernoz
779m

260     270     280     290     300

Extra day: The Bauges Mountains are criss-crossed by a number of quiet roads that are perfect for cycling. The easiest way to visit this area is to traverse from Annecy to Chambéry via the Col de Leschaux, Lescheraines and the Col de Plainpalais. There are trains back to Annecy every 30 to 60 minutes, depending on the time of day. If you are looking for a more challenging day out, turn right just after the Col de Plainpalais, go over Mont Revard (magnificent views) and head back to Annecy via Trévignin, Cusy and Gruffy.

| Distance | Location | Directions |
|---|---|---|
| 0.0 | Annecy *hôtel de ville* | Come out of the *hôtel de ville* and turn R |
| 0.4 | Jtn: Ave D'Albiny/Rue Louis Revon | Turn L onto Rue Louis Revon (Hôtel du Département) – start of intermittent cycle lane |
| 0.6 | Jtn | Turn R onto Ave de Parmelan. Follow (Annecy-le-Vieux) |
| 1.7 | Annecy-le-Vieux | Go straight on along Ave des Carrés. Continue straight on to pick up and follow (Thônes – Les Aravis) |
| 2.7 | Start of cycleway | Follow cycleway uphill – more or less parallel to road |
| 5.1 | Roundabout | Leave the cycleway and turn L at the roundabout (Thônes – Les Aravis) |
| 5.8 | Roundabout | Turn L onto D5 (Naves Parmelan). Follow D5 to Thorens-Glières |
| 20.8 | Thorens-Glières: D5/D2 | Go straight on – D2 |
| 25.8 | Groisy-Le Plot | Go under N203 and through Le Plot – D2D |
| 26.1 | D2D/D2 | Turn R – D2 (Groisy) |
| 28.7 | Groisy: D2/D23 | Turn R – D23 – 2nd of two Jtns (Cruseilles) |
| 37.4 | Cruseilles: T-Jtn | Turn R and then immediately L onto Rue de l'Arthaz |
| 37.9 | Crossroads | Go straight on – D41A (Le Salève) |
| 50.2 | High point | Go straight on |
| 54.4 | La Croisette: D41A/D45 | Turn L – D45 |
| 59.0 | Le Coin: D45/D145 | Turn R – D145 and follow this road to Collonges-sous-Salève |
| 61.7 | Collonges | Turn L – one-way – then turn R onto Rue Lamartine |
| 61.9 | T-Jtn | Turn R and go over motorway and railway |
| 62.3 | Traffic lights | Go straight on to Franco–Swiss border |
| 62.5 | Franco-Swiss border | For directions to airport, see Appendix 1 |
| 74.9 | Geneva airport | |

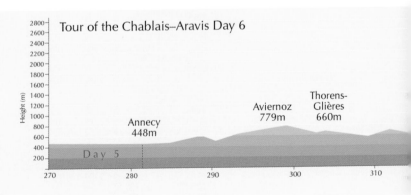

*Admiring Lake Annecy from one of the many pontoons along the edge of the lake*

## FACILITIES AND SERVICES

| Location | Distance (km) | Water | Shops | Café | Campsite | B&B | Hotel | Bank | Bike Shop |
|---|---|---|---|---|---|---|---|---|---|
| Annecy | 0.0 | x | x | x | x | x | x | x | x |
| Naves Parmelan | 10.0 | x | — | x | x | x | x | — | — |
| Thorens-Glières | 20.8 | x | x | x | x | — | x | x | — |
| Groisy | 28.7 | — | x | x | — | — | — | x | — |
| Cruseilles | 37.4 | x | x | x | x | — | x | x | x |
| Le Salève (La Croisette) | 54.4 | — | — | x | — | — | — | — | — |
| Collonges-sous-Salève | 61.7 | x | x | x | x | — | — | x | — |
| Geneva | 75.9 | — | x | x | x | x | x | x | x |

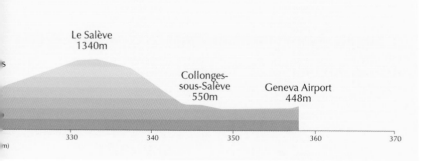

Le Salève
1340m

Collonges-
sous-Salève
550m

Geneva Airport
448m

330    340    350    360    370

# ACCOMMODATION

## Geneva

**Campsites**

Camping d'Hermance, in Hermance, 14km from Geneva on the lakeside road to Thonon (April to end Sept), Tel. (022) 751 14 83

Bois de Bay, in Satigny, 4km west of Geneva airport (all year), Tel. (022) 341 05 05

Val de l'Allondon, in Satigny, 4km west of Geneva airport (early April to end Oct), Tel. (022) 753 15 15

**Bed & Breakfast**

Geneva youth hostel, Tel. (022) 732 62 60

There are also several bed & breakfasts in and around Geneva. Contact TO for details.

**Hotels**

There are more than 100 hotels in Geneva. Contact TO for details.

## Thonon-les-Bains

**Campsites**

Le Lac Noir, 3km south of Thonon, on the D903 (June to Sept), Tel. 04 50 71 12 46

Le Morcy, 3km west of Thonon, at Morcy (Easter to mid-Sept), Tel. 06 82 27 51 50

Saint Disdille, 3km north of Thonon, near Port Ripaille (early April to end Sept), Tel. 04 50 71 14 11

Le Disdillou, 3km north of Thonon, near Port Ripaille (dates not known), Tel. 04 50 26 13 59

**Bed & Breakfast**

La Clématite, Tel. 04 50 71 85 95

Centre International de Séjour (hostel, sleeps 200), Tel. 04 50 71 77 80

**Hotels**

There are 13 hotels in Thonon-les-Bains. Contact TO for details.

## Chatel

**Campsites**

L'Oustalet (mid-June to end August), Tel. 04 50 73 21 97

**Bed & Breakfast**

Le P'tit Cornillon, Tel. 04 50 81 35 49

Chalet l'Etringa, Tel. 04 50 81 31 48

La Couqueille, Tel. 04 50 73 31 89

La Savoyarde, Tel. 04 50 73 23 17

Chalet des Arbres, Tel. 04 50 73 86 54

**Hotels**

There are more than 25 hotels in Chatel. Contact TO for details.

## Samoêns

**Campsites**

Le Giffre (all year), Tel. 04 50 34 41 92

**Bed & Breakfast**

There are several bed & breakfasts and *gites d'étapes* in and around Samoens. Contact TO for details.

**Hotels**

There are 14 hotels in Samoêns. Contact TO for details.

## La Clusaz

### Campsites

Domaine du Fernuy (early June to early Sept), Tel. 04 50 02 44 75

At St Jean-de-Sixt: Le Cret (early June to mid-Sept), Tel. 04 50 02 38 89

### Bed & Breakfast

Youth hostel, Tel. 04 50 02 41 73

La Chuitta, Tel. 04 50 02 43 34

Les Groseilliers, Tel. 04 50 02 63 29

La Sence, Tel. 04 50 02 42 81

La Ferme du Var, Tel. 04 50 02 26 56

La Trace, Tel. 04 50 02 46 76

### Hotels

There are more than 20 hotels in La Clusaz. Contact TO for details.

## Annecy

### Campsites

Le Belvedere (end March to mid-Oct), Tel. 04 50 45 48 30

The Belvedere is the only campsite in Annecy, but there are others along the lakeshore. Contact TO for details.

### Bed & Breakfast

Youth hostel, Tel. 04 50 45 33 19

Mr Michel, Tel. 04 50 45 72 28

### Hotels

There are more than 40 hotels in Annecy. Contact TO for details.

## TOURIST INFORMATION

### Regional Information

| | Telephone | Website |
|---|---|---|
| Haute-Savoie | 04 50 51 32 31 | www.savoie-mont-blanc.com |

### Tourist Information Offices

| Location | Telephone | Website |
|---|---|---|
| Geneva | 022 909 70 00 | www.geneve-tourisme.ch |
| Yvoire | 04 50 72 80 21 | http://yvoire.free.fr/ |
| Thonon-les-Bains | 04 50 71 55 55 | www.thononlesbains.com |
| Abondance/Chatel | 04 50 73 02 90 | www.valdabondance.com |
| Chatel | 04 50 73 22 44 | www.chatel.com |
| Morzine | 04 50 74 72 72 | www.morzine.com |
| Samoëns | 04 50 34 40 28 | www.samoens.com |
| Cluses | 04 50 98 31 79 | www.cluses.fr |
| Le Grand Bornand | 04 50 02 78 00 | www.legrandbornand.com |
| Saint Jean-de-Sixt | 04 50 02 70 14 | www.saintjeandesixt.com |
| La Clusaz | 04 50 32 65 00 | www.laclusaz.fr |
| Manigod | 04 50 44 92 44 | www.manigod.com |
| Faverges | 04 50 44 60 24 | www.pays-de-faverges.com |
| Annecy | 04 50 45 00 33 | www.lac-annecy.com |
| Thorens-Glières | 04 50 22 40 31 | www.paysdefilliere.com/office-de-tourisme |
| Cruseilles | 04 50 44 81 69 | www.cruseilles.fr |

# ROUTE THREE

# TOUR OF MONT BLANC

| Day | Route | Distance | Height Gain |
|---|---|---|---|
| 1 | Martigny to Chamonix | 44.0km | 1434m |
| 2 | Chamonix to Beaufort | 81.6km | 1526m |
| 3 | Beaufort to Bourg St Maurice | 45.7km | 1407m |
| 4 | Bourg St Maurice to Aosta | 85.7km | 1375m |
| 5 | Aosta to Martigny | 83.7km | 1889m |
| | **Totals** | **340.7km** | **7631m** |

As the highest mountain in western Europe, Mont Blanc attracts millions of visitors every year. Most come to just look at the Roof of Europe, a small minority actually climb to the top and an increasing number choose to do a circuit round the entire massif, either under their own steam (on foot or by bike) or by car, coach or motorbike. The classic circuit by road, via Martigny, Chamonix and Aosta, goes over some of the most famous passes in the Alps including the Grand St Bernard, the highest point on the circuit. Obviously, the roads around such a famous tourist honey-pot are not going to be deserted, especially during the holiday season. Where possible, the itinerary avoids the major tourist routes, but this is still a tour that is best enjoyed outside the main mid-July to mid-August holiday period.

The most obvious attraction of this area is the scenery, which is quite simply breathtaking, especially in the spring and the autumn, when the light is often at its sharpest. For a large part of the circuit it is Mont Blanc itself that dominates the horizon, a massive but shapely lump of rock and ice that dwarfs even the loftiest of its neighbours. On cloudless days, when deep blue skies hover over the pristine white of the summit snowfields and the vivid greens of the surrounding pastures, Mont Blanc is an invitation to climb towards the heavens. But seen in the lowering orange-grey light of an approaching storm, the mountain exudes a terrible menace that would discourage all but the (fool-) hardiest of climbers; local folklore long believed that only

the damned were drawn towards the summit!

The tour is described starting from Martigny, as this is the easiest place to get to by public transport. (If you are driving to France, Sallanches would be a more convenient place to start). By travelling in a clockwise direction, the height of the passes that you go over gradually increases from day to day, and the tour finishes with a superbly enjoyable descent from the Grand St Bernard Pass.

Martigny may not be the most architecturally distinguished town in Switzerland, but it does boast an extremely impressive array of museums. Art lovers and historians could easily spend several days browsing through all the treasures the town has to offer. The most outstanding museum, for both the eclectic range of subjects that it covers (Roman history, fine art, classic cars) and the quality of its permanent and temporary exhibitions, is the Pierre Gianadda Foundation. Martigny is surrounded by vineyards, many of which cultivate Chasselas grapes, which are thought by many to be the first grape variety cultivated by man. The local wine is called Fendant, as, when ripe, the grapes split if pressed between finger and thumb (*fendre*: to split). Fendant is usually drunk as an aperitif or to accompany fish or cheese dishes, especially fondue.

Although the first stage of the tour is only 44km, it is worth making an early start as the lower slopes of the Col de la Forclaz offer no shade whatsoever: in the middle of summer the road can feel like a furnace. In marked contrast, the upper part of the road runs

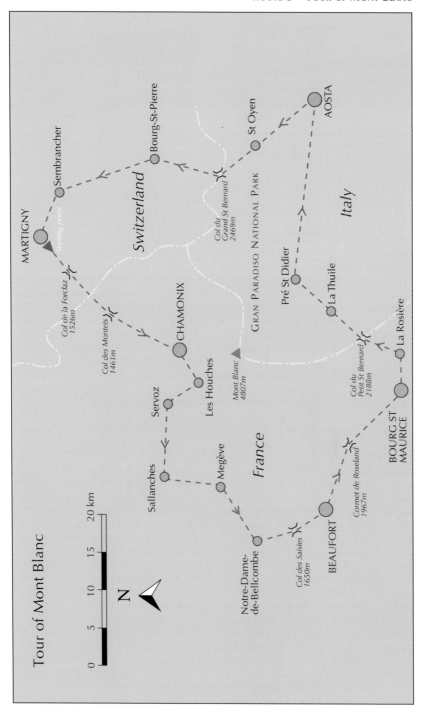

Tour of Mont Blanc

through dense forest, that cuts out the sun and blocks any view. Once over the pass, this corridor of trees opens out to reveal the spectacularly chaotic Glacier du Trient, a foretaste of the scenic delights to come. An all-too-brief descent through the steep-sided Trient Valley takes you to the Franco–Swiss border at Le Châtelard, an excellent place to stock up on chocolate!

Being the main route from Martigny to Chamonix, the road over the Forclaz Pass can be very busy, especially during the summer holidays. The only way to avoid the Forclaz is to go through the Trient Gorge. Unfortunately, a 5km section of this route is on an unpaved, but well maintained, forest track.

As long as your legs are not too tired after the Col de la Forclaz, the climb up to the Col des Montets should not feel too difficult and there is always the added incentive of knowing that from the pass it is downhill all the way to Chamonix and the end of this first stage. Needless to say, the scenery is magnificent: few valleys can boast such a spectacular mix of snowy domes, tortured glaciers and towering rock spires. Chamonix has used its position at the foot of Europe's highest mountain to transform itself from a tiny village into the undisputed mountaineering capital of the world. However, Mont Blanc does not 'belong' to Chamonix: the summit actually lies within the boundaries of St Gervais, and it is from here that most climbers start their ascent. Despite the cost (37 Euros in 2007) and the queues, every visitor to Chamonix should take the cable car to the top of the Aiguille du Midi. Rising 2800 metres above the town centre, the cable car itself is an engineering marvel and the panorama from the top is unbeatable.

Day 2 of the tour starts quite gently, following minor roads through Les Houches, from where the views of the Chamonix Aiguilles are arguably even better than those from Chamonix itself, to Sallanches, a bustling market town on the banks of the Arve. On leaving Sallanches, the tempo changes dramatically as the road climbs steeply (gradients of up to 15%) out of the valley. This road takes you through the village of Combloux, and on to the very chic and exclusive resort of Megève. At the beginning of 2005, Megève

became the first ski resort in the *département* of Haute-Savoie to be connected to a resort in Savoie. This fact is only particularly noteworthy when you consider that these neighbouring *départements* created links with Switzerland (Portes du Soleil) and Italy (La Rosière/La Thuile) many years ago, but had never before managed to overcome the intense rivalry between themselves.

From Megève, a 10km descent along the N212 leads to the foot of the Col des Saisies. This is the longest climb of the day, but the ascent is divided into two sections by a short descent, with the first section being longer and steeper than the second. For once, Mont Blanc cannot be seen, being hidden behind the Aiguille Croche, however the view of the Aravis Range to the north provides ample compensation. As every cycle ride in the mountains should, the day ends with a long and enjoyable descent to Beaufort, a truly authentic and unspoilt mountain village. Beaufort has given its name to the 'Prince of Gruyere Cheeses', the best variety of which is Beaufort d'alpage. Cheese lovers are sure to enjoy a visit to the local cooperative dairy, although they won't be able to taste Beaufort d'alpage here, as this form of the cheese can only be made in the alpine pastures. Beaufort also boasts a bakery that sells the best homemade ice cream you will find this side of Italy.

The third stage of the tour heads south to the village resort of Arèches, an excellent example of how to reap the benefits of tourism without destroying the landscape. From Arèches, the road rises very steeply, through picture-postcard alpine pastures and past traditional wooden chalets to the Col du Pré, which, rather unusually, is neither the geographical col nor the highest point of the road. During the descent from the pass, Mont Blanc once again comes into view, but it tends to be the extremely picturesque Roselend Reservoir that draws the eye. The road goes over the dam and around the northern end of the reservoir before once again striking uphill to the Cormet de Roselend. This area has one of the highest snowfalls in the French Alps, and it is not unusual to see two-metre-high walls of snow beside the road in the middle of May. As this stage is quite short, during the descent I

*The pleasant pedestrianised streets of Aosta*

recommend making a short detour to Les Chapieux, an excellent place to have lunch whilst admiring the majestic Aiguille des Glaciers, which reigns over the northern end of the valley.

Day 3 ends at the busy little town of Bourg St Maurice. Being the gateway to several of the biggest ski resorts in Europe (such as Tignes, Val d'Isère, Les Arcs), Bourg St Maurice's economy is very much dependent on tourism. However, it is not really a resort itself and has few tourist attractions of its own. The little minerals museum is quite interesting and, if you are still hungry for cheese, the town's co-operative dairy is open to visitors.

The Col du Petit St Bernard, which has been a point of passage between the Tarentaise and Aosta Valleys for at least three millennia, provides the objective for day four. Despite following a *route nationale*, traffic levels are rarely a problem as long as you are not on the road on the 20th August. This is Saint Bernard's Day, the occasion for a huge gathering at the summit of the pass, during which pedestrian and vehicle traffic can be so dense that cycling becomes impossible! In around 25BC, the Romans built a temple and a column

to the glory of Jupiter, naming the pass Columna Jovis. After the fall of the Roman Empire, cutthroats and brigands overran the area, curtailing the lucrative trans-alpine trade in wine and minerals. This sorry state of affairs was attributed to the evil powers exercised by the garnet carbuncle at the top of the Jupiter column, so, at the beginning of the 11th century, Bernard of Menthon, then Archdeacon of Aosta, was petitioned to exorcise the column. He quickly cast out the demons and toppled the malevolent stone. The base of the column and other archaeological remains can still be seen on either side of the road.

The pass is also the border between France and Italy, although there are few obvious signs that you have changed country. In fact, from 1032 until the unification of Italy in the second half of the 19th century, the Aosta Valley was governed by the house of Savoie, an historical connection to France that is still seen in many place names such as La Thuile and Pré St Didier. The valley retains a great deal of autonomy and French is still an official language alongside Italian. Aosta is an extremely pleasant city to explore with a great deal to see. There are too many places of interest to mention all of them here, but the

Roman amphitheatre and the Sant'Orso cloisters should not be missed. The city's tourist office provides an excellent free monument guide and map (in English).

All too soon, it is time to leave Aosta and head up to the second of the St Bernard Passes. Like it is smaller brother, the Grand St Bernard Pass has been used by travellers since pre-historic times. Julius Caesar is known to have crossed the pass in 57BC on his way to conquer the pagans of Martigny. The lawlessness into which the area

**Getting off the train in Bourg St Maurice**

descended towards the end of the first millennium AD was brought under control by King Canute of Denmark and Rudolph III of Burgundy, allowing Bernard of Menthon to build a hospice to provide shelter and a safe haven for merchants and pilgrims. Nearly a thousand years later the hospice still provides board and lodging for travellers all year round. In May 1800 Napoleon took his army across the pass into Italy, running up an enormous bill at the hospice, a debt that remained unsettled until it was symbolically repaid by President Mitterand in May 1984. You can learn more about the pass's fascinating history at the museum at the summit. Although no longer used for mountain rescue, the hospice still maintains a kennel for its famous Saint Bernard dogs. The kennel breeds about 15 pedigree puppies a year and sells them for around 1000 Euros each. This is not the only business carried out at the pass as the numerous souvenir stalls, shops and cafés testify.

The pass is also the border between Italy and Switzerland and, as Switzerland is not part of the European Union, the border is well policed. Once you have cleared customs, all that remains is the magnificent 40km descent to Martigny, 2000 metres below: a fitting finale to a spectacular tour.

## GETTING THERE

### By car
For cyclists driving from the UK, Sallanches is a more convenient town than Martigny from which to start the tour. If you start in Sallanches, the first day of the tour would be from Sallanches to Beaufort (52km), and the last day would be from Martigny to Sallanches (75km). Sallanches is 800km from Calais.

### By plane
**Via Geneva:** There is a train every hour (that will accept bikes) from Geneva Airport to Martigny, via Lausanne. The journey takes around 2 hours.

**Via Lyon:** If you fly into Lyon Airport, the easiest place to start the tour from is Bourg St Maurice. However, even this 'easiest' of options can still be very time consuming.

Shuttle bus/train: If the shuttle bus will accept your bike, there is a direct service from Lyon airport to Bourg St Maurice, or you can take the bus to Chambéry and the train from Chambéry to Bourg St Maurice. (Chambéry coach station is next to the railway station.) For both of these routes, there are only two to five buses per day, depending on the exact time of year and the day of the week.

**Cycle/Train:** To take the train you have to cycle to Bourgoin Jallieu (see Appendix 1 for route details). There are only three or four trains per day and the journey takes three to four hours.

**Via Turin:** The tour could also be started from Aosta by flying to Turin. Contact Turin airport (**www.aeroportoditorino.it**) and/or Italian railways (**www.trenitalia.com**) for information about connections from Turin to Aosta.

## WHEN TO GO

The ideal time to do this circuit is June or September as the roads over both of the St Bernard Passes are closed from late November to the end of May and some of the roads, especially those between Martigny and Chamonix, can be very busy during the summer holidays.

## MAPS

No single map covers the entire area in enough detail for comfortable navigation. A combination of the Michelin Local Map, Sheet 328: Ain, Haute-Savoie, and the Italian Istituto Geografico Centrale 1:50,000 scale map for the *Massiccio del Monte Bianco*, which can be bought in Italy, works well.

# Day 1 – Martigny to Chamonix

Like most high mountains, Mont Blanc 'creates' its own weather and the summit is often battered by raging blizzards while the surrounding peaks bask under clear blue skies. However, according to local lore, the mountains can give you a good weather forecast: when there is a lenticular cloud covering Mont Blanc and the other summits are clear, it will stay fine; but if the Aiguille Verte is also shrouded in cloud, storms are brewing.

| Distance | Location | Directions |
|---|---|---|
| 0.0 | Martigny station | Come out of the station and go straight ahead past 'Helvetia Patria'. Keep going straight on, first following (Centre Ville), and then (Forclaz) |
| 3.0 | Roundabout | Go straight on (Col de la Forclaz) 13.3km at 8% |
| 16.3 | Col de la Forclaz | Go straight on through Trient to the Franco–Swiss border |
| 25.1 | Le Châtelard: customs post | Go straight on – N506 6.7km at 4.5% |
| 31.8 | Col des Montets | Go straight on and down through Argentière (Chamonix) |
| 41.1 | Les Praz | Turn R (Les Praz) |
| 43.6 | Chamonix: jtn | Go straight on |
| 43.8 | Go straight on | Pedestrian sign for TO (Do not follow road signs to TO) |
| 43.9 | Jtn | Turn R – pedestrian sign for TO |
| 44.0 | Chamonix TO | TO is on your L |

| FACILITIES AND SERVICES | | | | | | | | |
|---|---|---|---|---|---|---|---|---|
| Location | Distance (km) | Water | Shops | Café | Campsite | B&B | Hotel | Bank | Bike Shop |
| Martigny | 0.0 | x | x | x | x | x | x | x | x |
| Col de la Forclaz | 16.3 | x | x | x | x | x | x | — | — |
| Trient | 19.4 | x | x | x | — | x | — | — | — |
| Le Châtelard | 25.1 | x | x | x | — | — | x | — | — |
| Vallorcine | 27.5 | x | x | x | x | x | x | — | — |
| Argentière | 35.1 | x | x | x | x | x | x | x | — |
| Chamonix | 44.0 | x | x | x | x | x | x | x | x |

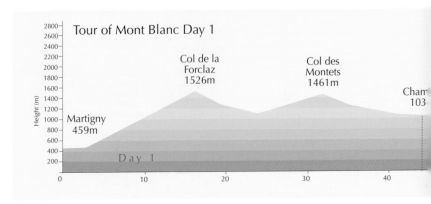

Tour of Mont Blanc Day 1

Col de la Forclaz 1526m

Col des Montets 1461m

Martigny 459m

Cham 103

Day 1

*Chamonix and the statue commemorating Balmat and Saussure's ascent of Mont Blanc*

Chamonix has become so synonymous with Mont Blanc that the town has officially changed its name to Chamonix-Mont Blanc. The highest mountain in Western Europe was first climbed by Michel-Gabriel Paccard and Jacques Balmat in 1786. Their ascent took two days, following a route from Chamonix (now called the Grands Mulets Route). Today, the most popular route to the summit starts in Saint Gervais (via the Nid d'Aigle mountain railway), but most mountaineers still take two days to get to the top. The current record for climbing Mont Blanc from the church in the centre of Chamonix was set in 1990. Pierre-André Gobet took 3hrs 38mins to reach the summit and 1hr 32mins to get back to Chamonix. In 2003, the record was attempted on skis by Stéphane Brosse and Pierre Gignoux. Carrying their skis over the bottom section, where there was no snow, they did the climb in 4hrs 04mins and completed the descent in 1hr 08mins.

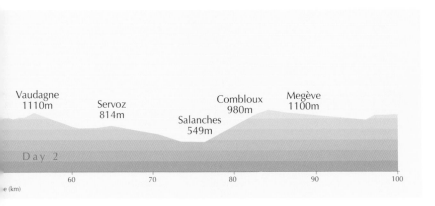

Vaudagne
1110m

Servoz
814m

Salanches
549m

Combloux
980m

Megève
1100m

Day 2

60      70      80      90      100

e (km)

# Day 2 – Chamonix to Beaufort

The ski resort at Les Saisies owes its existence not to a Frenchman but to an Austrian. Erwin Eckl came to the region from the Tyrol in 1935 to teach skiing at Hauteluce. The following year he bought a barn at Les Saisies and turned it into a hotel, thereby launching the new resort.

| Distance | Location | Directions |
|---|---|---|
| 0.0 | Chamonix TO | Come out of the TO and turn L |
| 0.1 | Roundabout | Turn L (Toutes Directions) |
| 0.6 | Jtn | Turn R – second of two parallel roads (Les Bossons) |
| 5.0 | Roundabout | Go straight on – D243 (Les Houches) |
| 6.4 | Mini-roundabout | Bear L onto Ave des Alpages |
| 8.0 | Jtn | Go straight on – Rue de Bellevue |
| 8.9 | Roundabout | Turn L – Route des Chavants |
| 9.4 | Jtn | Follow Route de Vaudagne through Vaudagne (Annecy) |
| 15.1 | Bridge over dual-carriageway | Go over dual-carriageway – D13 (Chamonix/Servoz). Follow D13 to (Sallanches) |
| 29.4 | Sallanches: roundabout | Turn L (Centre Ville) |
| 30.1 | Traffic lights | Go straight on – Ave St Martin |
| 30.3 | Sallanches main square | Turn R at traffic lights, then take first L (Combloux) |
| 30.5 | Jtn | Turn L (Combloux) |
| 30.6 | Jtn | Turn R – D113 (Cordon) then immediately L (Combloux par ancienne route) 5.3km at 8% |
| 35.9 | Combloux: jtn | Turn R (La Cry-Cachet) 2.5km at 7% |
| 36.9 | Jtn | Turn L (Mégeve) |
| 40.6 | Jtn N212 | Turn R – N212 and go through Megève and Praz-sur-Arly (Albertville) |
| 50.2 | N212/D218A | Turn L – D218A (Les Saisies) and go up to Les Saisies 8km at 6.5%, short descent, then 5km at 4% |
| 64.2 | Col des Saisies | Go straight on |
| 72.1 | D218/D218E | Turn L onto D218E (Hauteluce) |
| 72.2 | D218E/D70 | Go straight on along D218E |
| 73.0 | Hauteluce | Turn R – D70 (Beaufort) |
| 80.2 | D70/D925 | Turn R – D925 |
| 81.6 | Beaufort TO | |

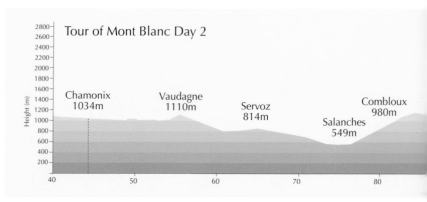

Tour of Mont Blanc Day 2

*The fabulous view of the Chamonix Aiguilles from Les Houches*

## FACILITIES AND SERVICES

| Location | Distance (km) | Water | Shops | Café | Campsite | B&B | Hotel | Bank | Bike Shop |
|---|---|---|---|---|---|---|---|---|---|
| Chamonix | 0.0 | x | x | x | x | x | x | x | x |
| Les Houches | 8.2 | x | x | x | x | x | x | x | — |
| Passy | 26.8 | x | x | x | x | x | x | x | — |
| Sallanches | 31.2 | x | x | x | x | x | x | x | x |
| Combloux | 36.8 | x | x | x | x | x | x | x | x |
| Megève | 42.0 | x | x | x | x | x | x | x | x |
| Praz-sur-Arly | 46.5 | x | x | x | x | — | x | x | — |
| Notre Dame de Bellecombe | 54.0 | x | x | x | — | x | x | — | x |
| Les Saisies | 65.1 | x | x | x | — | x | x | x | — |
| Hauteluce | 73.9 | x | x | x | — | x | x | x | — |
| Beaufort | 82.5 | x | x | x | x | x | x | x | (1) |

(1) Nearest bike shop is in Albertville, 20km southwest of Beaufort

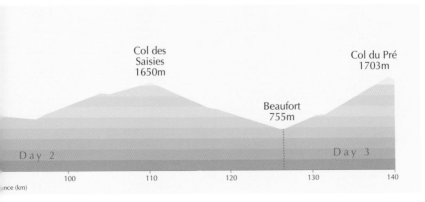

# Day 3 – Beaufort to Bourg St Maurice

Extra day: Beaufort provides an excellent base from which to add an extra day (or days) to the tour. The village is at the centre of a superb network of cycling circuits, which were set up at the instigation of a group of local cyclists in order to develop cycling tourism in this wonderfully beautiful area. Thirteen different routes, of all levels of difficulty, have now been clearly signposted and a small descriptive brochure has been published (available from local tourist offices, price 5 Euros). The most challenging circuit is the 155km-long Grand Tour of the Beaufortain, which includes 3850 metres of height gain.

| Distance | Location | Directions |
|----------|----------|------------|
| 0.0 | Beaufort TO | Come out of TO and turn L – D218 (Arêches-Le Planay) 4km at 6.5% |
| 5.0 | Arêches: D218/D85 | Go straight on – D218 (Col du Pré) 7.3km at 9% |
| 12.3 | Col du Pré | Go straight on |
| 15.7 | Low point | Go straight on |
| 17.7 | Col de Meraillet: D217/D925 | Turn R – D217 (Bourg Saint Maurice) Short descent then 5.9km at 6.5% |
| 25.9 | Cormet de Roseland | Go straight on (D217 becomes D902) |
| 45.6 | Bourg St Maurice: roundabout: D902/N90 | Turn R – N90 (Aime) |
| 45.7 | Bourg St Maurice TO | TO is on the R |

## FACILITIES AND SERVICES

| Location | Distance (km) | Water | Shops | Café | Campsite | B&B | Hotel | Bank | Bike Shop |
|----------|---------------|-------|-------|------|----------|-----|-------|------|-----------|
| Beaufort | 0.0 | x | x | x | x | x | x | x | (1) |
| Arêches | 5.0 | x | x | x | x | x | x | — | — |
| Col du Pré | 12.3 | — | — | x | — | — | — | — | — |
| Col de Meraillet | 17.7 | — | — | x | — | — | — | — | — |
| Bourg St Maurice | 45.7 | x | x | x | x | — | x | x | x |

(1) Nearest bike shop is in Albertville, 20km southwest of Beaufort

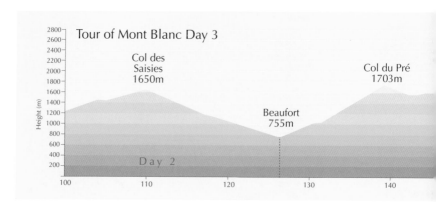

76

*Looking down on the hamlet of Boudin,
below the Col du Pré*

Although 80% of France's electricity is produced by nuclear power stations, the country's hydropower plants are a key part of the electricity network. Unlike nuclear plants, hydropower stations can be switched on and off in minutes to respond to peaks and troughs in demand and they are very economical: hydro-electricity is 50% cheaper than nuclear electricity. Water from Roseland Reservoir is fed to a generating plant in the Tarentaise Valley via a 13km penstock. Due to the 1km height difference between the dam and the power plant, the water has enough power to produce more than 500MW of electricity. Positioning the gener-ating plant at the bottom of an industrial valley also helps to minimise the installation's impact on the mountain environment.

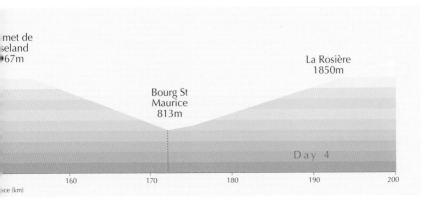

Aosta is surrounded by four of Europe's highest and most famous mountains: Mont Blanc, Monte Rosa, the Matterhorn and the Gran Paradiso.

| Distance | Location | Directions |
|---|---|---|
| 0.0 | Bourg St Maurice TO | Come out of the TO and turn R – N90 |
| 0.1 | Roundabout | Go straight on – N90 (Italy) 31.2km at 4.5% |
| 0.8 | Roundabout | Go straight on – N90 (La Rosière) |
| 2.9 | Séez N90/D902 | Bear L – N90 (Aosta) |
| 22.4 | La Rosière | Go straight on |
| 31.3 | Col du Petit St Bernard | Go straight on |
| 54.4 | Pré St Didier S26/S26D | Turn R – S26 (Aosta) |
| 83.0 | Entrance to Aosta | Bear R – Rue de Petit St Bernard (Aosta) |
| 84.5 | Aosta: roundabout | Turn R – Rue de Chambéry (Centre Ville) |
| 85.4 | Jtn Rue de Chambéry/Ave des Maquisards | Get into LH lane and turn L – Ave des Maquisards |
| 85.5 | Jtn Ave des Maquisards/Place de la République | Turn R – Place de la République (*hôtel de ville*). Go through the pedestrian area to the *hôtel de ville* and TO |
| 85.7 | Aosta: Place Emilio Chanoux | TO is on the L |

## FACILITIES AND SERVICES

| Location | Distance (km) | Water | Shops | Café | Campsite | B&B | Hotel | Bank | Bike Shop |
|---|---|---|---|---|---|---|---|---|---|
| Bourg St Maurice | 0.0 | x | x | x | x | — | x | x | x |
| Séez | 2.9 | x | x | x | x | x | x | — | — |
| La Rosière | 22.4 | x | x | x | — | — | x | x | — |
| Col du Petit St Bernard | 31.3 | — | x | x | — | — | — | — | — |
| La Thuile | 44.1 | x | x | x | x | x | x | x | — |
| Pré St Didier | 54.4 | x | x | x | — | — | x | x | — |
| Aosta | 85.7 | x | x | x | x | x | x | x | x |

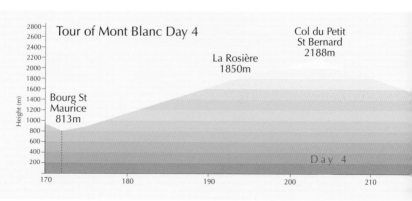

Tour of Mont Blanc Day 4

*The statue of St Bernard just before the pass that bears his name*

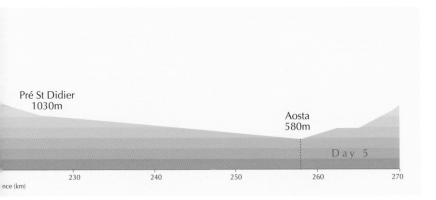

Pré St Didier
1030m

Aosta
580m

Day 5

230    240    250    260    270

nce (km)

Cycling long distances burns enormous quantities of fuel, but huge midday meals are not a good idea. After a leisurely climb over the Grand Saint Bernard Pass, my wife and I were feeling strong, so we decided to keep going to Argentière. However, we needed to eat first and the open-air restaurants in Martigny were just too inviting. After a generous three-course lunch, we were back on the bikes grinding up to the Forclaz under the blazing afternoon sun. We made it over the pass – just – and checked into a hotel at Le Châtelard. Our laziness was punished by the weather gods and we woke to rain hammering against the bedroom window. We quickly covered the 10km to Argentière, but it was two very wet and very cold cyclists that rolled into the village.

| Distance | Location | Directions |
|---|---|---|
| 0.0 | Aosta TO | Come out of the TO and turn L. Go to Rue Xavier Maistre and turn L, 4.4km at 4.5% |
| 0.3 | Traffic lights | Go straight on. Rue Xavier Maistre becomes Ave Pierre Laurent |
| 0.5 | Traffic lights | Go straight on along Ave Pierre Laurent |
| 0.7 | Ave Pierre Laurent/ Rue Roma | Go straight across Rue Roma (underpass for pedestrians and cyclists) and up the very steep Chemin des Capucins – no street name sign |
| 0.7 | Chemin des Capucins/ Ave Grand St Bernard | Turn R onto Ave Grand St Bernard |
| 4.4 | Variney | Turn R (Valpelline) |
| 7.7 | Castello | Bear L (Allein) 8.5km at 4.5% |
| 12.5 | Jtn | Turn L (Allein) |
| 14.3 | Jtn | Turn R: no signs |
| 16.2 | Allein "chef-lieu" | Bear L (Etroubles) |
| 20.8 | Etroubles | Turn R – S27 18.1km at 6.5% |
| 24.1 | Jtn | Turn R (Martigny): the main road goes through the Grand St Bernard tunnel |
| 38.4 | Italian border post | Go straight on |
| 38.9 | Col du Grand St Bernard | Go straight on and follow N21 to Martigny |
| 80.7 | Martigny: roundabout | Turn R (Martigny) |
| 81.2 | Roundabout | Go straight on (Centre Ville). Go straight through town centre to station |
| 83.7 | Martigny station | Station is in front of you |

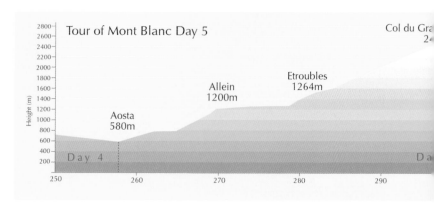

*In summer, the Col du Grand St Bernard is overrun with souvenir stalls*

## FACILITIES AND SERVICES

| Location | Distance (km) | Water | Shops | Café | Campsite | B&B | Hotel | Bank | Bike Shop |
|---|---|---|---|---|---|---|---|---|---|
| Aosta | 0.0 | x | x | x | x | x | x | x | x |
| St Oyen | 22.0 | x | x | x | x | x | — | — | — |
| Col du Grand St Bernard | 38.9 | — | x | x | — | — | — | — | — |
| Bourg St Pierre | 51.5 | x | x | x | x | x | x | — | — |
| Liddes | 58.0 | — | x | x | — | — | x | x | — |
| Orsières | 65.4 | — | x | x | — | x | x | x | — |
| Martigny | 83.7 | x | x | x | x | x | x | x | x |

d

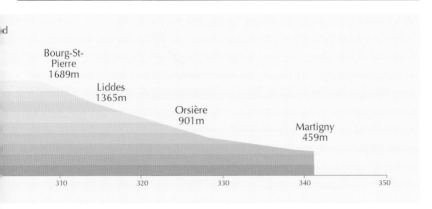

Bourg-St-Pierre 1689m

Liddes 1365m

Orsière 901m

Martigny 459m

310  320  330  340  350

# ACCOMMODATION

## Martigny

**Campsites**

TCS (all year round), Tel. 02 77 22 45 44

**Bed & Breakfast**

Mrs Troillet, Tel. 02 77 22 72 16

Mrs Maury, Tel. 02 77 22 77 57 or 02 77 21 26 33

Mrs Peyla, Tel. 02 77 22 17 57

**Hotels**

There are 12 hotels in Martigny. Contact TO for details.

## Chamonix

**Campsites**

There are 11 campsites in Chamonix. Contact TO for details.

**Bed & Breakfast**

There are more than 20 bed & breakfasts/*gites d'étapes* in Chamonix. Contact TO for details.

**Hotels**

There are more than 60 hotels in Chamonix. Contact TO for details.

## Beaufort

**Campsites**

Le Domelin (June to end Sept), Tel. 04 79 38 33 88

**Bed & Breakfast**

Chalet de Bernoline, Tel. 04 79 38 05 56

Mr and Mrs Quiot, Tel. 04 79 38 09 22

**Hotels**

Le Doron (**), Tel. 04 79 38 33 18

Hotel du Grand Mont (**), Tel. 04 79 38 33 36

La Cascade (**) 3km west of Beaufort on D925, Tel. 04 79 38 70 00

Hotel de la Roche (*), Tel. 04 79 38 33 31

## Bourg St Maurice

**Campsites**

Le Versoyen (mid-May to end Oct), Tel. 04 79 07 03 45

**Bed & Breakfast**

There are no bed & breakfasts in Bourg St Maurice

**Hotels**

There are seven hotels in Bourg St Maurice. Contact TO for details.

## Aosta

**Campsites**

Milleluci (all year round), Tel. (0165) 23 52 78

Ville d'Aoste (early June to end Oct), Tel. (0165) 26 72 13

**Bed & Breakfast**

There are nine bed & breakfasts in Aosta. Contact TO for details.

**Hotels**

There are 27 hotels in Aosta. Contact TO for details.

## TOURIST INFORMATION

**Regional Information**

| | Telephone | Website |
|---|---|---|
| Haute-Savoie | 04 50 51 32 31 | **www.savoie-mont-blanc.com** |
| Savoie | 04 79 85 12 45 | **www.savoie-mont-blanc.com** |
| Aosta Valley | 01 65 23 66 27 | **www.regione.vda.it** |

**Tourist Information Offices**

| Location | Telephone | Website |
|---|---|---|
| Martigny | 02 77 21 22 20 | **www.martignytourism.ch** |
| Vallorcine | 04 50 54 60 71 | **www.vallorcine.com** |
| Chamonix | 04 50 53 00 24 | **www.chamonix.com** |
| Passy | 04 50 58 80 52 | **www.ot-passy.com** |
| Sallanches | 04 50 58 04 25 | **www.sallanches.com** |
| Combloux | 04 50 58 60 49 | **www.combloux.com** |
| Megève | 04 50 21 27 28 | **www.megeve.com** |
| Praz-sur-Arly | 04 50 21 90 57 | **www.prazsurarly.com** |
| Notre Dame de Bellecombe | 04 79 31 61 40 | **www.notredamedebellecombe.com** |
| Les Saisies | 04 79 38 90 30 | **www.lessaisies.com** |
| Arêches-Beaufort | 04 79 38 37 57 | **www.areches-beaufort.com** |
| Bourg Saint Maurice | 04 79 07 04 92 | **www.lesarcs.com** |
| La Rosière | 04 79 06 80 51 | **www.larosiere.net** |
| La Thuile | 0165 88 30 49 | **www.lathuile.net** |
| Bourg Saint Pierre/Liddes/Orsières | 02 77 83 32 48 | **www.saint-bernard.ch** |

*The Cormet de Roseland in the middle of May (Day 3)*

# TOUR OF THE CHARTREUSE–BAUGES

| Day | Route | Distance | Height Gain |
|---|---|---|---|
| 1 | Grenoble to Aiguebelette-le-Lac | 71.9km | 1060m |
| 2 | Aiguebelette-le-Lac to Le Bourget-du-Lac | 71.5km | 740m |
| 3 | Le Bourget-du-Lac to Annecy | 75.0km | 1600m |
| 4 | Annecy to St Pierre d'Albigny | 60.5km | 640m |
| 5 | Bauges circuit from St Pierre d'Albigny | 68.4km | 1300m |
| 6 | St Pierre d'Albigny to Les Echelles | 61.3km | 1050m |
| 7 | Les Echelles to Grenoble | 44.0km | 1010m |
| | **Totals** | **453.1km** | **7400m** |

The Chartreuse and Bauges Regional Parks lie between Grenoble and Annecy, with Chambéry, the former capital of the Dukes of Savoie, sandwiched between them. Despite the proximity of these three regional centres, the two parks have remained relatively quiet backwaters where tourism, although an important part of the local economy, has not completely superseded more traditional industries such as agriculture and forestry. The Regional Park authorities continue to promote these industries whilst also encouraging the growth of new economic activities compatible with the conservation of the environment. As in all areas of outstanding natural beauty, tourism is seen as an important element in the Parks' economic survival, with the emphasis being put on low-impact tourism. Visitor numbers are increasing but car traffic remains light, even in the height of summer.

Many people are familiar with the name Chartreuse, either through the monastic order that Saint Bruno founded here in 1084, or through the famous Chartreuse liqueur (the 'elixir of long-life') that was invented by the monks in 1737. When Saint Bruno founded his monastery, he was looking for a place where he could devote himself to a life of contemplation, undisturbed by the hustle and bustle of the outside world. It is easy to see why he chose the Chartreuse: the mountainous interior of the massif, protected by an almost unbroken ring of high cliffs and only accessible via steep mountain passes or through deep, dark gorges, would have been particularly forbidding to most 11th-century travellers. In many ways, little has changed since Saint Bruno's day; modern transport has made access much easier, but the roads are just as spectacular and the landscape just as rugged.

The Bauges is perhaps the least known of the Pre-Alpine massifs. Even in France, when you mention the 'Bauges' to people from outside the area, they often think that you have simply mispronounced 'Vosges'! Typically for a country where gastronomy is such an important part of everyday life, when people do think of the Bauges it is in terms of food or, to be more exact, cheese. Tome des Bauges (one M) is the pride of local cheese-makers and woe betide anyone who confuses it with the 'Tomme' (two Ms) cheeses from other areas. Whereas the Chartreuse is characterised by spectacular cliffs and dramatic gorges, the Bauges has a gentler landscape of verdant U-shaped valleys, dotted with tiny villages that don't seem to have changed for centuries. The whole area has a very peaceful, pastoral atmosphere: this is a place in which to relax and enjoy the simple things in life.

The tour starts in Grenoble, which though a city surrounded by mountains is also the flattest city in France, making it ideal for cycling. (Plans of the city's well-developed network of

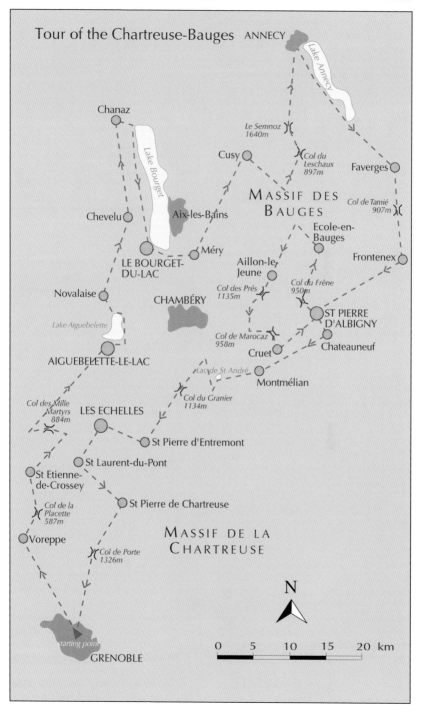

Tour of the Chartreuse-Bauges

ANNECY

Lake Annecy

Chanaz

Lake Bourget

Le Semnoz
1640m

Cusy

Col du
Leschaux
897m

Faverges

MASSIF DES
BAUGES

Col de Tamié
907m

Chevelu

Aix-les-Bains

Ecole-en-
Bauges

Méry

LE BOURGET-
DU-LAC

Aillon-le-
Jeune

Frontenex

Col du Frêne
950m

Novalaise

CHAMBÉRY

Col des Prés
1135m

ST PIERRE
D'ALBIGNY

Lake Aiguebelette

Col de Marocaz
958m

Cruet

Chateauneuf

AIGUEBELETTE-LE-LAC

Lac de St André

Montmélian

Col du Granier
1134m

Col des Mille
Martyrs
884m

LES ECHELLES

St Pierre d'Entremont

St Laurent-du-Pont

St Etienne-
de-Crossey

Col de la
Placette
587m

St Pierre de Chartreuse

Voreppe

MASSIF DE LA
CHARTREUSE

Col de Porte
1326m

N

0    5    10    15    20  km

starting point

GRENOBLE

cycleways and cycle lanes can be obtained from the 'Download brochures' page on the Grenoble tourist office website.) Grenoble is a determinedly forward-looking city and has carved itself a niche as France's 'silicon valley'. The old town, which remains the vibrant heart of the city, reflects Grenoble's long and illustrious history and, as befits an important regional centre, is home to many interesting museums. These include the Musée de l'Ancien Eveché (local history), the Musée de la Résistance et de la Déportation (Grenoble was a very important centre for the Resistance during the Second World War), the Musée de Grenoble (considered one of the best fine arts museums outside Paris) and the Natural History Museum.

An easy 15km cycle along the flat roads between Grenoble and Voreppe leads to the Col de la Placette: the first pass of the day and the gateway to the western part of the Chartreuse Park. To the north of the pass the very pleasant, rolling countryside is dominated by the spectacular limestone cliffs that form the western ramparts of the Chartreuse mountains. There are few outstanding landmarks along these quiet roads, but a 360° loop in the road – Le Tourniquet – between St Etienne-de-Crossey and Meribel-les-Echelles is quite an unusual feature. Once over the highest point on the day's circuit, the Col de la Croix des Mille Martyrs, 30km of quite easy cycling takes you to the shores of Lake Aiguebelette, and the end of this first stage. Lake Aiguebelette is a wonderful place to go swimming as the water is exceptionally clean and warm.

Day 2 continues along the shores of the lake to the village of Novalaise and the southern edge of the Avant-Pays Savoyard. This is an area of traditional farms and rolling hills between the pre-Alps and the River Rhone: truly *La France profonde* and a delightful area for cycling. Wine production is an increasingly important part of the local economy – unlike many areas of France, where the wine industry is in crisis – and vineyards are taking over larger and larger areas of the countryside. Wines from Jongieux are particularly worth looking out for. Chanaz, the next port of call, is a picturesque village on the banks of the Rhone and a favourite haunt for artists who come to paint the river, the boats and the waterside houses.

A few kilometres from the village you get your first glimpse of Lake Bourget, the largest natural lake in France and currently the subject of a huge development programme aimed at protecting the natural beauty of the area. The route follows the lakeshore from Portout to Conjux, before heading inland to St Pierre-de-Curtille. From just after Conjux, it is possible to make a 10km detour to visit Hautecombe Abbey, the traditional last resting place for members of the House of Savoie. Guided visits, which provide an interesting insight into the history of Savoie, are available in several languages. The steep hillsides that drop directly into the lake prevent the road following the water's edge, so to reach Le Bourget-du-Lac you have to leave the lakeshore and climb Mont de la Charvaz. As this is the most difficult ascent of the day, it is easy to justify a short break at the highest point of the road to admire the bird's-eye view of the Abbey, the lake and the mountains to the east. The day ends at Le Bourget-du-Lac, a small lakeside village with an exceptional range of restaurants, from unpresuming family affairs to luxurious two-star Michelin establishments.

Day 3 starts by following the Chambéry-Aix-les-Bains cycleway around the southern end of Lake Bourget. The route then leaves the lakeshore, to avoid the busy roads through Aix-les-Bains (one of the aims of The Great Lake Project is to reduce traffic along the eastern shore of the lake), and climbs up into the Bauges across the foot of Mont Revard. The Revard was one of France's first purpose built ski resorts and the remains of the cable-car that serviced the resort from 1935 to 1969 can still be seen above the village of Mouxy. The route rejoins the main road just before Cusy, the last place to stock up on calories before the climb to the Col de Leschaux. It is possible to go straight down to Annecy from the col, but, if you have the strength in your legs, it is worth continuing up to the Semnoz, as the views from the top, especially of Mont Blanc, are magnificent. It is not often that you have the opportunity to cycle to the top of a mountain and enjoy a 360° panorama! The long descent into the centre of Annecy is also great fun.

Early morning light on the harbour at Le Bourget-du-Lac

Annecy is generally considered the most beautiful city in the French Alps and is therefore a very popular tourist destination (book accommodation in advance for July and August!). During the summer months, the city entertains its visitors with a wide range of events, from ambulatory street theatre to the Fête du Lac firework display. Even without the added entertainment, just wandering through the narrow, cobbled streets of the old town is a delight. For more information about Annecy, see Route 2.

The route now heads south, along the Annecy cycleway – a much more pleasant alternative to the congested roads out of the city, especially in the morning before the cycleway itself becomes busy. The cycleway continues all the way to Ugine, but you leave it at Faverges, approximately 24km from Annecy. Interesting diversions along the lakeshore include the bell foundry and museum (Musée de la Cloche) at Sévrier and the village of Duingt with its *vieux château*. Faverges marks the start of the climb up to the Col de Tamié, the only pass on the day's itinerary. About 2km before the pass, you go past Tamié Abbey which, as well as marking the border between Haute-Savoie and Savoie, is home to one of the region's lesser-known cheeses (called Tamié, surprisingly enough).

The southern slopes of the Col de Tamié open out into the Combe de Savoie – the heart of Savoie's wine-growing industry. Savoie does not have the prestige of many of France's other wine-producing areas, but many of its wines are very pleasant and well worth tasting. The day ends at St Pierre d'Albigny, a small town dominated by the impressive silhouette of Miolans Castle. This castle-prison, which most famously held the Marquis de Sade in 1772, is open to the public and is worth a visit.

Up until now, the tour has skirted around the edge of the Bauges, but St Pierre d'Albigny provides an excellent starting point from which to explore the heart of the massif. As this is a circular trip, you can leave your luggage behind and enjoy a day of 'lightweight', although still quite strenuous, cycling. The day starts with a stiff climb from the centre of St Pierre up to the Col du Frêne. On the other side of the pass the landscape changes completely: the green fields of the wide valley floor lead the eye to the majestic summit of Mont Trélod at the northern end of the valley. In the middle of this valley lies Ecole-en-Bauges, home to the Bauges Regional Park Flora and Fauna Centre as well as a famous bakery that has exported its bread to hotels as far a-field as London and Paris. The gastronomic theme continues in Aillon-le-Jeune, where the local dairy produces some excellent cheeses, including Tome des Bauges and its own speciality, Bleu des Aillons. You can also visit the dairy to see how the cheese is made. After Aillon-le-Jeune, the circuit goes over two more passes: the Col des Prés, and the Col du Marocaz. It is worth making a short detour (less than 1km) just before the Col de Marocaz to visit La Thuile and its beautiful lake. The day ends with a steep descent into the Combe de Savoie, followed by 8km of gentle cycling back to St Pierre d'Albigny.

The penultimate day of the tour takes you across the River Isére to Chateauneuf, and then follows the eastern flank of the Combe de Savoie to Montmélian. The old town of Montmélian is small but attractive and the Vine and Wine Museum gives you an opportunity to learn more about Savoie's wines. Five kilometres to the west of Montmélian lies Lake St André, the smallest lake on the tour and a popular picnic spot for the inhabitants of Chambéry. (To visit Chambéry, the former capital of the Dukes of Savoie, follow the

*The peaceful shores of Lac de St André and Mont Granier*

'Boucle du Lac de St André' cycling signs into the city centre, and then follow the D912 to rejoin the main route at the Col du Granier. This adds about 15km to the circuit). The lake lies in the shadow of the forbidding north face of Mont Granier, a 700m-high wall of grey limestone which was formed in 1248 by a massive landslide that devastated an area of 20sq km, burying several villages. There are two roads to the Col du Granier from Lake St André, both of which are very steep; the route described here follows the easier and quieter of the two. From the pass, a very pleasant descent leads through Entremont-le-Vieux, with its interesting cave-bear museum, to St Pierre d'Entremont and the spectacular Gorges du Guiers Vif. This penultimate stage ends at Les Echelles/Entre-Deux-Guiers, two adjoining villages that straddle the Guiers Vif. The only hotel is in Les Echelles, the campsite is in Entre-Deux-Guiers.

The final leg takes you through another deep defile and back into the heart of the mountains. Of all the places of interest in the area, the most famous is undoubtedly the Grand Chartreuse Monastery. The monastery itself, which is set well back from the road, is closed to the public, but the adjoining museum provides a fascinating insight into the Spartan lives of the monks. If you have the time (and muscles) to make another short detour, why not visit St Pierre-de-Chartreuse, the 'capital' of the region and home to the Regional Park Visitor Centre, and/or the church at St Hugues, which has a striking collection of modern religious art. There is now only one more major pass to go over, the Col de Porte, before heading back down into the brouhaha of Grenoble.

hour and the journey takes around 1hour 10mins.

### Via Geneva
Take the train from the airport to Geneva central station (Cornavin). From Cornavin there is a train every 2–3 hours, either direct or via Culoz and Chambéry. The direct journey takes around 2 hours 15mins.

### Via Grenoble
See directions in Appendix A

### Via Chambéry
The tour can be started directly from Chambéry airport. Come out of the airport terminal and follow the road to the junction with the N202 (roundabout). Go straight on along the D17 ('Voglans'). Where the D17 turns right, go straight on along a cycle lane ([Boucle de Voglans], no entry for cars) to join the third stage of the tour at Viviers-du-Lac – junction D17/D17B (2.2km from the airport). To get back to the airport from Le Bourget-du-Lac, follow the directions for the start of stage three as far as the roundabout at the junction of the N211 and D17. Turn right here ('Chambéry') onto N202. Turn right at the next roundabout ('Chambéry–Voglans airport') to get to the airport.

### WHEN TO GO
All of the passes crossed by this tour are kept open all year round, but it is usually only warm enough for enjoyable cycling from April to October. The roads are never too busy, even during the peak holiday months of July and August but, if you come at this time, it is advisable to book accommodation in advance.

### GETTING THERE
**By car**
Grenoble is 870km from Calais

**By plane**
**Via Lyon St Exupéry**
*Bus:* There is a shuttle bus every hour
*Train:* To take the train you have to cycle to La Verpillière (see Appendix A for route details). On average, there is one train every

### MAPS
**Michelin:** Local – Sheet 333, Isère, Savoie
 **Michelin:** Regional – Sheet 244, Rhône-Alpes
 **IGN:** Top 100 – Sheet 53: Grenoble, Mont Blanc (the area around Voreppe is not shown on this map. For this you need Sheet 51: Lyon, Grenoble, but the navigation here is easy and this map is not essential).

| Distance | Location | Directions |
|---|---|---|
| 0.0 | Grenoble station | Leave station via (Centre Ville) exit. Go straight across street in front of station to Rue Casimir Brenier, which is followed to Place Hubert Dubedout |
| 0.4 | Place Hubert Dubedout | Go across square (easiest on foot). Cross River Isère and then turn L to go to gap in fence that leads down to cycleway |
| 0.6 | Cycleway | Turn R onto cycleway and follow it for 2km |
| 2.6 | Bridge over cycleway | Turn 180° R and go up under motorway |
| 2.9 | St Martin-le-Vinoux: roundabout | Go straight on to join cycleway alongside N75 Follow this cycleway/lane for 11.5km |
| 13.4 | Voreppe: N75/D520A | Turn R – D520A (Voreppe – Centre) then (Toutes Directions) to get to roundabout in centre of Voreppe |
| 14.9 | Voreppe: roundabout D520A/D520E | Go straight on – D520A (Col de la Placette): 5.5km at 6% |
| 20.4 | Col de la Placette | Go straight on |
| 24.5 | D520A/D520 | Turn L – D520 (Voiron) |
| 28.2 | St Etienne-de-Crossey: D520/D49D | Turn R – D49D (St Aupre) |
| 28.7 | D49D/D49 | Turn R – D49 (becomes D28) (Miribel-les-Echelles). Go through Miribel to Col de la Croix des Mille Martyrs: 5.2km at 6% |
| 42.8 | Col des Mille Martyrs | Go straight on |
| 46.1 | D28/D49C | Turn 180° R – D49C (Merlas) then (St Bueil) |
| 54.0 | Jtn just before St Bueil | Turn R (Voisant) – sign well hidden in hedge on RHS of road. Go through Voissant and down to D82A |
| 58.3 | D82K/D82A | Turn R – D82A (becomes D203) (St Béron). Follow D203 through St Béron to La Bridoire |
| 63.6 | La Bridoire | Turn R – D921E (Lac d'Aiguebelette): 2.2km at 5% |
| 65.8 | D921E/D921B | Turn R – D912B (Le Gué des Planches) |
| 66.4 | D921B/D921 | Turn L – D921 (Lac d'Aiguebelette) |
| 66.7 | D921/D921B | Turn R – D921D (Lépin-le-Lac) and follow road to Aiguebelette-le-Lac |
| 71.9 | Aiguebelette-le-Lac | Village church on RHS of road (Chef Lieu) |

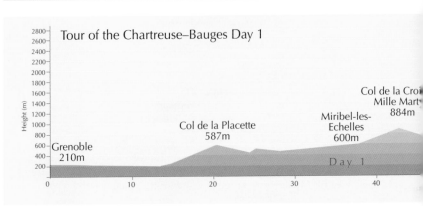

Tour of the Chartreuse–Bauges Day 1

*The Chartreuse from Col de la Croix des Mille Martyrs*

## FACILITIES AND SERVICES

| Location | Distance (km) | Water | Shops | Café | Campsite | B&B | Hotel | Bank | Bike Shop |
|---|---|---|---|---|---|---|---|---|---|
| Grenoble | 0.0 | x | x | x | x | x (1) | x | x | x |
| St Egrève | 4.5 | — | x | x | — | — | x | x | — |
| Voreppe | 14.9 | x | x | x | — | x | x | x | — |
| St Etienne-de-Crossey | 28.2 | x | x | x | x | x | x | — | (2) |
| Miribel-les-Echelles | 38.7 | x | x | x | x | x | x | — | — |
| Merlas | 50.0 | x | — | x | — | — | — | — | — |
| St Béron | 60.8 | — | — | x | x | — | — | — | — |
| La Bridoire | 63.6 | — | x | x | — | x | — | — | — |
| Lépin-le-Lac | 66.7 | x | x | x | x | x | x | — | — |
| Aiguebelette-le-Lac | 71.9 | x | — | — | x | — | x | — | (3) |

(1) At La Tronche on the north-east edge of Grenoble (about 4km from the station)

(2) At Voiron, 5km west of St Etienne-de-Crossey

(3) Nearest bike shop: Pont de Beauvoisin, 14km from Aiguebelette-le-Lac

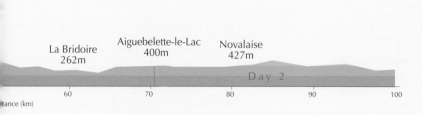

La Bridoire 262m    Aiguebelette-le-Lac 400m    Novalaise 427m

Day 2

Distance (km) — 60 — 70 — 80 — 90 — 100

## Day 2 – Aiguebelette-le-Lac to Le Bourget-du-Lac

As well as being an idyllic place for swimming, Lake Aiguebelette is also renowned as a rowing centre. Like cyclists, rowers prefer wind-free conditions and Aiguebelette boasts 300 windless days per year. As the third largest natural lake in France (after Bourget and Annecy), it regularly hosts international rowing competitions and was the venue for the World Rowing Championships in 1997.

| Distance | Location | Directions |
| --- | --- | --- |
| 0.0 | Aiguebelette-le-Lac: Chef Lieu | From in front of church head north along D921D |
| 6.5 | D921D/D41: roundabout | Go straight on (Novalaise) |
| 7.1 | D41/D921: roundabout | Turn R – D921 (Novalaise) |
| 10.8 | Novalaise: D921/D916 | Go straight on – D921 (Yenne) |
| 17.3 | D921/D921C | Bear R – D921C (St Paul-sur-Yenne). Follow this road to Chevelu |
| 25.8 | Chevelu: D921C/ N504 | Go straight on – D210 (Jongieux) |
| 26.8 | Jtn | Turn L, and then bear R 100 metres further on |
| 27.5 | Jtn | Bear L |
| 29.5 | D210/D44 | Turn L (Jongieux) |
| 30.2 | Billième: D44/D210 | Turn R – D210 (Jongieux) and go through Jongieux to D921 |
| 36.0 | D210/D921 | Turn R – D921 (Chanaz) |
| 44.4 | Chanaz: D921/D18 | Go straight on – D18 (Conjux) |
| 47.5 | Portout: D18/D914 | Turn R – D914 (Conjux) |
| 50.5 | D914/D18 | Follow D914 (St Pierre de Curtille): 9.1km at 4% |
| 52.2 | St Pierre de Curtille: D914/D210 | Turn L – D914 (Col du Chat) |
| 64.0 | D914/D914A | Turn L – D914 (Le Bourget-du-Lac) |
| 67.7 | D914/N504 | Go straight on (Bourdeau) |
| 67.8 | Jtn | Turn R [Chambéry] |
| 68.2 | Jtn | Bear L. Do not follow (Le Bourget-du-Lac) |
| 68.5 | D13/D14 | Turn R – D14 |
| 71.5 | Le Bourget-du-Lac: Port des Mouettes | Information point/snack bar is on L |

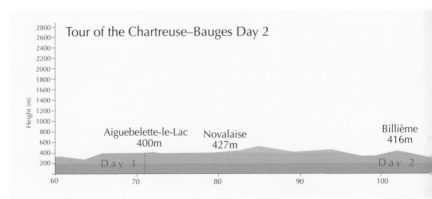

Tour of the Chartreuse–Bauges Day 2

*Lake Bourget and the Belledonne Mountains
from the Col du Chat*

## FACILITIES AND SERVICES

| Location | Distance (km) | Water | Shops | Café | Campsite | B&B | Hotel | Bank | Bike Shop |
|---|---|---|---|---|---|---|---|---|---|
| Aiguebelette-le-Lac | 0.0 | x | — | — | x | — | x | — | (1) |
| Novalaise | 10.8 | x | x | x | — | — | x | x | — |
| Chevelu | 25.8 | x | x | x | x | — | x | — | — |
| Billième | 30.2 | x | — | — | — | — | — | — | — |
| Jongieux | 32.3 | x | — | — | — | x | — | — | — |
| Chanaz | 44.4 | x | x | x | x | — | — | — | — |
| Portout | 47.5 | — | — | — | — | — | x | — | — |
| Conjux | 50.0 | x | — | — | x | — | — | — | — |
| St Pierre-de-Curtille | 52.2 | x | — | x | x | x | — | — | — |
| Le Bourget-du-Lac | 71.5 | x | x | x | x | x | x | x | (2) |

(1) Nearest bike shop: Pont de Beauvoisin, 14km from Aiguebelette-le-Lac

(2) Nearest bike shop: Aix-les-Bains, 10km from Le Bourget-du-Lac or La Motte Servolex, 9km from Le Bourget-du-Lac

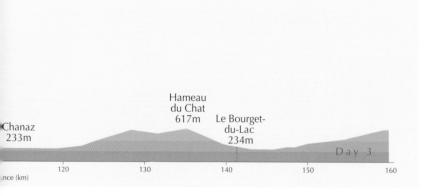

## Day 3 – Le Bourget-du-Lac to Annecy

Savoie has a flourishing wine industry, largely due to a sales policy that is known as 'in-situ exports': nearly all of the region's wine is sold locally, but a large percentage is drunk elsewhere, taken home as a souvenir by visiting tourists. Of the area's wines, Chignin-Bergeon has the best reputation and is correspondingly expensive. Marestel from Jongieux is another pleasant white wine; if you prefer red, you might like to try a Mondeuse.

| Distance | Location | Directions |
|---|---|---|
| 0.0 | Le Bourget-du-Lac: Port des Mouettes | Turn L in front of information point/snack bar |
| 0.1 | Carpark entrance | Turn L into car park then turn R in front of Ecole Française de Voile to join start of cycleway [Aix-les-Bains] |
| 0.7 | Bridge | Turn L and go over river [Aix-les-Bains] |
| 3.2 | Port entrance | Leave cycleway to join N211. Follow this road to roundabout |
| 3.4 | Roundabout: N211/D17B | Go straight on – D17B (Viviers-du-Lac). |
| 4.4 | D17B/D17 Jtn with road from Chambéry airport. | Go straight on through Viviers-du-Lac to reach D991 |
| 5.0 | D17B/D991 | Turn R – D991 (Méry) |
| 5.7 | D991/D51 | Turn L (Méry): 11.9km at 3% |
| 7.5 | Méry: D51/D211 | Turn L – D211. Go through Drumettaz and Mouxy |
| 12.1 | D211/D913 | Bear R – D913 (Le Revard). Go through Trévignin |
| 16.9 | D913/D211 | Turn L – D211 (St Offenge) |
| 19.9 | Montcel: D211/D211A | Turn R– D211A (St Offenge) |
| 23.8 | St Offenge Dessous | Go straight on – D211B–D103 (Cusy) |
| 27.5 | D103/D911 | Turn R – D911 and go through Cusy |
| 37.4 | D911/D912 | Turn L – D912 (Col de Leschaux): 6.8km at 6% |
| 44.2 | Col de Leschaux: D912/D110 | Turn L – D110 (Le Semnoz): 13.8km at 5.5% |
| 58.0 | Le Semnoz | Go straight on – D41 |
| 74.2 | Jtn | Turn R (Centre Ville) |
| 74.6 | Roundabout | Turn L – Rue des Marquisats (Centre Ville) |
| 75.0 | Annecy *hôtel de ville* | *Hôtel de ville* is on R |

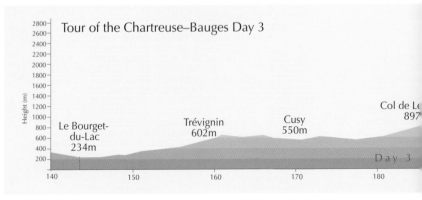

Tour of the Chartreuse–Bauges Day 3

*Lake Annecy from the Semnoz*

## FACILITIES AND SERVICES

| Location | Distance (km) | Water | Shops | Café | Campsite | B&B | Hotel | Bank | Bike Shop |
|---|---|---|---|---|---|---|---|---|---|
| Le Bourget-du-Lac | 0.0 | x | x | x | x | x | x | x | (1) |
| Viviers-du-Lac | 4.7 | x | x | x | — | x | x | x | — |
| Mouxy | 11.7 | x | — | — | — | — | — | — | — |
| Trévignin | 16.2 | — | — | x | x | — | x | — | — |
| Montcel | 19.9 | — | — | x | x | — | x | — | — |
| Cusy | 28.1 | — | x | x | x | x | — | — | — |
| Col de Leschaux | 44.2 | x | — | x | — | x | — | — | — |
| Le Semnoz | 58.0 | — | — | x | — | x | x | — | — |
| Annecy | 75.0 | x | x | x | x | x | x | x | x |

(1) Nearest bike shop: Aix-les-Bains, 10km from Le Bourget-du-Lac or La Motte Servolex, 9km from Le Bourget-du-Lac

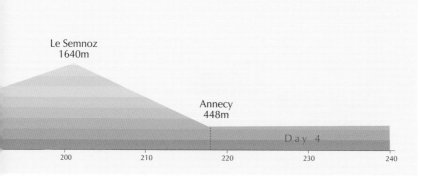

Le Semnoz
1640m

Annecy
448m

Day 4

200   210   220   230   240

## Day 4 – Annecy to St Pierre d'Albigny

| Distance | Location | Directions |
|---|---|---|
| 0.0 | Annecy *hôtel de ville* | Come out of *hôtel de ville* and turn L onto Quai E. Chappuis – Rue des Marquisats |
| 0.4 | Roundabout | Go straight on – N508 (Faverges) |
| 0.9 | Start of cycleway | Cross N508 to follow cycleway on L side of road |
| 23.8 | Jtn on cycleway | Turn R to leave cycleway (no signs) |
| 24.0 | Traffic lights | Turn L – Route d'Annecy |
| 24.7 | Traffic lights | Go straight on |
| 25.2 | Faverges N508/D12 | Turn R – D12 (Col de Tamié) |
| 35.5 | Col de Tamié | Go straight on – D201C: 10.3km at 4% |
| 45.0 | Frontenex: D201C/D201 | Turn R – D201. Follow D201 to St Pierre d'Albigny |
| 60.2 | St Pierre d'Albigny: D201/D911 | Go straight on – D201 |
| 60.5 | Place Charles Albert | TO is on R |

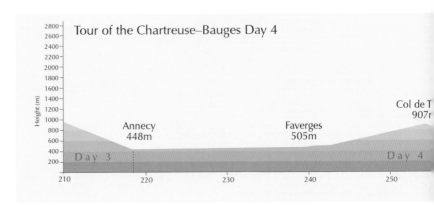

| **FACILITIES AND SERVICES** | | | | | | | | | |
|---|---|---|---|---|---|---|---|---|---|
| Location | Distance (km) | Water | Shops | Café | Campsite | B&B | Hotel | Bank | Bike Shop |
| Annecy | 0.0 | x | x | x | x | x | x | x | x |
| Sevrier | 2.6 | — | x | x | x | — | x | x | — |
| Doussard | 19.0 | — | x | — | x | x | x | x | — |
| Faverges | 25.2 | x | x | x | — | x | x | x | x |
| Col de Tamié | 36.0 | x | — | x | — | — | — | — | — |
| Frontenex | 45.5 | — | x | x | — | — | — | x | — |
| St Vital | 46.8 | x | — | — | — | x | — | — | — |
| Freterive | 56.1 | x | — | — | — | — | — | — | — |
| St Pierre d'Albigny | 61.0 | x | x | x | x | — | x | x | (1) |

(1) Nearest bike shop: Albertville, 21km from St Pierre d'Albigny

**Tour of the Chartreuse–Bauges Day 4**

Annecy 448m

Faverges 505m

Col de T
907r

Day 3

Day 4

*The imposing form of Miolans Castle, whose prison once held the Marquis de Sade*

With the exception of an occasional snake, the Bauges and Chartreuse Regional Parks, with their neat little villages and well-kept pastures, are the last places you would expect to encounter potentially dangerous wildlife. Chamois, foxes and hares are common, and there are a few, very discreet lynxes, but nothing to worry these pastoral communities. So, an immense shock-wave spread through the area when wolves were found to have returned. The reintroduction of wolves into the Abruzzi (Italy) and Mercantour (France) National Parks has sparked a bitter argument between environmentalists and shepherds, so the authorities tend not to broadcast the whereabouts of these animals. However, when a wolf is run over by a car, as occurred in the Combe de Savoie, and when wolves attack cattle, as happened a few kilometres from Grenoble, it is hard to keep their presence a secret.

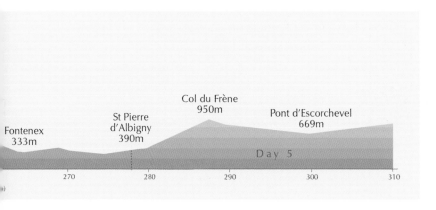

Col du Frène
950m

St Pierre
d'Albigny
390m

Pont d'Escorchevel
669m

Fontenex
333m

Day 5

270    280    290    300    310

To visitors, the boundaries of the 96 *départements* that make up mainland France and Corsica seem to have been rather arbitrarily drawn. For example, part of the Vaucluse *département* forms an enclave within the Drôme and many geographically distinct mountain areas are split between two *départements*. The reasons for this are very varied and often quite complex. The boundary between Isère and Savoie, which runs through the middle of the Chartreuse Mountains, follows the border between France and the Piedmont, of which Savoie was a part. In 1860, when the *département* of Mont Blanc was divided into Haute-Savoie and Savoie, the new *départementale* border followed the boundary between the dioceses of Annecy and Chambéry, splitting the Bauges in two.

| Distance | Location | Directions |
|---|---|---|
| 0.0 | St Pierre d'Albigny TO | Turn L and follow Rue Louis Blanc Pinget to D201/D911 jtn |
| 0.3 | D201/D911 | Turn L – D911 (Col du Frêne): 7.9km at 6% |
| 8.2 | Col du Frêne | Go straight on through Routhenes and Ecole-en-Bauges to Pont d'Escorchevel |
| 20.4 | Pont d'Escorchevel: D911/D206 | Turn L – D206 |
| 31.6 | D206/D59 | Turn R – D206 (Col des Prés) and go through Aillon-le-Jeune to Col des Prés: 4.0km at 6% |
| 35.6 | Col des Prés | Go straight on to Les Chavonettes |
| 42.0 | Les Chavonettes: D206/D21 | Turn L – D21 |
| 44.0 | D21/D21E | Turn L – D21E and go through Arvey: 3.4km at 5.5% |
| 48.5 | D21E/D11 | Turn L – D11: 4.5km at 4% |
| 53.0 | Col de Marocaz | Go straight on |
| 60.6 | Cruet: D11/D201 | Turn L and follow D201 (St Pierre d'Albigny) |
| 67.8 | St Pierre d'Albigny: roundabout | Turn L at roundabout (Centre Ville) |
| 68.2 | Roundabout | Go straight on to church and Place Charles Albert (Centre Ville) |
| 68.3 | Town centre | Turn L at T-jtn at top of Place CharlesAlbert |
| 68.4 | TO | TO is on R |

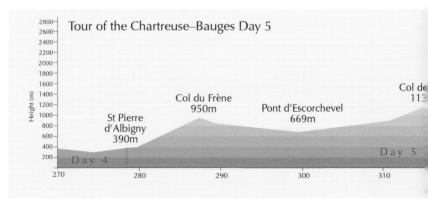

*Looking north towards Mont Trélod from below the Col du Frêne*

## FACILITIES AND SERVICES

| Location | Distance (km) | Water | Shops | Café | Campsite | B&B | Hotel | Bank | Bike Shop |
|---|---|---|---|---|---|---|---|---|---|
| St Pierre d'Albigny | 0.0 | x | x | x | x | — | x | x | (1) |
| Ste Reine | 10.0 | x | — | x | — | — | — | — | — |
| Ecole-en-Bauges | 17.0 | x | x | x | — | x | — | — | — |
| Aillon-le-Vieux | 17.8 | x | — | — | — | x | — | — | — |
| Aillon-le-Jeune | 31.8 | x | x | x | x | x | x | — | — |
| Puygros | 47.0 | x | — | — | — | — | — | — | — |
| Cruet | 60.6 | x | — | — | — | — | — | — | — |
| St Pierre d'Albigny | 68.4 | x | x | x | x | — | x | x | (1) |

(1) Nearest bike shop: Albertville, 21km from St Pierre d'Albigny

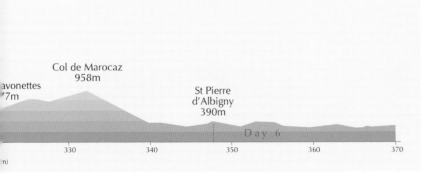

# Day 6 – St Pierre d'Albigny to Les Echelles

Despite its modest height (1933m), Mont Granier boasts its own glacier, but it is not a glacier many people see – it is inside the mountain!

| Distance | Location | Directions |
|---|---|---|
| 0.0 | St Pierre d'Albigny TO | Turn L and go to Place Charles Albert |
| 0.1 | Place Charles Albert | Turn R and go down to L of church |
| 0.2 | Roundabout | Turn L – Chemin du Pré de la Cure |
| 0.5 | Roundabout | Turn R (1st exit) – D911 |
| 1.0 | Roundabout | Turn L – D911 (A43). Follow (A43) to traffic lights at D911/N6 jtn |
| 3.5 | D911/N6: traffic lights | Go straight on along D202 (Chateauneuf): 1.8km at 5.5% |
| 5.3 | Chateauneuf – *Eglise* D202/D31 | Turn R – D31 (Coise) |
| 7.6 | D31/D31E | Turn L – D31 (Coise Chef-lieu) |
| 8.5 | D31/D204 | Turn R – D204 (Montmélian) |
| 17.4 | Roundabout | Go straight on – D204 (Montmélian) |
| 17.7 | Roundabout | Turn R – D923 |
| 17.9 | Roundabout | Go straight on – D204 (Montmélian Centre) |
| 18.6 | Montmélian: roundabout | Go straight on (Centre Ville) |
| 18.7 | Roundabout | Turn L – D201 (Francin) |
| 19.0 | Roundabout | Go straight on – D201E (Francin) |
| 19.6 | Roundabout | Turn L – D201 (Les Marches) |
| 23.1 | Les Marches: D201/N90 traffic lights | Turn L – N90 (Lac de St André) |
| 23.5 | N90/D12 | Turn R – D12 (Lac de St André). Follow D12 past Lac de St André and through St André |
| 28.5 | D12/D12E | Turn L – D12E (Col du Granier): 7.6km at 8% |
| 36.1 | D12E/D912 | Turn L – D912 (Col du Granier): 3.0km at 6% |
| 39.1 | Col du Granier | Go straight on |
| 49.3 | St Pierre d'Entremont: D912/D520C | Turn R – D520C (Les Echelles) |
| 61.0 | Entre-Deux-Guiers | Turn R and go through Entre-Deux-Guiers to Les Echelles |
| 61.3 | Les Echelles | TO is on L |

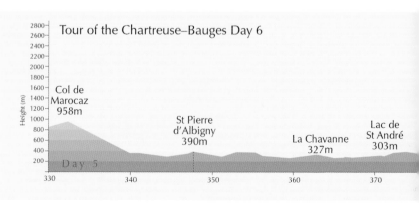

*Vineyards at the foot of Mont Granier (Day 6)*

## FACILITIES AND SERVICES

| Location | Distance (km) | Water | Shops | Café | Campsite | B&B | Hotel | Bank | Bike Shop |
|---|---|---|---|---|---|---|---|---|---|
| St Pierre d'Albigny | 0.0 | x | x | x | x | — | x | x | (1) |
| Chateauneuf | 5.3 | x | — | — | — | — | — | — | — |
| La Chavanne | 16.3 | x | x | x | — | — | — | — | — |
| Montmélian | 18.6 | — | x | x | x | — | x | x | — |
| Les Marches | 23.1 | — | x | x | — | x | — | — | — |
| Lake St André | 24.6 | x | — | x | x | — | — | — | — |
| Col du Granier | 39.1 | — | — | x | — | x | — | — | — |
| Entremont-le-Vieux | 44.0 | x | x | x | x | x | x | — | — |
| St Pierre- d'Entremont | 49.3 | x | x | x | x | x | x | x | — |
| St Christophe-sur-Guiers | 59.3 | x | — | x | — | x | — | — | — |
| Les Echelles | 61.3 | x | x | x | x | — | x | x | x |

(1) Nearest bike shop: Albertville, 21km from St Pierre d'Albigny

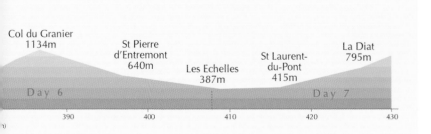

There are many very fit retired people in Savoie, so I was somewhat surprised that an ascent of the Col du Granier by an octagenarian should be deemed interesting enough to merit a story on the local TV news – until I found out that he did it on a unicycle!

| Distance | Location | Directions |
|---|---|---|
| 0.0 | Les Echelles | Come out of TO and turn R. Go across River Guiers Vif and into Entre-Deux-Guiers |
| 0.3 | Entre-Deux-Guiers | Turn R – Rue de la Poste |
| 0.6 | Traffic lights | Go straight on at lights and then take 1st L – D28B (Villette) |
| 5.2 | Villette | Bear L – D28. Follow this road to St Laurent-du-Pont |
| 7.0 | St Laurent-du-Pont D28/D520 | Turn L – D520 (St Pierre de Chartreuse) |
| 7.2 | D520/D520B | Turn R – D520B (St Pierre de Chartreuse): 10.1km at 3.8% |
| 17.3 | La Diat D520B/D512 | Turn R – D512. Follow this road to Col de Porte: 8.5km at 6% |
| 25.8 | Col de Porte | Go straight on |
| 28.3 | D512/D57 | Turn R – D57 (Sarcenas). Follow D57 to jtn with N75 |
| 43.1 | St Martin-le-Vinoux D57/N75 | Turn R – N75 |
| 43.3 | Place Aristide Briand | Cross River Isère and then Place Hubert Dubedout to get to Rue Casimir Brenier. Go along Rue Casimir Brenier to station |
| 44.0 | Grenoble station | |

| Location | Distance (km) | Water | Shops | Café | Campsite | B&B | Hotel | Bank | Bike Shop |
|---|---|---|---|---|---|---|---|---|---|
| **FACILITIES AND SERVICES** | | | | | | | | | |
| Les Echelles | 0.0 | x | x | x | x | — | x | x | x |
| St Laurent-du-Pont | 7.0 | x | x | x | x | x | x | x | x |
| La Diat (St Pierre de Chartreuse) | 17.3 | x | x | x | — | x | x | — | — |
| Col de Porte | 25.8 | — | — | x | — | — | — | — | — |
| Grenoble | 44.0 | x | x | x | x | x | x | x | x |

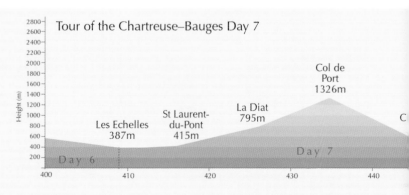

*St Hugues and the Grand Som*

Extra day: Le Bourget-du-Lac is at the foot of the Mont du Chat, one of the most challenging climbs in the French Alps. The ascent is just over 14km long, with an average gradient of almost 10% for the last 12km. After admiring the view from the summit café, head down the western side of the mountain, turning left after about 7km to go through Vacheresse and over the Col de l'Epine. From the Col de l'Epine, go through St Sulpice and La Motte Servolex to follow the Balcons du Bourget cycling route back to the lake. The circuit can be made a little easier by going back round to Le Bourget-du-Lac via St Paul-sur-Yenne, Chevelu and the Col du Chat.

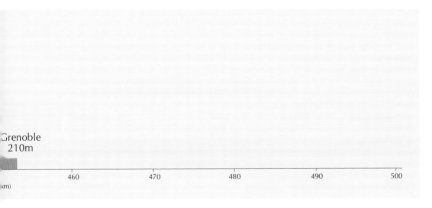

Grenoble
210m

| | 460 | 470 | 480 | 490 | 500 |

(km)

# ACCOMMODATION

## Grenoble

**Campsites**

The nearest campsite is at Seyssins, on the southwest edge of Grenoble:

Les Trois Pucelles (all year), Tel. 04 76 96 45 73

**Bed & Breakfast**

Mr Cohen, La Tronche, Tel. 04 76 44 78 98

**Hotels**

There are more than 50 hotels in Grenoble. Contact TO for details.

## Lépin-le-Lac/Aiguebelette-le-Lac

**Campsites**

Le Mont Grêle, Tel. 04 79 36 06 64

Ferrand (early May to end Oct), Tel. 04 79 36 01 50

Le Curtelet (early May to end Sept), Tel. 04 79 44 11 22

Les Peupliers (early April to end Oct), Tel. 04 79 36 00 48

**Bed & Breakfast**

La Clairière du Moulin, Tel. 04 79 36 30 05

La Grange du Rossignolet, Tel. 04 79 36 09 62

La Bageatière, Tel. 04 79 65 95 61

**Hotels**

La Combe (**), Tel. 04 79 36 05 02

Auberge du Lac (**), Tel. 04 79 36 03 27

Les Sirenes (**), Tel. 04 79 36 05 09

La Diligence, Tel. 04 79 44 12 45

## Le Bourget-du-Lac

**Campsites**

L'Ile aux Cygnes (end April to end Sept), Tel. 04 79 25 01 76

Le Lamartine (Bourdeau) (mid-June to mid-Sept): 04 79 25 03 41 (town hall)

**Bed & Breakfast**

Mr and Mrs Van der Hoeven, Tel. 04 79 25 27 72

Mr and Mrs Prud'homme, Tel. 04 79 25 24 19

Mrs Gonay, Tel. 04 79 25 01 72

**Hotels**

Ombremont (***), Tel. 04 79 25 00 23

Beaurivage (**), Tel. 04 79 25 00 38

Atmosphères, Tel. 04 79 25 01 29

Hotel du Port (**), Tel. 04 79 25 00 21

Hotel du Lac, Tel. 04 79 25 00 10

L'Orée du Lac, Tel. 04 79 26 22 20

## Annecy

**Campsites**

Le Belvedere (end March to mid-October), Tel. 04 50 45 48 30

This is the only campsite in Annecy itself, but there are many others along the lakeshore. Contact TO for details.

**Bed & Breakfast**

Youth hostel, Tel. 04 50 45 33 19

Mr Michel, Tel. 04 50 45 72 28

**Hotels**

There are more than 40 hotels in Annecy. Contact TO for details.

## St Pierre d'Albigny

**Campsites**

Lac de Carouge (early June to mid-Sept), Tel. 04 79 28 58 16

L'Arclusaz (July/August), Tel. 04 79 28 53 39

**Bed & Breakfast**

Château des Allues, Tel. 04 79 71 48 96

Mrs Lamare, Tel. 06 21 20 76 11

**Hotels**

Hotel Central (**), Tel. 04 79 28 50 05

Relais des 3 Vallées, Tel. 04 79 44 27 68

## Les Echelles/Entre-Deux-Guiers

**Campsites**

L'Arc-en-ciel (early March to end Oct), Tel. 04 76 66 06 97

**Bed & Breakfast**

There are no bed & breakfasts in Les Echelles

**Hotels**

Auberge du Morge (**), Tel. 04 79 36 62 76

## TOURIST INFORMATION

### Regional Information

| | Telephone | Website |
|---|---|---|
| Isere | 04 76 54 34 36 | www.isere-tourisme.com |
| Savoie | 04 79 85 12 45 | www.savoie-mont-blanc.com |
| Haute-Savoie | 04 50 51 32 31 | www.savoie-mont-blanc.com |

### Tourist Information Offices

| Location | Telephone | Website |
|---|---|---|
| Grenoble | 04 76 42 41 41 | www.grenoble-isere-tourisme.com |
| Voiron | 04 76 05 00 38 | www.paysvoironnais.info |
| Lépin-le-Lac | 04 79 36 00 02 | www.avant-pays-savoyard.com |
| Yenne | 04 79 36 71 54 | www.avant-pays-savoyard.com |
| Le Bourget-du-Lac | 04 79 25 01 99 | www.bourgetdulac.com |
| Aix-les-Bains | 04 79 88 68 00 | www.aixlesbains.com |
| Annecy | 04 50 45 00 33 | www.lac-annecy.com |
| Faverges | 04 50 44 60 24 | www.pays-de-faverges.com |
| St Pierre d'Albigny | 04 79 25 19 38 | www.saintpierredalbigny.fr |
| Aillon-le-Jeune | 04 79 54 63 65 | www.lesaillons.com |
| Montmélian | 04 79 84 07 31 | www.montmelian.com |
| St Pierre d'Entremont | 04 79 65 81 90 | www.chartreuse-tourisme.com |
| Les Echelles | 04 79 36 56 24 | www.avant-pays-savoyard.com |
| St Laurent-du-Pont | 04 76 06 22 55 | perso.wanadoo.fr/st-laurent-du-pont |
| St Pierre de Chartreuse | 04 76 88 62 08 | www.st-pierre-chartreuse.com |

# TOUR OF THE BELLEDONNE

| Day | Route | Distance | Height Gain |
|-----|-------|----------|-------------|
| 1 | Grenoble to Allevard | 75.8km | 1710m |
| 2 | Allevard to Albertville | 68.6km | 1130m |
| 3 | Albertville to La Chambre | 64.0km | 1660m |
| 4 | La Chambre to Bourg d'Oisans | 60.8km | 1670m |
| 5 | Bourg d'Oisans to Grenoble | 90.8km | 1080m |
| | **Totals** | **360.0km** | **7250m** |

For the purposes of this tour, the name Belledonne has been used in its widest sense to describe the westernmost ramparts of the true Alps between Albertville, Grenoble and La Mure. A closer look at the geography of the area shows that the Arc and Romanche Rivers divide the chain into three separate massifs – from north to south: the Lauzière, the Belledonne and the Taillefer. Three names that may be more familiar to keen cyclists and followers of the Tour de France are the Madeleine, Glandon and Ornon passes, all of which are found along the eastern flank of the Belledonne. Rising to almost 2000m, the Col de la Madeleine and the Col du Glandon are undoubtedly the 'stars' of the Tour of the Belledonne, however they are far from being the only difficulties in this short but strenuous five-day circuit.

Talk to any local cyclist/walker/skier and you will be regaled with stories of how wonderful the Belledonne is. At first sight it is difficult to see what could engender such enthusiasm, as there are few individually striking summits, spectacular cliffs or dramatic gorges; nothing that instantly inspires awe and admiration. This is probably part of the attraction; in a society that increasingly proposes instant gratification and where pleasures are correspondingly fleeting, the Belledonne offers the greatest rewards to those who take the time to get to know it well. Because it has avoided intensive tourist development and never been subject to the restrictions deemed necessary to protect neighbouring national

parks and nature reserves, the Belledonne has retained an unusual degree of authenticity. As could be expected in an area that does not attract a lot of tourists, hotels and campsites can be few and far between and there is only a limited number of potential overnight stopping places.

The Tour of the Belledonne starts and finishes in Grenoble, the self-styled capital of the Alps. Whether or not you agree with such a bold statement, it must be admitted that Grenoble has a unique location, nestled at the foot of three different massifs: the Chartreuse, the Vercors and the Belledonne. Many major cities – of which Grenoble is undoubtedly one, being home to 700,000 people – are unpleasant to cycle around because of the amount of traffic on the roads. However, Grenoble is doubly fortunate in having a well-developed network of cycleways and in being surrounded by steep mountains that funnel most of the traffic along the valley floors. With the exception of one or two roads to the more popular resorts, as soon as you head up into the hills you will rarely be bothered by cars. For more information about Grenoble see the introduction to Route 4.

Day 1 starts quite gently, following the banks of the River Isère, mostly on cycleways well away from the traffic of the city centre. After about 10km, the rhythm abruptly changes as you leave the valley to climb up into the foothills of the Belledonne, but the hard work is soon rewarded with fantastic views of the Chartreuse Mountains on the

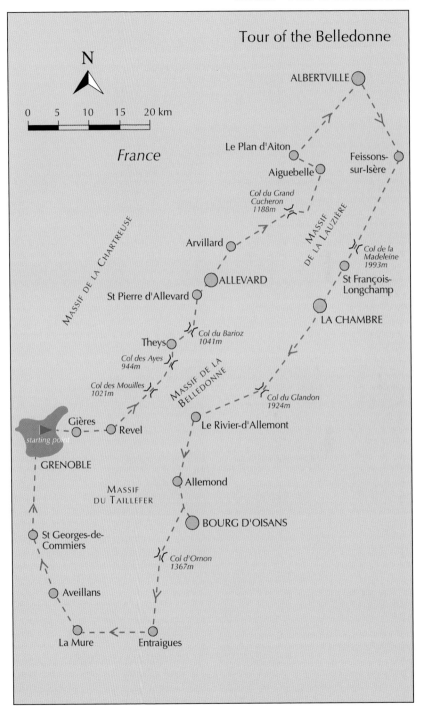

## Tour of the Belledonne

N

France

0  5  10  15  20 km

ALBERTVILLE

Le Plan d'Aiton

Aiguebelle

Feissons-sur-Isère

Col du Grand
Cucheron
1188m

Arvillard

MASSIF DE LA CHARTREUSE

MASSIF DE LA LAUZIÈRE

ALLEVARD

St Pierre d'Allevard

Col de la
Madeleine
1993m

St François-
Longchamp

Col du Barioz
1041m

LA CHAMBRE

Theys

Col des Ayes
944m

Col des Mouilles
1021m

MASSIF DE LA
BELLEDONNE

Col du Glandon
1924m

Gières

Revel

Le Rivier-d'Allemont

starting point

GRENOBLE

Allemond

MASSIF
DU TAILLEFER

BOURG D'OISANS

St Georges-de-
Commiers

Col d'Ornon
1367m

Aveillans

La Mure

Entraigues

The Belledonne seen from near Le Naysord

opposite side of the Grésivaudan Valley. The road goes through a succession of traditional farming villages, following what the French call a 'balcony route' (a traverse across the flanks of a mountain with many good viewpoints along the way). However, the road is by no means flat; you will go over a total of four passes (although one, the Col du Lauteret, is so insignificant that it isn't even marked on most maps) before getting to Allevard.

Although there is little sign of it today, for many centuries Allevard's prosperity was based on the exploitation of iron ore from the nearby Bréda Valley, with the surrounding forests providing fuel for the smelters. Every visitor to Paris will have seen at least one example of Allevard iron as it was used to make the girders with which the Eiffel Tower was built. At the end of the 18th century, the focus of the town's economy began to change with the discovery of the medicinal properties of the local sulphur-rich waters. Allevard-les-Bains is still a spa resort, but it had its heyday at the beginning of the 20th century when it attracted the rich and famous from far and wide. The Musée de Jadis (Museum of Yesteryear) should satisfy the curiosity of those who would like to know more about the history of this surprising and pleasant little town.

From Allevard, the route continues northwards to the village of Arvillard and then through the idyllically pastoral Vallée des Huiles to the Col du Grand Cucheron. Apart from the last 2.5km below the pass, the cycling is quite easy, allowing your legs to warm up gently after the previous day's exertions. The slopes around the pass are very densely forested, but there is one small clearing at the top that gives an excellent view of the Lauzière Mountains to the north. From the pass, the road drops down into St George des Hurtières, a former iron, silver and copper mining village, although cycling through the forests and pastures that surround the village today, it is difficult to imagine it as a mining community. The harsh lives of the miners are vividly portrayed in the village's excellent museum. From St George the road winds down to Aiguebelle, where you cross the Maurienne Valley before climbing back up to Aiton. After a short descent to Le Plan d'Aiton, 13km of easy cycling through the Combe de Savoie takes you to Albertville.

Albertville is a relatively new town which was built in 1856 at the foot of the mediaeval citadel of Conflans. For almost 150 years, this was just another anonymous small town, but, in 1992, Albertville was thrust under the international spotlight when it hosted the 16th Winter Olympics. The Games were a huge success for Albertville, but the biggest rewards, in terms of publicity and international tourism, went to the ski resorts of the Tarentaise Valley (such as Courchevel, La Plagne and Val d'Isère). The story of Albertville's Olympic adventure is told at the Maison des Jeux Olympiques. Despite the large sums of money spent preparing the town for the Olympics, Albertville has little to attract passing tourists, but it is the only town in the area to offer a reasonable range of accommodation. However, Conflans, on the eastern edge of the town, is well worth a visit.

The third stage of the tour takes you south-east along the Tarentaise Valley to the foot of the Col de la Madeleine. Most of the traffic through the valley uses the RN90 dual-carriageway, which was built for the Winter Olympics, so the other roads tend to be very quiet. Once again the day starts gently with less than 250 metres of height gain in the first 20km: a good warm up before you attack the steep initial slopes of the Col de la Madeleine. The climb to the Madeleine is long (25km), but the gradient is quite variable and every few kilometres there are flatter sections where your legs can relax a little. From a tourism marketing point of view it seems to be very important for a pass to be at least 2000 metres high, so a prominent signpost at the top announces 'Col de la Madeleine 2000m', despite the actual height being only 1993 metres. The fact that the pass does not quite make the 2000-metre mark does nothing to spoil the view, especially when it can be enjoyed from the terrace of one of the col's roadside cafés. From the pass it is downhill all the way to La Chambre: a superb but quite technical 18km descent.

La Chambre is only 2km from the foot of the Col du Glandon, the second big climb on the circuit, so your legs have much less time to get warmed up. This is a much stiffer challenge than the Col de la Madeleine, as, apart from 1km through the village of St Colomban-des-Villards, the gradient is unrelenting and the steepest part is right at the top. Up to St Colomban, the road rises through dense forest, so the views are limited.

Above the village, the trees thin out allowing you to appreciate the fabulous countryside around you. Unusually for such a high pass, there are no cafés or refreshment stands at the top, so, outside the holiday season, when the camper vans have gone home, the Glandon has a very wild and isolated atmosphere. If you are in desperate need of refreshment, don't worry, there is a café on the south side of the pass, a few hundred metres from the top. However, you can't afford to relax too much as the hard work is not all over yet: the descent is broken by two short uphill sections. The first, alongside Grand Maison reservoir, is not too difficult, but the second, going up to Le Rivier d'Allemont, has an average gradient of around 10%. To look on the positive side, these two uphill sections mean that the descent will take longer, giving you more time to appreciate one of the most beautiful valleys in the northern Alps. The view of the Grand Pic de la Belledonne from just before Le Rivier d'Allemont is particularly impressive.

Day 4 ends at Bourg d'Oisans, one of the gateways to the Ecrins National Park. Bourg d'Oisans is a pleasant place that has developed as a tourism centre whilst retaining the charm of a traditional French provincial town. Every year the town is the venue for a major international mineral fair that attracts collectors from all over the world, so it is not surprising that the Mineral and Wildlife Museum should have such a good collection of crystals. Bourg's proximity to so many famous cols (such as Glandon, Croix de Fer and Galibier) has also made it a honey-pot for cyclists. Many of the hotels do special packages that include the sort of substantial breakfast that is so essential before a long day on the bike. The magnet that draws thousands of cyclists to Bourg d'Oisans is Alpe d'Huez, perhaps the most famous mountain stage of the Tour de France. Route 6 includes a circuit that starts with the climb to 'L'Alpe'.

The final day of the tour takes you back to Grenoble via the Col d'Ornon and the Valbonnais, a much more pleasant alternative to the direct route along the very busy N91. Although this stage is very long, once over the Col d'Ornon most of the cycling is

Looking up towards the final hairpins below the Col de la Madeleine

easy; there are no more long or steep climbs. For me, the Col d'Ornon also marks the boundary between the northern and the southern Alps. There is no sudden change in the landscape, but there is a subtle change in the atmosphere, which now has a sunnier, more relaxed Provençale feel. The atmosphere changes once again as you get to La Mure, once an important regional crossroads, but now struggling to come to terms with the decline of the coalfields just to the north of the town. La Mure was a strategic centre during the religious wars of the 16th and 17th centuries, first as a Protestant stronghold and later as a Catholic base for the conversion and persecution of the Calvinist heretics. You can learn more about the town's history, from prehistoric times to the mining era, at the Musée Matheysin. However, if you would like to get a real feel for what life was like for local miners, the place to visit is the Mine-image museum at La Motte-d'Aveillans, which includes an impressive reconstruction of a coalface.

Once past La Motte-Aveillans, the road goes down over the River Vaulx and then up onto the Corniche du Drac, high above the River Drac. The views from here, across to the Vercors Mountains and the tower-like Mont Aiguille, are superb. A 10km descent takes you through the mediaeval village of St Georges-de-Commiers to the valley floor and the industrial complexes around Jarrie. Despite appearances, the enjoyable cycling is not over yet; after a short sprint along the RN85, you leave the factories behind to climb out of the valley and up to the village of Champagnier, from where there is a fabulous panorama across Grenoble to the Chartreuse. Champagnier is only a few short kilometres from the suburbs of Grenoble and the cycleway that will lead you back to the city centre and the end of this superbly varied tour.

## GETTING THERE

### By car
Grenoble is 870km from Calais

### By plane
#### Via Lyon St Exupéry
*Bus:* Shuttle bus every hour.

*Train:* To take the train you have to cycle to La Verpillière (see Appendix 1 for route details). On average, there is a train to Grenoble every hour and the journey takes around an hour and ten minutes.

#### Via Geneva
Take the train from the airport to Geneva central station (Cornavin). From Cornavin there is a train to Grenoble every two to three hours, either direct or via Culoz and Chambéry. The direct journey takes around 2hrs 15mins.

#### Via Grenoble
See directions in Appendix 1

#### Via Chambéry
Directions to Chambéry station are given in Appendix 1. There is a very frequent train service from Chambéry to Grenoble with trains every 20mins to one hour, depending on the time of day. The journey takes around 45mins.

## WHEN TO GO

This tour can be done at any time from early May to the end of September. In October, it is usually too cold to cycle over such high passes as the Col de la Madeleine and the Col du Glandon and they are closed from mid-November to early May. At the beginning of May, even if the roads are officially still closed, it is usually possible to get through on a bike.

## MAPS

**Michelin:** Local – Sheet 333, Isère, Savoie
**Michelin:** Regional – Sheet 244, Rhône-Alpes
**IGN:** Top 100 – Sheet 53: Grenoble, Mont Blanc

# Day 1 – Grenoble to Allevard

Grenoble's tram system provides a fast and efficient way of getting round the city, but its rails can present quite a hazard for the unwary cyclist. Riding across Place Grennette, Grenoble's main shopping square, one day, I tried to cross the tramlines at too acute an angle. My front wheel slipped into the gap between the rail and the pavement and stopped dead resulting in a very spectacular dismount. The bike went flying, but somehow I managed to stay on my feet, catapulted into a thirty-metre sprint. Fortunately, it was a Sunday and the appreciative audience was not too large.

| Distance | Location | Directions |
|---|---|---|
| 0.0 | Grenoble station | Leave the station via the (Centre Ville) exit and go straight across the street in front of the station. Go down Rue Casimir Brenier to Place Hubert Dubedout |
| 0.4 | Place Hubert Dubedout | Go across the square (easiest on foot) and the follow Quai Crequi along the (true) L bank of River Isère. Go straight on to Place Emile de Marcieu |
| 1.3 | Place Emile de Marcieu | Turn L at the traffic lights and go across Place Emile de Marcieu to join the cycle lane along Quai Jonkind |
| 2.2 | Rue Poilus | Turn L onto the cycleway and follow it alongside the Isère (short sections not paved) |
| 10.7 | Junction | Turn R and go across the level crossing |
| 10.8 | D523 | Turn L – D523 |
| 11.8 | D523/D291 | Turn R – D291 (La Pererée): 6km at 6% |
| 20.5 | D291/D280b | Turn L – D208b (Revel) |
| 22.8 | Revel D208b/D11 | Go straight on – D11 |
| 24.2 | D11/D280 | Turn L – D280 (Allevard) Follow this road to St Pierre d'Allevard: a total of 47.9km |
| 46.3 | Col des Mouilles | 4.1km at 6.5% – up to the pass |
| 53.8 | Col des Ayes | 1.1km at 6% – up to the pass |
| 64.2 | Col du Barioz | 6.2km at 7% – up to the pass |
| 72.1 | D280/D525 | Turn R – D525 (Allevard) |
| 75.0 | Roundabout | Go straight on (Centre Ville) |
| 75.8 | Allevard | Place de la Resistance |

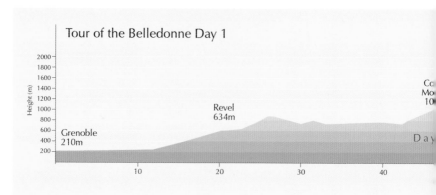

*Roadside sculptures near Le Mollard*

## FACILITIES AND SERVICES

| Location | Distance (km) | Water | Shops | Café | Campsite | B&B | Hotel | Bank | Bike Shop |
|---|---|---|---|---|---|---|---|---|---|
| Grenoble | 0.0 | x | x | x | x | (1) | x | x | x |
| Revel | 22.8 | x | x | x | — | x | — | — | — |
| Le Neysord | 30.0 | — | — | — | x | x | — | — | — |
| St Mury-de-Monteymond | 39.1 | x | — | x | x | — | — | — | — |
| Col des Mouilles | 46.3 | — | — | x | — | — | — | — | — |
| Col des Ayes | 53.8 | x | — | — | x | — | — | — | — |
| Theys | 58.0 | x | — | x | x | x | x | — | — |
| Col du Barioz | 64.2 | — | — | x | — | — | — | — | — |
| Allevard | 75.8 | x | x | x | x | x | x | x | (2) |

(1) Nearest B&B: La Tronche on the northeast edge of Grenoble (approx 4km from station)

(2) Nearest bike shop: Goncelin, 10km southwest of Allevard

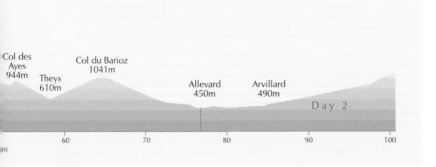

There are three ways in which this second day can be made a little more challenging: **1** – Turn right in the middle of Aiton to go through Bonvillard (D102, D69). The road climbs quite steeply gaining 370m in less than 5km, but the views of the Bauges Mountains to the west are truly spectacular. **2** – Cross the Combe de Savoie just after Ste. Hélène-sur-Isère and follow the D201C to the Col de Tamié, 570m above the valley floor. Turn right just before the pass to follow the D104, D104A and D63 down into the centre of Albertville. **3** – From Albertville, follow the D105 (signposted Conflans at first) to go past the Fort du Mont and over the Col des Cyclotouristes (not marked on most maps). This is a very stiff 13km/ 1000m climb. Return to Albertville via Molliessoulaz and the D925.

| Distance | Location | Directions |
|---|---|---|
| 0.0 | Allevard: Place de la Resistance | Turn R in front of church onto Rue du Grand Pont. Go over the river then turn L onto Rue Bir Hakeim |
| 1.1 | Roundabout | Bear R – D209 (Arvillard) |
| 7.0 | Arvillard | Go through the centre of the village |
| 7.2 | D209/D207E | Turn R – D207E (Presle) |
| 8.8 | D207E/D207 | Turn R – D207 (Presle) then (Col du Grand Cucheron): 13.7km at 3.5% then 2.6km at 9% just before the pass |
| 25.1 | Col du Grand Cucheron | Go straight on |
| 34.8 | D207/D73 | Turn L – D73 (Aiguebelle) |
| 42.6 | Aiguebelle: D73/N6 | Turn R – N6 |
| 42.8 | N6/D72 | Turn L – D72 (Randens) then R to go over the River Arc |
| 43.3 | Junction | Turn L – D72 (Aiton). Go straight through Aiton and down to Le Plan d'Aiton |
| 49.9 | Le Plan d'Aiton: D72/D925 | Turn R – D925 (Albertville) |
| 63.4 | Grignon: roundabout D925/D64 | Turn L – D64 (Gilly-sur-Isère) |
| 65.6 | Gilly-sur-Isère: D64/D990 | Turn R – D990 (Albertville). |
| 68.6 | Albertville | Railway station |

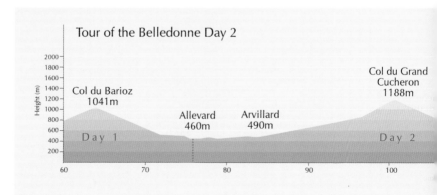

Tour of the Belledonne Day 2

*Le Bourget-en-Huile*

## FACILITIES AND SERVICES

| Location | Distance (km) | Water | Shops | Café | Campsite | B&B | Hotel | Bank | Bike Shop |
|---|---|---|---|---|---|---|---|---|---|
| Allevard | 0.0 | x | x | x | x | x | x | x | (1) |
| Arvillard | 7.0 | x | x | x | — | — | x | — | — |
| Bourget-en-Huile | 18.0 | x | — | — | — | — | — | — | — |
| St George-des-Hurtières | 36.0 | x | — | x | — | x | — | — | — |
| Aiguebelle | 42.6 | x | x | x | — | — | x | x | — |
| Le Plan d'Aiton | 49.9 | — | x | — | — | — | — | — | — |
| Gilly-sur-Isère | 65.6 | — | x | x | — | — | — | — | — |
| Albertville | 68.6 | x | x | x | x | x | x | x | x |

(1) Nearest bike shop: Goncelin, 10km southwest of Allevard

```
Georges-
Hurtières
80m        Aiguebelle        Le Plan                Albertville
            320m             d'Aiton                337m
                             300m
                                                                      Day 3

        120              130              140              150              160
km)
```

115

In spite of all his engineering skills, man's achievements are no match for the forces of nature. Even such sturdy structures as roads sometimes lose the struggle against gravity. A massive landslide at the end of the 1990s swept away one of the roads to the Col de la Madeleine. If you look to your left from La Thuile, you can still see where the road ends abruptly in a very steep scree slope. Unsurprisingly, there are no plans to rebuild this road!

| Distance | Location | Directions |
|----------|----------|------------|
| 0.0 | Albertville station | Come out of the station and go straight on along Ave Jean Jaurès. Continue straight on at three sets of traffic lights and at a roundabout – Ave du 8 Mai 1945, and then Route de Tours/D990. Go through La Bathie to Langon Gare |
| 12.5 | Langon Gare: roundabout | Turn R to go over the motorway and the River Isère |
| 13.8 | D66B/D66 | Turn L – D66. Follow the D66 past Feissonnet – D66–D97 |
| 19.1 | D97/D94 | Turn R – D94 (Col de la Madeleine) |
| 44.4 | Col de la Madeleine | Go straight on: 25.3km at 6% |
| 64.0 | La Chambre | |

| FACILITIES AND SERVICES | | | | | | | | | |
|-------------------------|--|--|--|--|--|--|--|--|--|
| Location | Distance (km) | Water | Shops | Café | Campsite | B&B | Hotel | Bank | Bike Shop |
| Albertville | 0.0 | x | x | x | x | x | x | x | x |
| La Bathie | 9.0 | — | x | x | x | — | x | x | x |
| Celliers | 35.0 | x | — | x | — | — | x | — | — |
| Col de la Madeleine | 44.4 | — | — | x | — | — | — | — | — |
| St François-Longchamp | 49.0 | — | x | x | — | x | x | x | — |
| La Chambre | 64.0 | x | x | x | x | — | x | x | (1) |

(1) Nearest bike shop: St Jean-de-Maurienne, 10km southeast of La Chambre

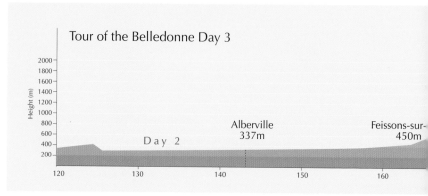

Tour of the Belledonne Day 3

_Mont Blanc from the Col de la Madeleine_

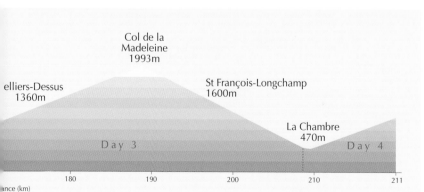

Col de la
Madeleine
1993m

elliers-Dessus
1360m

St François-Longchamp
1600m

La Chambre
470m

Day 3

Day 4

180     190     200     210     211

ance (km)

## Day 4 – La Chambre to Bourg d'Oisans

| Distance | Location | Directions |
|---|---|---|
| 0.0 | La Chambre | Turn L – D76 |
| 0.4 | Roundabout | Turn R |
| 0.7 | Roundabout | Go straight on |
| 1.2 | Roundabout | Go straight on |
| 1.4 | Roundabout | Turn R (Col du Glandon) |
| 1.8 | Roundabout | Turn L (Col du Glandon): 10.8km at 6% |
| 12.6 | St Colomban-des-Villards | Go straight on: 10.4km at 8% |
| 23.0 | Col du Glandon | Go straight on |
| 23.3 | D927/D926 | Turn R – D926-D526 (Allemont) |
| 39.2 | Le Rivier-d'Allemont | Go straight on |
| 48.9 | D526/D44 | Turn R along D526 and go over the dam (Allemont) |
| 50.2 | Allemond | Go straight on |
| 53.6 | Rochetaillée: D526/N91 | Turn L – N91 (Bourg d'Oisans) |
| 60.8 | Bourg d'Oisans TO | TO is on the left |

| FACILITIES AND SERVICES | | | | | | | | | |
|---|---|---|---|---|---|---|---|---|---|
| Location | Distance (km) | Water | Shops | Café | Campsite | B&B | Hotel | Bank | Bike Shop |
| La Chambre | 0.0 | x | x | x | x | — | x | x | (1) |
| St Etienne-de-Cuines | 2.5 | x | x | x | — | — | x | x | — |
| St Colomban-des-Villards | 12.6 | x | x | x | x | x | x | — | — |
| Col du Glandon | 23.0 | — | — | x | — | — | — | — | — |
| Le Rivier-d'Allemont | 39.2 | x | x | x | — | x | x | — | — |
| Allemond | 50.2 | x | x | x | x | x | x | — | — |
| Rochetaillée | 53.6 | — | — | — | x | — | — | — | — |
| Bourg d'Oisans | 60.8 | x | x | x | x | x | x | x | x |

(1) Nearest bike shop: St Jean-de-Maurienne, 10km southeast of La Chambre

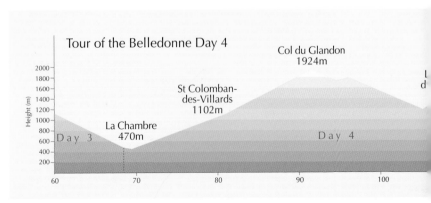

Tour of the Belledonne Day 4

Col du Glandon 1924m

St Colomban-des-Villards 1102m

La Chambre 470m

Day 3    Day 4

*The V-shaped Villards Valley below the Col du Glandon*

Buying and selling minerals has become big business, so much so that people are prepared to risk their lives in decaying mineshafts to collect them. At the beginning of 2005 and after a seven-month inquiry by 45 *gendarmes*, nine people were arrested and charged with illegally extracting minerals from the abandoned mines around Bourg d'Oisans. On searching their homes and garages, the police found a large quantity of dynamite and more than 50 tonnes of minerals. The suspects had even installed rail-mounted wagons in some of the shafts to extract their bounty. As the state is responsible for safety in former mine-workings, it was decided to blow up the mine entrances to seal them permanently. However, voices were immediately raised decrying an act of vandalism that would destroy a vital element in the region's industrial heritage. A petition was signed by 1500 people, including the mayor of Bourg d'Oisans ... and several of the people who had been arrested!

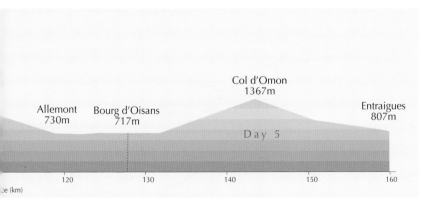

Allemont
730m

Bourg d'Oisans
717m

Col d'Omon
1367m

Entraigues
807m

Day 5

120   130   140   150   160

ce (km)

Extra day: the most obvious way to extend the tour is to do the circuit through Alpe d'Huez, as described in Route 6. For a less difficult ride, I would recommend the 60km round trip to La Bérarde up the Véneon Valley, arguably one of the most beautiful valleys in the Alps. Apart from short sections after Bourg d'Arud and around St Christophe, the gradient is quite gentle, allowing you to relax and soak up the magnificent surroundings. On the way back, it is worth making a short detour to visit the picturesque village of Venosc.

| Distance | Location | Directions |
|---|---|---|
| 0.0 | Bourg d'Oisans TO | Come out of the TO and turn R – N91 |
| 2.3 | N91/D526 | Turn L – D526 (Col d'Ornon): 11.6km at 5.5% |
| 13.9 | Col d'Ornon | Go straight on |
| 28.8 | Entraigues: D526/D117 | Turn R – D526 (La Mure) |
| 36.3 | D526/D26 | Go straight on along D26 (La Mure) |
| 47.5 | La Mure: D26/N85 | Turn R – N85 (Grenoble) |
| 48.2 | Roundabout | Go straight on |
| 48.4 | N85/D529 | Turn L – D529 and go through La Motte d'Aveillans and St George de Commiers (Vizille) |
| 71.8 | Roundabout: D529/D63A | Turn R – D529 (Grenoble) |
| 76.3 | Roundabout: D529/N85 | Turn L – N85 (Grenoble) |
| 77.5 | N85/D64 | Turn R – D64 (Champagnier) then (Grenoble) |
| 82.8 | Echirolles: roundabout | Go straight on – D269 (Grenoble) |
| 83.1 | Roundabout | Turn R onto cycleway parallel to tramway |
| 85.7 | Jtn: cycleway turns R at jtn with Rue de Bretagne | Go across road to go up path that leads to main road and big roundabout. Turn L at roundabout – Ave Edmond Esmonin (Lyon) |
| 86.4 | Traffic lights | Go straight on then bear R to go to R of fly-over |
| 86.8 | Jtn | Turn R – Ave Paul Verlaine. Follow cycle lane parallel to railway |
| 88.7 | Traffic lights | Turn L to follow cycleway between road and railway |
| 89.0 | Jtn | Turn L – Rue Colonel Lanoyerie |
| 89.7 | Fork | Bear L (Gare SNCF) |
| 90.2 | Grenoble station | Station is on the L |

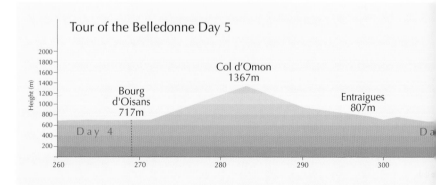

Tour of the Belledonne Day 5

Mt Aiguille, one of the most impressive mountains in the pre-Alps, as seen from La Motte d'Aveillans

| Location | Distance (km) | Water | Shops | Café | Campsite | B&B | Hotel | Bank | Bike Shop |
|---|---|---|---|---|---|---|---|---|---|
| Bourg d'Oisans | 0.0 | x | x | x | x | x | x | x | x |
| La Paute | 8.6 | x | — | — | — | — | — | — | — |
| Col d'Ornon | 13.9 | — | — | x | — | x | — | — | — |
| Les Daurens | 21.2 | x | — | x | — | x | — | — | — |
| Le Perrier | 23.9 | x | x | x | x | — | — | — | — |
| Entraigues | 28.8 | x | x | x | x | x | — | — | — |
| Valbonnais | 32.7 | x | — | — | x | x | — | — | — |
| La Mure | 47.5 | x | x | x | — | — | x | x | — |
| Aveillans | 54.0 | x | x | x | — | — | x | — | — |
| Notre Dame-de-Commiers | 72.7 | x | — | — | — | — | — | — | — |
| St George-de-Commiers | 76.4 | x | — | — | — | — | — | — | — |
| Grenoble | 90.8 | x | x | x | x | (1) | x | x | x |

**FACILITIES AND SERVICES**

(1) Nearest B&B: La Tronche on the northeast edge of Grenoble (approx 4km from station)

La Mure 855m

Aveillans 964m

St Georges-de-Commiers 384m

Grenoble 210m

320   330   340   350   360

e (km)

# ACCOMMODATION

## Grenoble

**Campsites**

Les Trois Pucelles, at Seyssins on the southwest edge of Grenoble (all year), Tel. 04 76 96 45 73

**Bed and Breakfast**

Mr Cohen, La Tronche, Tel. 04 76 44 78 98

**Hotels**

There are more than 50 hotels in Grenoble. Contact TO for details.

## Allevard

**Campsites**

Idéal Camping (early May to end Sept), Tel. 04 76 97 50 23

Clair Matin (1st May to mid-Oct), Tel: 04 76 97 55 19

**Bed & Breakfast**

There are no bed & breakfasts in Allevard

**Hotels**

There are eight hotels in Allevard. Contact TO for details.

## Albertville

**Campsites**

La Maladière (all year), Tel. 04 79 37 80 44

Les Adoubes (mid-June to mid-Sept), Tel. 04 79 32 06 62

**Bed & Breakfast**

Mr Boisneau, Tel. 04 79 31 23 23

Mrs Excoffon, Tel. 04 79 31 38 75

Mrs Verité, Tel. 04 79 32 29 68

Mr and Mrs Duet, Tel. 04 79 32 29 81

Mr Blanc, Tel. 04 79 32 39 10

**Hotels**

There are 10 hotels in Albertville. Contact TO for details.

## La Chambre

**Campsites (St Martin-sur-La Chambre)**

Le Bois Joli (early April to mid-October), Tel. 04 79 56 21 28

Le Petit Nice (all year) Tel. 04 79 56 37 12

**Bed & Breakfast**

There are no bed & breakfasts or *gites d'étapes* in La Chambre

**Hotels**

L'Eterlou ** Tel. 04 79 56 20 39

(Etape Hotel, at Saint Marie-de-Cuines, 3km south of La Chambre, Tel. 08 92 70 03 52)

## Bourg d'Oisans

**Campsites**

There are six campsites in Bourg d'Oisans. Contact TO for details.

**Bed & Breakfast**

Chalet 'La Source', Tel. 04 76 79 16 08

Other B&B-style accommodation exists around Bourg d'Oisans. Contact TO for details.

**Hotels**

There are 9 hotels in Bourg d'Oisans. Contact TO for details.

## TOURIST INFORMATION

### Regional Information

| | Telephone | Website |
|---|---|---|
| Isère | 04 76 54 34 36 | **www.isere-tourisme.com** |
| Savoie | 04 79 85 12 45 | **www.savoie-mont-blanc.com** |

### Tourist Information Offices

| Location | Telephone | Website |
|---|---|---|
| Grenoble | 04 76 42 41 41 | **www.grenoble-isere-tourisme.com** |
| Revel | 04 76 89 82 09 | **www.revel-belledonne.com** |
| Theys | 04 76 71 05 47 | no website |
| Allevard | 04 76 45 10 11 | **www.allevard-les-bains.com** |
| Aiguebelle | 04 79 36 29 24 | **www.ot-aiguebelle.com** |
| Albertville | 04 79 32 04 22 | **www.albertville.com** |
| St Francois-Longchamp | 04 79 59 10 56 | **www.saintfrancoislongchamp.com** |
| La Chambre | 04 79 56 33 58 | **www.tourisme-la-chambre.com** |
| St Colomban-des-Villards | 04 79 56 24 53 | **www.saint-colomban.com** |
| Allemont | 04 76 80 71 60 | **www.allemont.com** |
| Bourg d'Oisans | 04 76 80 03 25 | **www.bourgdoisans.com** |
| Valbonnais | 04 76 30 25 26 | **www.ot-valbonnais.fr** |
| La Mure | 04 76 81 05 71 | **www.ville-lamure.com** |
| La Motte d'Aveillans | 04 76 30 72 75 | no website |

*The Véneon Valley (Extra day)*

123

# ROUTE SIX

# TOUR OF THE ECRINS AND GRANDES ROUSSES

| Day | Route | Distance | Height Gain |
|-----|-------|----------|-------------|
| 1 | St Jean-de-Maurienne to Valloire | 26.4km | 1129m |
| 2 | Valloire to Briançon | 55.5km | 1241m |
| 3 | Briançon to Embrun | 61.3km | 726m |
| 4 | Embrun to St Bonnet-en-Champsaur | 64.3km | 1340m |
| 5 | St Bonnet-en-Champsaur to Bourg d'Oisans | 82.0km | 1686m |
| 6 | Bourg d'Oisans to Bourg d'Oisans | 58.2km | 1975m |
| 7 | Bourg d'Oisans to St Jean-de-Maurienne | 79.1km | 1962m |
| | **Totals** | **426.8km** | **10,059m** |

Although not a classic circuit in itself, the Tour of the Ecrins and Grandes Rousses includes some of the most famous mountain passes in the annals of cycling. There cannot be many keen cyclists who do not dream of following in the tracks of Mercx, Hinault and Armstrong on the roads to the Col du Galibier, Col de la Croix de Fer and Alpe d'Huez. Every year, thousands of cyclists attempt to do all three of these climbs in a single day as part of the famous Marmotte event, a 174km circuit with 5000 metres of height gain. Such long-distance challenges can be fun, but at the more gentle pace of the cycle-tourist you have much more time (and energy) to enjoy the surrounding countryside.

Grandes Rousses is the name given to the mountains between the Col du Galibier and the Col de la Croix Fer. It is an area that attracts relatively few visitors despite containing some of the most strikingly elegant summits in the Alps in the shape of the Aiguilles d'Arves. The neighbouring Ecrins Massif, the second highest range of mountains in France and a national park, is much more famous than the Grandes Rousses. The towns of Bourg d'Oisans, Briançon, Embrun and Gap mark the four corners of the massif, which culminates in the 4102 metre-high Barre des Ecrins. During the summer months this area is an extremely popular tourist destination and traffic levels on the main roads

often reach saturation point. Fortunately, with the exception of the descent from the Col du Lautaret to Briançon, cyclists are well served by a network of secondary roads that rarely see much traffic.

The tour starts in St Jean-de-Maurienne, Savoie's third largest city and the birthplace of the House of Savoie. The dynasty was founded by Humbert of the White Hands, who became the first Count of Savoie at the beginning of the 11th century. At its height, the family ruled lands that extended from Bourg-en-Bresse to Turin and from Geneva to Sardinia. Savoie itself became part of France in 1860, but the dynasty lived on with Victor-Emmanuel II becoming King of Italy in 1861. St Jean-de-Maurienne's first cathedral was built in the 6th century to provide a fitting resting-place for the diocese's sacred relics of John the Baptist. The original building was destroyed at the end of the first millennium and replaced in the 11th century by a building that has been greatly modified over the centuries, but which still stands today.

If you arrive in St Jean before the middle of the afternoon, you should have time to reach Valloire that same day. The classic route is through St Michel-de-Maurienne and over the Col du Télégraphe (see Route 8), however, the only way to get to St Michel is along the main *route nationale* and the road over the Col du Télégraphe can itself be busy at times.

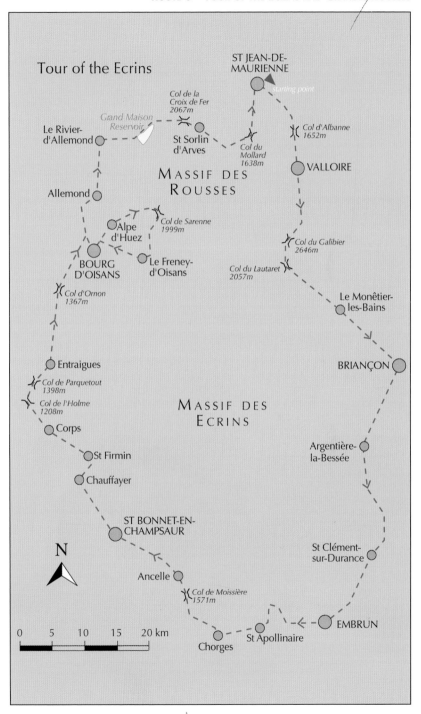

Tour of the Ecrins

ST JEAN-DE-MAURIENNE
*starting point*

Col de la
Croix de Fer
2067m

Grand Maison
Reservoir

Le Rivier-
d'Allemond

St Sorlin
d'Arves

Col du
Mollard
1638m

Col d'Albanne
1652m

VALLOIRE

MASSIF DES
ROUSSES

Allemond

Alpe
d'Huez

Col de Sarenne
1999m

Col du Galibier
2646m

BOURG
D'OISANS

Le Freney-
d'Oisans

Col du Lautaret
2057m

Le Monêtier-
les-Bains

Col d'Ornon
1367m

BRIANÇON

Entraigues

Col de Parquetout
1398m

MASSIF DES
ECRINS

Col de l'Holme
1208m

Corps

Argentière-
la-Bessée

St Firmin

Chauffayer

ST BONNET-EN-
CHAMPSAUR

St Clément-
sur-Durance

N

Ancelle

Col de Moissière
1571m

EMBRUN

St Apollinaire

Chorges

0   5   10   15   20 km

Fortunately, there is an alternative route, via Montricher and the Col de l'Albanne. The gradient is quite severe (an average of 7.5% for 12km) and there is a 2km section on an unpaved forest track (at least 80% can be ridden, even with a road bike), but you are rewarded with virtually deserted roads and a superb view from the pass.

Unlike many ski resorts, Valloire is as busy in summer as it is in winter, partly thanks to its location at the foot of the Col du Galibier. The Galibier has always been one of the great alpine passes and as such attracts tourists from far and wide. Although traffic is rarely a problem, the best time to cycle over the Galibier is the one morning in July (usually the first Thursday of the month) when the pass is closed to cars. However, Valloire also stages other events that may lead to the road being unpleasantly busy or completely closed, even to cyclists. Dates for these events can be found on the village's website.

Whether or not you have the road to yourself, cycling over the Galibier is always a challenge: there are few easy sections and the last kilometre is the steepest. The scenery is magnificent all the way, but very few mountain panoramas can rival the breath-taking view from the top of the pass. The chaotic glaciers and sombre cliffs of the north face of the Meije, just a stone's throw away, have a truly savage beauty that leaves no-one indifferent. The other high summits of the Ecrins seem to cower in the shadow of this monstrous wall of rock and ice. An even more grandiose spectacle is on offer to those who walk the short distance to the tiny summit just west of the pass, as the vista opens out to include the elegant spires of the Aiguilles d'Arves.

After an exhilarating descent to the Col du Lautaret, the route follows the main RN91 down the Guisane Valley to Briançon, the highest town in Europe. Given the number of forts surrounding the town, there can be no doubt as to the location's strategic importance. Many of these forts are open to visitors and guided tours are available. Briançon is a lively place and the town centre can be very busy, especially on a wet summer's day – it has to rain occasionally, even in a town that boasts 300 sunshine days a year! Come rain or shine, there are many interesting things to see including the old town, the forts and the Ski Museum at the Ecrins National Park Centre.

Stage three of the tour, along the Durance Valley from Briançon to Embrun, can be regarded as a semi-rest day as there are no long climbs to tackle. If you would like a more challenging day, the obvious alternative is to

*Argentière-la-Bessée: the biggest ice-axe in the world*

go over the Col d'Izoard (see Route 9) and rejoin the main itinerary just before St Clément-sur-Durance.

The first port of call after leaving Briançon is the former mining village of Argentière-la-Bessée. Without completely abandoning its industrial roots, Argentière has successfully turned itself into a centre for outdoor sports, building a white-water canoeing course and holding rock-climbing and ice-climbing competitions. Many of the village's streets have been named after famous mountaineers and the world's largest ice-axe stands proudly in front of the *marie*. A few kilometres south of Argentière lies the hardest climb of the day, a mere 1.5km long but with an average gradient of 12%. Although not completely flat, the rest of the stage is quite easy – time to relax and admire the marvellous scenery.

Embrun is a tiny cathedral city at the north-eastern end of the Serre-Ponçon Reservoir, the largest man-made lake in Europe. Work on the dam began in 1955, a century after the project was first mooted as a way to control the extremely variable flow-rate of the Durance River. The reservoir covers 2800 hectares and feeds 16 hydroelectricity plants, as well as providing irrigation water for 150,000 hectares of agricultural land via the Durance Canal. It is also a huge leisure resource that has transformed the economies of the surrounding villages. Embrun's gothic cathedral was built in the 12th and 13th centuries, but the city has been an archdiocese since the 9th century. The cathedral is one of the most imposing religious buildings in the Alps and well worth a visit. All that remains of the archbishop's palace is the Tour Brune, which now houses an interesting exhibition that explains the evolution of the surrounding landscape.

From Embrun the route follows quiet roads across the flanks of Mt Guillaume, turning left just before Réallon to take in the fabulous view of the lake from St Apollinaire. At this point there is no choice but to descend back into the valley to the pleasant little village of Chorges, and a final opportunity to stock up on calories before attacking the climb to the Col de Moissière. Once again it is possible to avoid the main road by following minor

roads around the northern edge of the village (not marked on either the IGN or Michelin maps). At this relatively low altitude, heat and dehydration can be your worst enemies, especially on the open, south-facing slopes you have to cross to get to the Col de Moissière. Fortunately, the last and steepest part of the ascent is through a cool(er) and shady forest.

The rest of the day's cycling is easy, a 12km descent followed by 11km on the flat. On the edge of the tiny resort of Ancelle, a pancake-smooth patchwork of fields covers the surface of a dried-up lake: an island of visual calm in the midst of this unrelentingly rugged landscape. St Léger-les-Mélèzes, a few kilometres north of Ancelle, is the last village with a full range of services before St Bonnet-en-Champsaur. It also has an excellent little natural history museum. St Bonnet is an attractive but very sleepy little place that seems to spring to life once a year when 300 villagers dress-up in period costumes to demonstrate the arts and crafts of their ancestors. This colourful Fête du Terroir takes place on the first Sunday in August.

Day 5 starts gently, through the rolling countryside north of St Bonnet, giving your legs time to warm up before tackling the three cols that bar the route to Bourg d'Oisans. The first climb, to the Col des Festraux, is not very long but the first 2km above St Firmin are very steep. After a short descent, the route turns right onto the main RN85, which takes you through Corps. This is the Route Napoléon, the road taken by Bonaparte when he returned from exile on the island of Elba to seize power. With Bonaparte's name splashed across the front of nearly every hotel, restaurant and bar, the visitor is left in no doubt as to the importance of this event in the area's history.

Just after Corps, the route once again leaves the main road to tackle the second major ascent of the day. There are in fact two passes to cross between Corps and Entraigues, but the descent between them is negligible. The road to the first pass, the Col de l'Holme, provides fabulous views of the 2790 metre-high Obiou and the other peaks of the Dévoluy. After the Col de l'Holme, the road very quickly rises again taking you up to

*The stunning pyramids of the Aiguilles d'Arves as seen from the Col du Mollard*

COMMUNE D'ALBIEZ-MONTROND
COL DU MOLLARD
Alt : 1638 m

(and above!) the Col de Parquetout. The descent from this second pass is very steep and narrow with a lot of blind corners, so be wary of vehicles coming the other way. The final climb of the day, over the Col d'Ornon, is long but quite easy, although the gradient increases slightly a few kilometres below the summit. If you are feeling too weary to continue, a night spent at the *gite d'étape* at Les Daurens is highly recommended. It was here that I first experienced a true *table d'hote*, where guests at a hotel or restaurant eat at the same table as their hosts. If you are lucky enough to have hosts like Mr and Mrs Marin, this is an excellent way to get a feel for French life. For those who make it all the way to the pass, the reward comes in the form of the wonderful descent to the Romanche Valley and Bourg d'Oisans.

Bourg d'Oisans is renowned amongst cyclists as the starting point for the climb to Alpe d'Huez. (see the introduction to Route 5 for more about Bourg d'Oisans). Every day during the summer, dozens if not hundreds of cyclists pit themselves against the 21 hairpins, 13km and 1120 metres of ascent. Alpe d'Huez is a must if only because of its legendary reputation, but you often have to share the road with a lot of tourist traffic, especially in July and August. The climb to

Alpe d'Huez is also the first part of a magnificent but strenuous circuit over the Col de Sarenne, one of the wildest passes in the Alps. The views of the Roche de Muzelle from the eastern side of the pass are truly spectacular, but the descent is very steep and care is needed as there is often a lot of gravel on the road. Just after Mizoën the route briefly joins the main RN91 before turning right at Le Freney-d'Oisans to follow the D211A above the Gorges de l'Infernet. The section across the Rochers d'Armentier is particularly dramatic: hanging 600 metres above the valley floor, the road seems to cling to the mountainside by its fingernails.

Day 7, over the Col de la Croix de Fer, is another long day, although when the roadworks on the direct route back to St Jean-de-Maurienne are completed (planned for 2008 – note that the road goes through three long tunnels), it will be possible to go straight down to St Jean-de-Maurienne, thus avoiding the steep climb to the Col du Mollard. Many people, including Lance Armstrong, consider the Croix de Fer to be one of the most beautiful passes in the Alps. At first the road runs through dense forest and it is only when you get to Le Rivier d'Allemond that the magnificent scenery is fully unveiled in all its glory. A roadside café 2.5km below the pass marks the junction with the road to the Col du Glandon, a mere 17 metres above you. If you are truly on your last legs, it is always possible to turn left here and go over the Col du Glandon to the railway station at La Chambre; otherwise, there is another café at the Col de la Croix Fer, giving you the opportunity to refuel before freewheeling down to the foot of the last climb of the tour. The road up to the Col du Mollard has the unwelcome characteristic of getting steeper and steeper as you approach the top, with the last 2.5km being at an average gradient of more than 10%. This time the compensation for your efforts is two-fold: a magnificent view of the Aiguilles d'Arves and a final exhilarating 18km descent back to St Jean-de-Maurienne.

## GETTING THERE

### By car
St Jean-de-Maurienne is 980km from Calais.

### By plane
#### Via Lyon
*Bus/Train:* Bus to Chambéry then train from Chambéry to St Jean-de-Maurienne. There are five or six busses per day and the journey takes about one hour. There is a train every two to three hours from Chambéry to St Jean-de-Maurienne and the journey takes 50mins to one hour.

*Cycle/Train:* You can also take the train by cycling to Bourgoin Jallieu (see Appendix 1 for route details), however, there are only two or three trains per day train – check the SNCF website to see if they are compatible with your flight times. The train journey takes between two and three hours, depending on connections.

#### Via Geneva
*Train:* Take the train from the airport to Geneva central station (Cornavin). There are only two or three trains per day from Cornavin to St Jean and you will always have to change at Chambéry and possibly Bellegarde and/or Culoz as well. The journey takes between three and four hours, depending on connections.

#### Via Chambéry
Directions to Chambéry station are given in Appendix 1. There are about five or six trains per day from Chambéry to St Jean-de-Maurienne. The journey takes around one hour.

## WHEN TO GO
This tour can only be done from the middle of June to October as the Col du Galibier is closed for the other seven months of the year. The Col de la Croix de Fer usually opens in early May, about one month before the Galibier. Apart from the section from Valloire to Briançon, the tour follows secondary roads that do not normally see a lot of traffic, even during the main holiday periods.

## MAPS
**Michelin:** Local – Sheet 333: Isère, Savoie; and Sheet 334: Alpes-de-Haute-Provence, Hautes-Alpes

**Michelin:** Regional – Sheet 244: Rhône-Alpes and Sheet 245: Provence, Côte d'Azur

**IGN:** Top 100 – Sheet 53: Grenoble, Mont Blanc and Sheet 54: Grenoble, Gap

Under the French Revolution all place-names with superstitious origins had to be changed, hence Saint Jean-de-Maurienne briefly became known as Arc.

| Distance | Location | Directions |
|---|---|---|
| 0.0 | St Jean-de-Maurienne Station | Come out of station, turn R then immediately L to go past the EDF office |
| 0.2 | Roundabout | Turn L – Rue Germain Sommeiller (Toutes Directions) |
| 0.3 | Jtn | Turn R – Quai de l'Arvan (Vallée de l'Arvan) |
| 0.9 | Jtn | Turn L – D906 (Torino) |
| 2.2 | Roundabout | Go straight on (Toutes Directions) |
| 2.3 | Roundabout | Turn L second exit  (Montricher–Albanne) |
| 3.9 | Roundabout D81/D80 | Go straight on – D81 (Montricher–Albanne) |
| 4.5 | Roundabout | Go straight on (Montricher–Albanne) |
| 6.6 | Le Bochet | Bear R towards centre of village |
| 6.7 | Jtn | Turn R – D81 (Montricher): 12.5km at 7.5% |
| 13.9 | Montricher: D81/D81B | Turn L – D81 (Albanne) |
| 19.2 | Col de l'Albanne | Go straight on |
| 20.3 | Albanne: jtn | Turn R (Albannette) |
| 22.6 | Jtn with forest track | Jtn is at apex of LH hairpin – go straight on along track [Valloire] |
| 24.5 | Jtn with paved road | Go straight on |
| 26.1 | Valloire | Take the road on the L, just after river, to town centre |
| 26.4 | Jtn | Turn R and TO is on R |

| Location | Distance (km) | Water | Shops | Café | Campsite | B&B | Hotel | Bank | Bike Shop |
|---|---|---|---|---|---|---|---|---|---|
| St Jean-de-Maurienne | 0.0 | x | x | x | x | — | x | x | x |
| Le Bochet | 6.6 | x | — | — | — | — | — | — | — |
| Montricher | 13.1 | x | — | x | — | — | x | — | — |
| Albanne | 20.1 | x | — | x | — | — | — | — | — |
| Valloire | 26.4 | x | x | x | x | x | x | x | x |

FACILITIES AND SERVICES

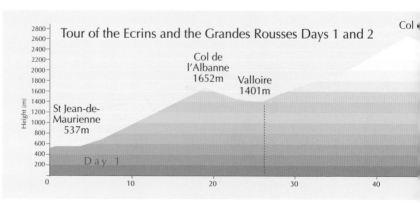

Tour of the Ecrins and the Grandes Rousses Days 1 and 2

*Looking down from Col du Galibier towards the Henri Desgrange Statue on Day 2 of the Ecrins and Grandes Rousses route*

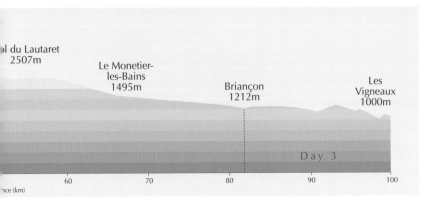

ol du Lautaret
2507m

Le Monetier-
les-Bains
1495m

Briançon
1212m

Les
Vigneaux
1000m

Day 3

60    70    80    90    100

ice (km)

Briançon's main street is known as 'La Grande Gargouille' after the open channel that runs down the middle. The channel's most important function was not as a drain, but as a way of supplying water to fight fires. La Grande Gargouille, which has an average gradient of 8% for 1km, has been the scene of many exciting finishes of stages of both the Tour de France and the Dauphiné Libéré.

*Looking across towards the Ecrins Mountains from the southern side of the Col du Galibier*

| Distance | Location | Directions |
|----------|----------|------------|
| 0.0 | Valloire TO | Come out of TO and turn R – D902: 17.5km at 7% |
| 17.5 | Col du Galibier | Go straight on |
| 26.2 | Col du Lauteret | Turn R – N91. Follow this, and then D994 into Briançon |
| 53.0 | Briançon – roundabout | Turn R (Gap) |
| 54.5 | Traffic lights | Turn L onto D2 (Gare SNCF) |
| 54.8 | Roundabout | Turn R |
| 55.0 | Roundabout | Go straight on |
| 55.5 | Briançon station | Station is on the R |

### FACILITIES AND SERVICES

| Location | Distance (km) | Water | Shops | Café | Campsite | B&B | Hotel | Bank | Bike Shop |
|----------|---------------|-------|-------|------|----------|-----|-------|------|-----------|
| Valloire | 0.0 | x | x | x | x | x | x | x | x |
| Col du Lautaret | 26.2 | — | x | x | — | — | — | — | — |
| Monêtier-les-Bains | 39.7 | x | x | x | — | x | x | x | x |
| Chantemerle | 48.0 | x | x | x | x | x | x | x | — |
| Briançon | 55.5 | x | x | x | x | (1) | x | x | x |

(1) At Villard St Pancrace, 2km south of Briançon

*Looking across towards the Ecrins Mountains from the southern side of the Col du Galibier*

| Distance | Location | Directions |
|---|---|---|
| 0.0 | Briançon station | Come out of the station and go straight on (Villar St Pancrace) |
| 0.1 | Roundabout | Turn R – D36 (Villar St Pancrace) |
| 0.3 | Roundabout | Go straight on (Villar St Pancrace) |
| 0.8 | Roundabout | Turn L (Villar St Pancrace) |
| 1.0 | Villard St Pancrace | Turn R at the roundabout (Centre Village) |
| 1.4 | Roundabout | Go straight on |
| 1.9 | Jtn | Go straight on along Routes des Espagnols |
| 7.8 | Roundabout | Turn L (Prelles) |
| 7.9 | Jtn | Turn L – N2094 (Prelles) |
| 8.2 | N2094/N94 | Turn R – N94 (Briançon) |
| 8.9 | N94/D4 | Turn L – D4 (Vallouise): 2.2km at 5% |
| 17.1 | D4/D994E | Turn L – D994E (Argentière) |
| 21.7 | Argentière-la-Bessée | Go straight through the village: D994E–D104 |
| 22.5 | Roundabout | Turn L – D104 |
| 23.5 | Roundabout | Go straight on – D138A (Champcella) |
| 26.7 | D138A/D38 | Go straight on – D38: 1.5km at 12% |
| 29.4 | Pallon | Turn L – D38 (Champcella) |
| 30.9 | Jtn | Bear L – D38 (St Crépin) |
| 35.4 | Jtn (after bridge) | Turn L |
| 35.7 | Jtn | Turn R along D38 (St Clément) |
| 39.6 | Jtn | Go straight on – D38 (St Clément) |
| 43.8 | D38/N94 | Turn L – N94 |
| 44.2 | N94/D994D | Turn R – D994D (St André-sur-Embrun) |
| 54.9 | D994D/D139 | Turn R – D994D (Embrun) |
| 58.8 | Jtn | Turn R over wooden bridge, and follow road round to L, and then to R to go up hill |
| 60.8 | Embrun | Turn L – N94 (Centre Ville) |
| 61.1 | Jtn | Turn L to go into pedestrian zone – Rue Clovis Hugues |
| 61.2 | Jtn | Turn R to get to TO |
| 61.3 | Embrun TO | TO is in front of you |

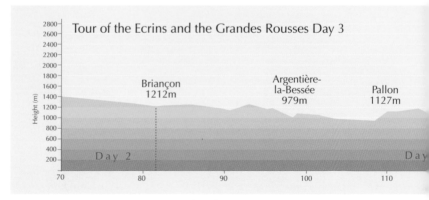

Tour of the Ecrins and the Grandes Rousses Day 3

Looking north from Chanteloube

## FACILITIES AND SERVICES

| Location | Distance (km) | Water | Shops | Café | Campsite | B&B | Hotel | Bank | Bike Shop |
|---|---|---|---|---|---|---|---|---|---|
| Briançon | 0.0 | x | x | x | x | (1) | x | x | x |
| Prelles | 8.9 | x | x | — | — | — | — | — | — |
| Les Vigneaux | 16.5 | x | x | — | x | x | — | — | — |
| Argentière-la-Bessée | 21.7 | x | x | x | x | x | x | x | x |
| Pallon | 29.5 | x | — | x | x | — | x | — | — |
| St Clément-sur-Durance | 43.8 | x | x | — | x | x | — | — | — |
| Embrun | 61.3 | x | x | x | x | x | x | x | x |

(1) At Villard St Pancrace, 2km south of Briançon

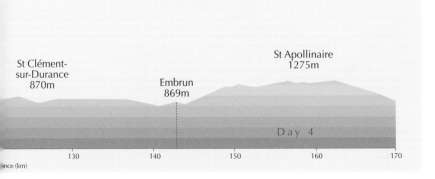

St Clément-sur-Durance 870m

Embrun 869m

St Apollinaire 1275m

Day 4

130      140      150      160      170

nce (km)

135

# Day 4 – Embrun to St Bonnet-en-Champsaur

In recent years, a great many ski resorts have pursued the 'big is beautiful' road to development, linking up with their neighbours to create immense ski areas with dozens of lifts. Other resorts, such as Ancelle, have decided to remain small and to use their 'traditional village' status to attract a new sort of clientele. Studies have shown that at least 20 percent of visitors to ski resorts come to the mountains to relax and soak up the scenery rather than to ski. The 'authentic mountain experience' these visitors are looking for is easier to provide when there are fewer ski lifts to mar the views.

| Distance | Location | Directions |
| --- | --- | --- |
| 0.0 | Embrun TO | Come out of the TO, turn R and then R again – Rue des Ecuries. This road leads to the N94. Turn L – N94 |
| 0.8 | N94/D9 | Turn R – D9 (Puy-Sanières) then (Réallon): 6.6km at 5.5%, and then 4km at 2.5% |
| 13.5 | Les Méans D9/D41 | Turn L – D9 (Chorges) |
| 27.0 | Jtn | Turn R (Briançon) |
| 27.6 | Chorges: jtn | Turn R (Le Bourget) |
| 27.8 | Jtn | Turn L (Gap) |
| 27.9 | Jtn | Turn R to go past car park (Le Martouret) then take first left: 5.5km at 2.5% |
| 30.0 | Jtn | Go straight on – D614 (no sign) |
| 33.7 | D614/D214 | Go straight on – D214 (Les Aubins): 7.5km at 8% |
| 41.2 | Col de Mossière | Go straight on |
| 45.3 | Ancelle: D214/D12 | Go straight on over bridge and then turn R – D13 (Pont du Fossé) |
| 50.2 | St Léger les Mélèzes: roundabout: D12/D113 | Turn L – D113 (St Bonnet) |
| 53.2 | D113/D944 | Turn L (St Bonnet) and then take the first R (Chabottes) |
| 53.8 | Jtn | Turn L – D945 (St Bonnet) |
| 54.6 | D945/D43A | Turn L – D945 (St Bonnet) |
| 63.9 | St Bonnet: jtn | Turn L (Centre Ville) |
| 64.1 | Jtn | Turn L and go down to Place Cheveril |
| 64.2 | Place Cheveril | Turn R beside fountain to get to Place Grenette |
| 64.3 | Place Grenette | TO is on L under covered market place |

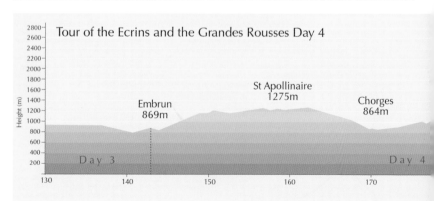

Tour of the Ecrins and the Grandes Rousses Day 4

*Ancelle, on the 'shores' of a dried-up lake.*

## FACILITIES AND SERVICES

| Location | Distance (km) | Water | Shops | Café | Campsite | B&B | Hotel | Bank | Bike Shop |
|---|---|---|---|---|---|---|---|---|---|
| Embrun | 0.0 | x | x | x | x | x | x | x | x |
| Les Truchets | 6.1 | x | — | — | — | — | — | — | — |
| Les Rousses | 15.3 | x | — | — | — | — | — | — | — |
| St Apollinaire | 19.1 | x | x | x | x | — | — | — | — |
| Chorges | 27.6 | x | x | x | x | x | x | x | — |
| Les Aubins | 35.6 | x | — | — | — | — | — | — | — |
| Ancelle | 45.3 | x | x | x | x | x | x | x | — |
| St Léger-les-Mélèzes | 50.2 | x | x | x | x | x | x | — | x |
| La Plaine | 53.8 | — | x | — | — | — | — | — | — |
| St Bonnet-en-Champsaur | 64.3 | x | x | x | x | x | x | x | x |

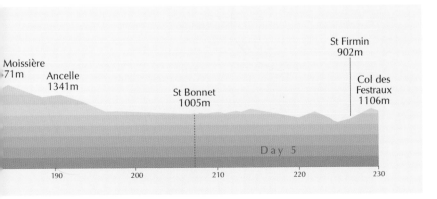

Bourg d'Oisans is one of the few places in the Alps where it is possible to rent road bikes that are of good enough quality for multi-day cycle touring in the mountains. Contact 'Cycles et Sports' (04 76 79 16 79) for prices and bookings. If you come to the Alps without a bike and you would like to start your tour in Bourg d'Oisans, there is a regular coach service from Grenoble (go to **www.vfd.fr for details**).

| Distance | Location | Directions |
|---|---|---|
| 0.0 | St Bonnet TO | Come out of TO and go past fountain. Turn L in front of Crédit Agricole onto Rue St Eusèbe |
| 0.1 | Jtn | Turn R (Autres Directions) |
| 6.2 | D23/D123 | Turn L – D23 (Chauffayer) |
| 12.6 | D23/D316 | Turn R – D316 (Les Blachus) |
| 16.4 | D316/D16A | Turn L – D16A (St Firmin) |
| 16.8 | D16A/D16 | Turn R – D16 (La Chapelle) |
| 16.9 | D16/D216 | Turn L – D216 (St Firmin): 4km at 6.5% |
| 18.9 | St Firmin: jtn | Go straight on (Les Reculas) |
| 19.6 | Jtn | Turn L – D58 (Aspres-les-Corps) |
| 21.4 | Col des Festraux | Go straight on |
| 26.5 | D58/N85 | Turn R – N85 Go through Corps |
| 30.6 | N85/D212 | Turn R – D212 (Ste Luce): 7.6km at 4% |
| 38.2 | Col de l'Holme | Go straight on |
| 41.0 | D212/D212F | Turn R – D212F (Valbonnais): 2.8km at 8% |
| 43.4 | Col de Parquetout | Go straight on |
| 43.8 | High point | Go straight on |
| 50.0 | Les Angelas: D212F/C9 | Turn R – D212F |
| 51.1 | D212F/D526 | Turn R – D526 |
| 53.2 | Entraigues: D526/D117 | Turn L – D526 (Bourg d'Oisans): 13.6km at 4% |
| 68.1 | Col d'Ornon | Go straight on |
| 79.7 | D526/N91 | Turn R – N91 (Bourg d'Oisans) |
| 82.0 | Bourg d'Oisans | TO is on the L |

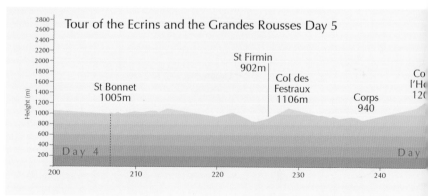

The Dévoluy Mountains as seen from the Col de l'Holme

## FACILITIES AND SERVICES

| Location | Distance (km) | Water | Shops | Café | Campsite | B&B | Hotel | Bank | Bike Shop |
|---|---|---|---|---|---|---|---|---|---|
| St Bonnet-en-Champsaur | 0.0 | x | x | x | x | x | x | x | x |
| Chauffayer | 12.6 | — | x | — | — | — | x | — | — |
| St Firmin | 18.9 | x | x | x | x | x | x | x | — |
| Corps | 29.6 | — | x | x | x | — | x | x | — |
| Ste Luce | 37.2 | x | — | — | — | — | — | — | — |
| Entraigues | 53.2 | x | x | x | x | x | — | — | — |
| Le Perrier | 58.1 | x | x | x | x | — | — | — | — |
| Les Daurens | 60.8 | x | — | x | — | x | — | — | — |
| Col d'Ornon | 68.1 | — | — | x | — | x | — | — | — |
| La Paute | 73.4 | x | — | — | — | — | — | — | — |
| Bourg d'Oisans | 82.0 | x | x | x | x | x | x | x | x |

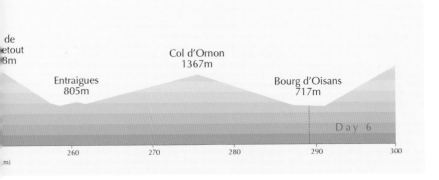

The climb to Alpe d'Huez was first included in the Tour de France in 1952, and has been part of the race 26 times (2008). It is renowned as the Dutch Mountain, as cyclists from that flat country tend to do extraordinarily well here; however, the country with the most victories is Italy. In 2004, and for the first time, Alpe d'Huez was ridden as a time-trial, giving Lance Armstrong the opportunity to seal his sixth victory in the Tour de France. He covered the 15.5km course in 39mins 41secs: an average speed of 23.4km/hr. However fast you do the climb, during the summer months a professional photographer will be waiting beside the road to immortalize your ascent of 'L'Alpe'.

| Distance | Location | Directions |
|---|---|---|
| 0.0 | Bourg d'Oisans TO | Come out of TO and turn L – N91 |
| 0.7 | N91/D211 | Turn L – D211 (Alpe d'Huez): 13.5km at 8.5% |
| 13.9 | Alpe d'Huez TO | Go straight on past TO and follow road around to L (Centre Station) |
| 14.2 | High point | Go straight on |
| 15.0 | Jtn | Turn R in front of La Belle Aurore (no sign) |
| 15.1 | Roundabout | Go straight on |
| 15.4 | Roundabout | Turn R past Residence Azur |
| 15.7 | Roundabout | Turn L (Col de Sarenne) |
| 16.1 | Jtn | Turn L and follow road up, past Club Med and altiport: 3.1km at 8% just before col |
| 24.1 | Col de Sarenne | Go straight on |
| 31.3 | Clavans-le-Haut | Turn R – D25A (Bourg d'Oisans) |
| 33.6 | D25A/D25 | Turn R – D25 (Bourg d'Oisans) |
| 37.1 | D25/N91 | Turn R – N91 (Grenoble) |
| 39.9 | Le Freney-d'Oisans: N91/D211A | Turn R – D211A (Auris-en-Oisans): 3.5km at 9%, short descent, and then 3.4km at 5.5% |
| 46.8 | Jtn | Turn L (Bourg d'Oisans) |
| 48.0 | Jtn | Go straight on – D211A (Bourg d'Oisans) |
| 54.1 | La Garde: D211A/D211 | Turn L – D211 (no sign) |
| 57.5 | D211/N91 | Turn R – N91 (Grenoble) |
| 58.2 | Bourg d'Oisans TO | TO is on the R |

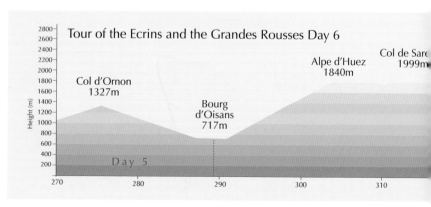

Tour of the Ecrins and the Grandes Rousses Day 6

*View of the Roche de
la Muzelle from
below the
Col de Sarenne*

## FACILITIES AND SERVICES

| Location | Distance (km) | Water | Shops | Café | Campsite | B&B | Hotel | Bank | Bike Shop |
|---|---|---|---|---|---|---|---|---|---|
| Bourg d'Oisans | 0.0 | x | x | x | x | x | x | x | x |
| La Garde | 4.1 | x | — | — | — | — | — | — | — |
| Huez | 10.0 | x | — | — | — | x | — | — | — |
| Alpe d'Huez | 13.9 | x | x | x | — | x | x | x | x |
| Clavans-le-Bas | 32.7 | x | — | x | — | — | x | — | — |
| Mizoën | 35.8 | x | x | x | x | x | — | — | — |
| Le Freney-d'Oisans | 39.9 | — | x | x | x | — | x | — | — |
| La Garde | 54.1 | x | — | — | — | — | — | — | — |
| Bourg d'Oisans | 58.2 | x | x | x | x | x | x | x | x |

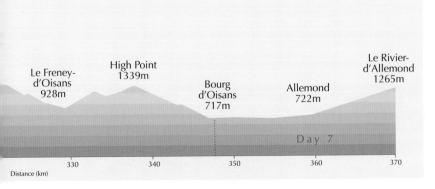

Extra day: If you would like to prolong your stay in Bourg d'Oisans, the ride up the Véneon Valley is an excellent day out (see route 5). However, if you prefer a change of scene, why not use St Bonnet as a base from which to explore the limestone plateaux and mountains of the Dévoluy. The circuit: St Bonnet–Col du Noyer–St Disdier–St Etienne-en-Dévoluy–Ambel–Le Glaizil–St Bonnet takes in some of the most beautiful scenery and avoids the busy route nationale as much as possible (approx 65km, 1100m height gain).

| Distance | Location | Directions |
|---|---|---|
| 0.0 | Bourg d'Oisans TO | Come out of the TO and turn R – N91 |
| 7.2 | Rochetaillée: N91/D526 | Turn R – D526 (Allemont). Go through Allemont and over the dam |
| 11.9 | D526/D44 | Turn L – D526 (Le Rivier d'Allemont) D526 later becomes D926. 7km at 7% |
| 21.6 | Le Rivier d'Allemont | Go straight on |
| 22.7 | High point | Go straight on |
| 24.2 | Low point | Go straight on 9.1km at 6.5%, short descent, and then 5.6km at 6% |
| 37.5 | D926/D927 | Go straight on |
| 40.2 | Col de la Croix de Fer | Go straight on through St Sorlin d'Arves and St Jean d'Arves |
| 54.5 | D926/D80 | Turn R – D80 (Albiez-le-Vieux): 5.9km at 7%* |
| 60.4 | Col du Mollard | Go straight on |
| 62.0 | Albiez-le-Vieux: D80/D110 | Turn L – D110 (St Jean-de-Maurienne) |
| 77.4 | Roundabout | Go straight on (no sign) |
| 77.6 | Roundabout | Go straight on (Toutes Directions) |
| 77.7 | Roundabout | Turn R (Gares) |
| 78.2 | Jtn | Turn R (Gare SNCF) |
| 78.3 | Jtn | Turn L (Gare SNCF) |
| 78.8 | Crossroads | Go straight on (Gares SNCF/Routière) |
| 79.1 | St Jean-de-Maurienne | Station is on the right |

* From 2008 onwards, it should once again be possible to follow the D926 all the way back to St Jean-de-Maurienne. This avoids the climb to the Col du Mollard; but be careful, there are three long tunnels on the D926.

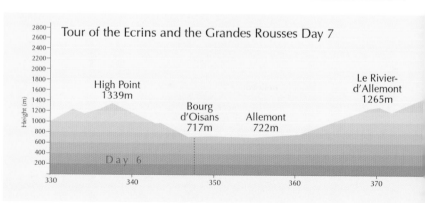

Tour of the Ecrins and the Grandes Rousses Day 7

The final slopes below the Col de la Croix de Fer, looking across towards the Belledonne mountains

## FACILITIES AND SERVICES

| Location | Distance (km) | Water | Shops | Café | Campsite | B&B | Hotel | Bank | Bike Shop |
|---|---|---|---|---|---|---|---|---|---|
| Bourg d'Oisans | 0.0 | x | x | x | x | x | x | x | x |
| Rochetaillée | 7.2 | — | — | — | x | — | — | — | — |
| Allemont | 13.0 | x | x | x | x | x | x | — | — |
| Le Rivier d'Allemond | 21.6 | x | x | x | — | x | x | — | — |
| Col de la Croix de Fer | 40.2 | — | — | x | — | — | — | — | — |
| St Sorlin d'Arves | 46.8 | x | x | x | x | x | x | x | — |
| St Jean d'Arves | 50.5 | x | — | — | — | x | x | — | — |
| Col du Mollard | 60.4 | x | x | x | — | x | — | — | — |
| Albiez-le-Vieuz | 62.0 | x | x | x | — | — | x | — | — |
| St Jean-de-Maurienne | 79.1 | x | x | x | x | — | x | x | x |

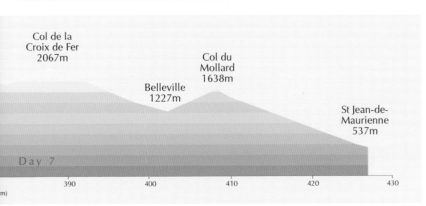

Col de la Croix de Fer 2067m

Col du Mollard 1638m

Belleville 1227m

St Jean-de-Maurienne 537m

Day 7

390   400   410   420   430

(km)

# ACCOMMODATION

## St Jean-de-Maurienne

**Campsites**

Camping des Grands Cols (end April to end Sept), Tel. 04 79 64 28 02

**Bed & Breakfast**

There are no bed & breakfasts in St Jean-de-Maurienne

**Hotels**

There are nine hotels in St Jean-de-Maurienne. Contact TO for details.

## Valloire

**Campsites**

Sainte Thecle (early June to end Sept), Tel. 04 79 83 30 11

**Bed & Breakfast**

Gite d'étape des Plans, Tel. 04 79 59 00 60

**Hotels**

There are 12 hotels in Valloire. Contact TO for details.

## Briançon

**Campsites**

Les Cinq Vallées (early June to end Sept), Tel. 04 92 21 06 27

**Bed & Breakfast**

Although there are no bed & breakfasts or *gites d'étapes* in the centre of Briançon, there are several in the surrounding hamlets. Contact TO for details.

**Hotels**

There are 17 hotels in and around Briançon. Contact TO for details.

## Embrun

**Campsites**

There are eight campsites in Embrun. Contact TO for details.

**Bed & Breakfast**

Le Vieux Chalet, Tel. 04 92 43 00 17

Le Pigeonnier, Tel. 04 92 43 89 63

Jennif'air, Tel. 04 92 43 37 80

Mrs Mathery, Tel. 04 92 43 39 76

**Hotels**

Le Lac (***), Tel. 04 92 43 11 08

Le Rex (**), Tel. 04 92 43 00 06

La Mairie (**), Tel. 04 92 43 20 65

Notre Dame (**), Tel. 04 92 43 08 36

Le Tourisme (*), Tel. 04 92 43 20 17

Du Commerce, Tel. 04 92 43 54 54

## St Bonnet-en-Champsaur

**Campsites**

Le Roure ('summer'), Tel. 04 92 50 01 86

Les Rives du Drac (mid-April to end Sept), Tel. 04 92 50 19 73

**Bed & Breakfast**

La Combe Fleurie, Tel. 04 92 50 53 97

Le Cairn, Tel. 06 08 64 86 09

**Hotels**

La Crémaillère (\*\*), Tel. 04 92 50 00 60

Auberge du Connetable, Tel. 04 92 49 00 62

## Bourg d'Oisans

**Campsites**

There are six campsites in Bourg d'Oisans. Contact TO for details.

**Bed & Breakfast**

Chalet 'La Source', Tel. 04 76 79 16 08

Other B&B-style accommodation exists around Bourg d'Oisans. Contact TO for details.

**Hotels**

There are 9 hotels in Bourg d'Oisans. Contact TO for details.

## TOURIST INFORMATION

### Regional Information

| | Telephone | Website |
|---|---|---|
| Savoie | 04 79 85 12 45 | www.savoie-mont-blanc.com |
| Hautes-Alpes | 04 92 53 62 00 | www.hautes-alpes.net |
| Isère | 04 76 54 34 36 | www.isere-tourisme.com |

### Tourist Information Offices

| Location | Telephone | Website |
|---|---|---|
| St Jean-de-Maurienne | 04 79 83 51 51 | www.saintjeandemaurienne.com |
| Valloire | 04 79 59 03 96 | www.valloire.net |
| Serre Chevalier | 04 92 24 98 98 | www.serre-chevalier.com |
| Briançon | 04 92 21 08 50 | www.ot-briancon.fr |
| L'Argentière-la-Bessée | 04 92 23 03 11 | no website |
| Embrun | 04 92 43 72 72 | www.ot-embrun.fr |
| Chorges | 04 92 50 64 25 | www.otchorges.com |
| Ancelle | 04 92 50 83 05 | www.ancelle.fr |
| St Léger-les-Mélèzes | 04 92 50 43 77 | www.st-leger05.fr |
| St Bonnet-en-Champsaur | 04 92 50 02 57 | www.saint-bonnet-en-champsaur.net |
| St Firmin | 04 92 55 23 21 | no website |
| Corps | 04 76 30 03 85 | www.corps-alpes.com |
| Valbonnais | 04 76 30 25 26 | www.ot-valbonnais.fr |
| Bourg d'Oisans | 04 76 80 03 25 | www.bourgdoisans.com |
| Allemont | 04 76 80 71 60 | www.allemont.com |
| St Sorlin d'Arves | 04 79 59 71 77 | www.saintsorlindarves.com |
| Albiez-le-Vieux | 04 79 59 30 48 | www.albiez-montrond.com |

Cyclists are made to feel welcome in Bourg d'Oisans (Day 6)

*The final hairpins below Alpe d'Huez*

# ROUTE SEVEN

# TOUR OF THE SOUTHERN PRE-ALPS

| Day | Route | Distance | Height Gain |
|-----|-------|----------|-------------|
| 1 | Grenoble to St Jean-en-Royans | 79.4km | 1030m |
| 2 | St Jean-en-Royans to Crest | 79.0km | 1390m |
| 3 | Crest to Vaison-la-Romaine | 85.9km | 1060m |
| 4 | Vaison-la-Romaine to Sault | 61.8km | 1780m |
| 5 | Sault to Serres | 74.0km | 990m |
| 6 | Serres to Corps | 67.1km | 1180m |
| 7 | Corps to Grenoble | 83.4km | 990m |
| | **Totals** | **530.6km** | **8420m** |

Of all the great mountains in the annals of cycling, Mont Ventoux reigns supreme. Although far from being the highest summit accessible by bike, it has a unique presence that makes any and every ascent a magnificent experience. Mont Ventoux forms the centre-piece of this circuit; however, there is much more to the Tour of the Southern pre-Alps than one legendary mountain: the breathtaking roads through the gorges of the Vercors are some of the most spectacular in Europe, and the barren combes and cliffs of the Dévoluy have a grandeur reminiscent of the mighty summits of the Dolomites. Between the two lies the rolling countryside of 'La Drôme Provençale', a region of picturesque red-tiled houses and olive groves. With such a variety of landscapes this is a tour that will delight even the most demanding of cycle tourists.

The tour starts in Grenoble, at the foot of the Vercors Mountains (for more information about Grenoble, see chapters four and five). Two roads lead directly from the city into the heart of the Vercors, but they can both be very busy, especially during the holiday season. Fortunately for cyclists, a newly extended bike path along the banks of the River Isère provides traffic-free access to the quieter roads on the northern flank of the massif. After 35km of flat cycling, the bike path ends near the village of St Gervais, a tiny farming community in the heart of the walnut groves for which the Isère

Valley is famous. Above St Gervais the road climbs steeply into the Vercors towards the seemingly impenetrable cliffs of the Gorges des Ecouges. Gazing up at the precipitous walls of the canyon, there doesn't seem to be a single line of weakness through which a road could pass. As you near the top of the gorge, the truth becomes startlingly apparent, there is no weakness: one lane tunnels through the mountain, while the lane open to cyclists teeters along the very edge of the cliff – vertical below, overhanging above! This is not a place for the faint hearted, as a very low wall is all that separates the narrow road from the vertiginous drop. Luckily, this section is very short and the road soon breaks through the cliff onto the gentler summit slopes of the Col de Romeyère.

The countryside surrounding the descent from the Col de Romeyère is much less harsh and forbidding than that of the Gorges des Ecouges, providing a respite for the spirit, as well as for the legs. However, this more pastoral atmosphere is short lived, as the route plunges into another rocky defile, the Gorges de la Bourne. Once again, the road is an engineering marvel, although mankind has not totally conquered the forces of nature, and rock falls large enough to cause road closures are quite common. A long, gentle descent through Choranche, famous for its spectacular show caves, leads to the 'perched houses' of

# Tour of the Southern Pre-Alps

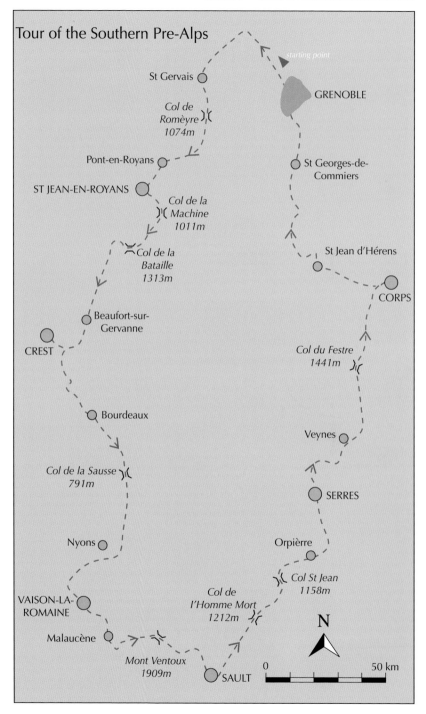

St Gervais

Col de
Romèyre
1074m

Pont-en-Royans

ST JEAN-EN-ROYANS

Col de la
Machine
1011m

Col de la
Bataille
1313m

Beaufort-sur-
Gervanne

CREST

Bourdeaux

Col de la Sausse
791m

Nyons

VAISON-LA-
ROMAINE

Malaucène

Mont Ventoux
1909m

SAULT

Col de
l'Homme Mort
1212m

Col St Jean
1158m

Orpièrre

SERRES

Veynes

Col du Festre
1441m

CORPS

St Jean d'Hérens

St Georges-de-
Commiers

GRENOBLE

*starting point*

N

0          50 km

St Gervais surrounded by walnut groves

Pont-en-Royans, one of the Vercors' best-known landmarks. Pont-en-Royans' Musée de l'Eau (Museum of Water) is also well worth a visit for the entertaining and educational insight it gives into one of the planet's most important resources.

From Pont-en-Royans, the route goes through two more 'en-Royans' villages – there are a total of nine – to St Jean-en-Royans, the final port of call for this first day. Although (perhaps because) it lacks any obvious tourist attractions, St Jean is a very pleasant little town in which to while away a few hours at the end of a hard day's cycling. It is also the ideal place to try the local speciality, *ravioles de royans*, small ravioli filled with cheese and seasoned with finely chopped parsley.

A cyclist heading south from St Jean-en-Royans has several options to choose from. The route described here goes through Combe Laval, one of the most awe-inspiring roads in the French Alps. Combe Laval is a truly breathtaking sight that attracts large numbers of tourists, so during the summer holidays an early start is advisable if you want to avoid the traffic. After Combe Laval, the route goes over the Col de la Machine, and then veers westwards to go over the Col de la Portette and the Col de la Bataille, before descending to Léoncel and the Drôme Valley. The other routes south from St Jean are very attractive but they are not as spectacular as Combe Laval. If you are looking for quiet roads but still want to do a challenging ride, going through Bouvante to join the main itinerary just after the Col de la Portette is recommended. If your legs are feeling a little weary after the previous day's exertions, the road through Oriol-en-Royans to Léoncel provides a less taxing alternative.

The climb through Combe Laval starts directly from St Jean, so there is little chance to warm up cold leg muscles before the hard work begins. During the first 8km, the gradient varies between 6 and 10% – good training for Mont Ventoux – but the slope relents as the road threads its way through the Rochers des Fécles, allowing you to ease off the pedals and soak up the magnificent spectacle. Built between 1893 and 1896 to service the forests of the Lente Plateau, the road's aesthetics were of little concern to the navvies and engineers who built it. Nevertheless, the cliff-edge road winding through a succession of arches and tunnels high above the valley floor is a truly breathtaking sight.

The road emerges from Combe Laval at the Col de la Machine, and then crosses the Lente Plateau before climbing easily up to the Col de la Portette and the first descent of the day. The cycling here is easy, but it is important not to use up too much energy on this section as there is still a lot of work to be done: there are three more climbs between the Col de la Portette and the Col de la Bataille. Most of this section is through thick forest; however, occasional clearings provide fabulous panoramas across the Bouvante Valley to the Royans region and the River Isère. The Col de la Bataille separates the Bouvante Valley to the north from the Gervanne Valley to the south, although the slopes on either side of the pass are so steep that the only direct access to these valleys is on foot. The road actually traverses the pass from east to west, contouring round the Roc de Toulau before tunnelling through the Rocher de la Sausse. This tunnel (there is a path to the top on its western side) provides the best views of the pass and the valleys below.

After the Col de la Bataille, there is still one more pass to cross, but the hard work for the day is already over, so you can relax and enjoy the fabulous descent to Léoncel – a pleasant hamlet with a friendly café and a beautiful Cistercian abbey. Once past Léoncel the road climbs very gently to the Col de Bacchus, before sweeping down into the Gervanne Valley. This southern flank of the Vercors already has a distinctly Provençale feel, as the vegetation becomes sparser and the first blue-shuttered, red-tiled houses appear. The sun also feels stronger, warming body and spirit as you sail down through Plan-de-Baix and Beaufort-sur-Gervanne to Mirabel-et-Blacons and, finally, Crest.

Crest is a bustling market town that grew up around its imposing tower, the highest keep in France. Visitors can climb to the battlements and appreciate the building's strategic importance for themselves: with almost unobstructed 360° views, the townspeople were sure to have plenty of warning of any approaching danger. Orientation tables at the top of the tower show all the major landmarks, and exhibitions within the tower explain the building's history (ask for the English translation at the ticket office). Scrambling up and down the higgledy-piggledy wooden staircases and narrow stone steps is fun in itself – especially if you have wobbly legs after a hard day's cycling. For those looking for a less strenuous way to round off the day, Crest has some great cafés in which to put up your feet and relax.

South of Crest lie the rolling hills of 'La Drôme Provençale', an area of isolated farms and tiny villages whose quiet charm provides a delightfully rural counterpoint to the brashness of the Vercors. Of course, the landscape is not without drama, as anyone who has passed beneath the spectacular cliffs of Saou on a stormy day will attest, but the overall impression is of a less aggressive landscape. The area is a paradise for cyclists as it has a dense network of mostly quiet roads and innumerable cols to explore. For anyone contemplating staying in the area for several days, Bourdeaux, La Motte-Chalancon and Buis-les-Baronnies are all excellent places to be based.

Day three starts gently, following the Drôme Valley to Aouste-sur-Sye, and then crossing the river to start the climb to the Col du Pas de Lauzens – perhaps the easiest pass on the entire circuit. To the south of the Pas de Lauzuns, the road sweeps down an impressive cliff-lined valley to the fabulous village of Saou. The area's hot, dry climate is ideal for keeping goats, and goat farming in France is synonymous with goat's cheese. The local variety is called Picodon, a small disc-shaped cheese that can be quite soft and mild, or hard and more pungent, depending on how long it has been allowed to mature. Picodon has been awarded AOC status, which means it can only be made in a restricted area (mostly in the Drôme and Ardèche *départements*) and that producers must follow a strict set of guidelines. Saou is so proud of its local cheese that every year it holds the Fête du Picodon, with a fair, concerts and, of course, a competition for the best cheese. The *fête*, which is always held on the third weekend in July, attracts around 10,000 visitors to a village of a mere 500 souls.

From Saou, the kilometres quickly fly by, the only difficulty being the final part of the ascent to the Col de la Sausse. Once over the pass, it is downhill all the way to Les Pilles, 7km to the west of the pretty market town of Nyons. If you would like to cut the stage short, Nyons has a wide range of accommodation and, if needed, there is a bike shop in Aubres, about halfway between Les Pilles and Nyons. However, the standard route bypasses Nyons by following a very quiet minor road over the Col de la Croix Rouge to Mirabel-aux-Baronnies, from where you will get your first views of the mighty Ventoux, towering above the surrounding countryside. From Mirabel the route makes another slight detour to avoid a busy main road and to visit Villedieu, a lovely Provençale village with an idyllic square, complete with traditional café – an excellent place to take a break before the descent into Vaison.

With its long and clearly visible history, Vaison-la-Romaine is one of the most interesting towns in this corner of Provence. Its two most obvious tourist attractions are its Roman remains, including a theatre, several extensive villas and the elegant bridge over the River Ouvèze, and the mediaeval quarter and castle above the modern town. It would be impossible to see everything Vaison has to offer in a single overnight visit, but one thing that should not be missed is the view from the 12th-century castle, reached via the narrow, cobbled streets of the 'Ville Haute'. If time allows, Vaison is also a good place to take a semi-rest day, combining a short bike ride around some of the Côte du Rhone's most famous vineyards (Beaumes de Venise, Gigondas, Rasteau) with a more leisurely exploration of the town. The tourist office will provide you with all the information you need about Vaison and its neighbouring vineyards. Unsurprisingly, Vaison is very popular with tourists, but even in the middle of the summer holidays it does not seem to get uncomfortably busy.

Of course, for cyclists the big attraction of Vaison-la-Romaine is that it lies at the foot of Mont Ventoux. Rising almost 1800m from the plains to the south and west, and towering 700m above the highest hills to the north and

As the heat saps the strength from their legs, most cyclists will be relieved that this is the last ascent of the day.

Orpierre is a pretty mediaeval village in a magnificent setting that has made an unusual choice in terms of developing its tourism economy. Surrounded by limestone cliffs that have long been popular with rock climbers, the village has decided to encourage climbing, thereby targeting what many other areas consider a very unprofitable clientele. However, Orpierre's singular policy has been a resounding success, with climbers flocking to the village from all over Europe. Of course, non-climbers are also welcome to enjoy the village's picturesque streets and shady cafés. From Orpierre, the route follows the orchard-lined Céans Valley to Eyguians, before heading north beside the River Buëch to Serres. The main road on the eastern side of the Buëch is the most direct route from Grenoble to the Mediterranean and therefore too busy to cycle safely. Fortunately, the minor road on the western side of the river sees very little traffic and provides a quiet, mostly flat and very scenic alternative.

Serres, your next port of call, has a long history of welcoming travellers. There has been a settlement here since at least 800BC, and the village was already a way station in Roman times, on the road from Rome to Avignon. However, modern-day Serres is a rather unpresuming place whose main attraction is the surrounding countryside. The road from Serres to Veynes is almost deserted and offers wonderful views across to the mountains of the Dévoluy. After a short climb through Sigottier, the route descends to Aspremont, and then follows minor roads above the Petite Buëch to bypass Veynes (which lies on a very busy main road) and enter the Dévoluy.

Despite having two regional capitals on its doorstep (Grenoble and Gap), the Dévoluy has not undergone the same tourism development as the neighbouring Vercors and Ecrins Massifs. The area does have a ski resort, Superdévoluy, but there are no well-known 'honeypots' to attract summer tourists. Most visitors are hikers, and it is very easy to see why they are drawn to the Dévoluy: the scenery is superb, and the area has some of the most spectacular summits in the pre-Alps. Arriving from the south, it is not until you reach the Col du Festre, the gateway to the Dévoluy, that the first clear views of the area's magnificent peaks appear. In all directions, the green pastures of the lower slopes rise up into narrow, scree-filled combes that culminate in impressive bastions of white rock. The architecture of these high places is much more reminiscent of the high summits of the true Alps than that of the other pre-Alpine massifs to which the Dévoluy is, in geological terms, more closely related.

From the pass, the road descends through Agnières-en-Dévoluy to St Disdier, a pretty hamlet with a fabulous *gite gastronomique* (**www.gite-devoluy.com**). The *gite* is run by a wonderful couple whose aim is to turn the *gite d'étape* experience into a gastronomic delight. Eric, a Frenchman of Italian origin who was born in Morocco, combines all these influences to produce dishes that are sometimes unusual, but always superb. And at 35 Euros per person for half-board accommodation in a double room (29 Euros for dormitory-style accommodation) you could not ask for better value for money.

Below St Disdier lies the Défilé de la Souloise, one of the few deep gorges in the Dévoluy and an uninviting place where the sun never seems to shine. However, the valley soon widens again as the road emerges onto the plain at Les Payas before plunging down to the Lac de Sautet, a huge reservoir that was built to feed the hydroelectric plants on the River Drac below. For once, the day ends on an uphill note, as Corps, the final stage town, sits 160m above the reservoir.

Corps has been a staging post for travellers for centuries and has seen the passage of many illustrious figures, the most celebrated being Napoleon on his return from exile on the island of Elba. In this modern age of motorways and bypasses, Corps is unusual in still relying on passing travellers for a large part of its trade. As a result, it has an extremely large number of hotels, restaurants and cafés for such a small village. It will be interesting to see how local trade fares should the planned motorway between Grenoble, Gap and

Sisteron ever see the light of day. As most visitors are passing through, they only see the shops, hotels and restaurants on the main street, never getting to explore the small but attractive historic centre of the village – a pleasant place for a pre- or after-dinner stroll.

Although the final stage of this long and strenuous journey does not go over any large mountains or high passes, the cycling is not easy, as there are numerous small hills to be climbed. From the Lac du Sautet, the road climbs up into the Trièves, an area of rolling hills sandwiched between the Vercors and the Ecrins. The Trièves is only 50km north of Serres, but the greenness of the countryside and the architecture of the villages show that the climate here is very different from that of Provence. The area is still far enough south for summers to be warm and dry, but winters tend to be cool and damp, creating a lush and leafy landscape that is somehow comforting to northern European eyes. However, more corporal comforts, such as cafés and shops, are rare in this sparsely populated area – there is not a single shop on the 55km leg from Corps to Monteynard – so ensure you have all the sustenance you need.

Approaching St Jean d'Hérans, the view extends across hills and valleys to Mont Aiguille, a 200m pillar of limestone and one of the most striking mountains in the Alps. The summit plateau is surrounded on all sides by vertical limestone walls and boasts a selection of flora and fauna found nowhere else. From St Jean, the route descends steeply to cross the River Drac, before ascending (also steeply) to the lovely hamlet of St Arey with its beautifully situated 12th-century church. The road from St Arey to St Georges-de-Commiers, known as the Cornice du Drac, offers several stunning panoramas across the river to the eastern ramparts of the Vercors, a reminder of your exploits earlier in the tour. Most of the Cornice road is a false flat, although it dips down to La Motte St Martin, and then climbs quite steeply to reach the D529 and one of the most exhilarating descents of the entire tour. At the end of the descent, the route goes through the industrial town of Champ-sur-Drac before bearing right to go up to Champagnier and then down through Echirolles to finish back at Grenoble station.

### By car
Grenoble is 870km from Calais.

### By plane
### Via Grenoble St Geoirs
The tour can be started directly from Grenoble airport. The route from the airport to Grenoble city centre (see Appendix 1, section 4A) meets the bike path 23.6km from Grenoble airport (24.3km from Grenoble station).

### Via Lyon St Exupéry
*Bus:* Shuttle bus to Grenoble every hour.

*Train:* To take the train you have to cycle to La Verpillière (see Appendix A for route details). On average, there is one train every hour and the journey takes around 1hr 10mins.

### Via Geneva
Take the train from the airport to Geneva central station (Cornavin). From Cornavin there is a train every 2–3 hours, either direct or via Culoz and Chambéry. The direct journey takes around 2hrs 15mins.

Most of the passes crossed by this tour are kept open all year round; however, the roads over Mont Ventoux are usually closed from late November until the middle of April. The best time to do this tour is May to early October. Although the Vercour and Ventoux areas attract a lot of tourists during the summer holiday period, the circuit mostly avoids the busiest roads and can therefore be enjoyed throughout the summer. If you come during the peak holiday months of July and August it is essential to book accommodation in advance.

**Michelin:** Local – Sheet 332: Drôme, Vaucluse

**Michelin:** Regional – Sheets 244: Rhône-Alpes and 245: Provence, Côte d'Azur

**IGN:** Top 100 – Three sheets are needed for this tour – 52: Grenoble, Valence; 54: Grenoble, Gap; and 60: Cavaillon, Digne-les-Bains

*The Obiou as seen from Les Moras*

# Day 1 – Grenoble to St Jean-en-Royans

There are several roads into the northern part of the Vercors. If you would like to try an alternative to the route described in this chapter, here are a few tips. **1** – The D106 through St Nizier is pleasant when quiet, although it is popular with motorists during the holiday period. **2** – Avoid the D531 from Sassenage, as it is by far the busiest road and it carries a lot of truck traffic. **3** – The D218 from St Quentin-sur-Isère is now a dead end as the Tunnel du Mortier has been closed (marked 'route coupée' on the Michelin maps). **4** – The D22 through the Gorges du Nant provides the final and most spectacular alternative: from St Gervais continue south to Cognin-les-Gorges, and then turn left towards Malleval. At the top of the gorge, cross the Coulmes Plateau and descend through Presles to Pont-en-Royans.

| Distance | Location | Directions |
|---|---|---|
| 0.0 | Grenoble station | Leave station via 'Centre Ville' exit. Go straight across street in front of station to Rue Casimir Brenier, and follow this to Place Hubert Dubedout |
| 0.4 | Place Hubert Dubedout | Go across square (easiest on foot). Cross River Isère and then turn L to go to gap in fence (easy to miss) that leads down to cycleway |
| 0.6 | Cycleway | Turn R onto cycleway |
| 2.9 | Jtn | Bear left to go under bridge |
| 24.3 | Jtn (just before D45) | Turn L (St Gervais) onto cycleway |
| 34.8 | End of cycleway | Turn L – D35 (St Gevais) |
| 35.5 | D35/N532 | Go straight on – D35 (Rencurel) 9km at 8%, followed by 3km at 3.5% |
| 44.2 | Tunnel | The road uphill goes through an unlit tunnel. Cyclists are directed to follow the left-hand lane along the edge of the cliff (no-entry sign for cars) – beware of oncoming vehicles |
| 49.1 | Col de Romèyre | Go straight on |
| 57.1 | Jtn (just before D531) | Bear R |
| 57.3 | La Balme-de-Rencurel | Turn R – D531 – no sign |
| 70.0 | Pont-en-Royans: D531/D54 | Go straight on – D54 (St Jean-en-Royans) |
| 76.5 | Roundabout: D54/D216 | Go straight on – D54 (St Jean-en-Royans) |
| 79.4 | St Jean-en-Royans | The TO is on the L (behind a prominent fountain) |

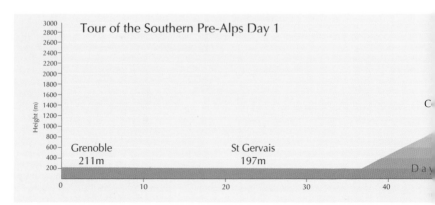

Tour of the Southern Pre-Alps Day 1

Height (m)

3000 2800 2600 2400 2200 2000 1800 1600 1400 1200 1000 800 600 400 200

Grenoble 211m    St Gervais 197m

0    10    20    30    40

*The perched houses of
Pont-en-Royans*

## FACILITIES AND SERVICES

| Location | Distance (km) | Water | Shops | Café | Campsite | B&B | Hotel | Bank | Bike Shop |
|---|---|---|---|---|---|---|---|---|---|
| Grenoble | 0.0 | x | x | x | x | (1) | x | x | x |
| Rencurel | 54.5 | x | — | x | — | x | x | — | — |
| La Balme-de-Rencurel | 57.3 | x | — | x | — | x | x | — | — |
| Choranche | 65.5 | x | — | x | x | x | x | — | — |
| Pont-en-Royans | 70.0 | x | x | x | x | x | x | x | — |
| Ste Eulalie-en-Royans | 72.4 | x | x | x | — | — | — | — | — |
| St Laurent-en-Royans | 74.9 | x | x | x | — | x | x | x | — |
| St Jean-en-Royans | 79.4 | x | x | x | x | x | x | x | x |

(1) At La Tronche on the northeast edge of Grenoble (about 4km from the station)

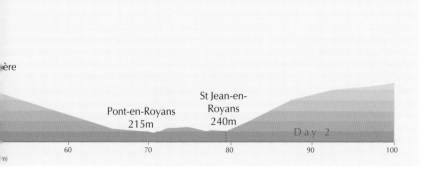

ère

Pont-en-Royans
215m

St Jean-en-
Royans
240m

D a y  2

60    70    80    90    100

m)

The roads in the Vercors are notorious for rockfalls and landslides. One of the most spectacular sections of road, through the Grands Goulets, had to be left out of the tour as it has been closed definitively and replaced by a 1.7km-long tunnel (due to open in 2008). Even the Gorges de la Bourne, a vital link for the area's economy, has been the scene of fatal accidents due to rockfalls, most recently in 2004 and in November 2007. The road was reopened after the 2007 tragedy, but extensive work to improve safety is planned.

| Distance | Location | Directions |
|---|---|---|
| 0.0 | St Jean-en-Royans TO | Turn L onto D70 |
| 0.5 | D70/D76 | Go straight on – D76 (Lente) |
| 0.8 | D76/D131 | Bear L – D76 (Lente): 8.1km at 7.5%, followed by 4.4km at 4% |
| 12.5 | Col de la Machine | Go straight on: false flat for 7.5km |
| 17.7 | D76/D199 | Turn R – D191 (Léoncel) |
| 20.5 | Col de la Portette | Go straight on: 1.2km descent, then 4km at 5%, 1.5km descent, short climb, 4.3km descent, then 2.8km at 6% |
| 34.8 | Col de la Bataille | Go straight on through the tunnel (high point) |
| 43.3 | Léoncel: D199/D70 | Turn L – D70 (Crest). Go through Léoncel, over the Col de Bacchus, and then down to Mirabel-et-Blacons |
| 73.3 | Mirabel-et-Blacons D70/D93 | Turn R – D93 (Crest) |
| 75.5 | Aouste-sur-Sye: roundabout | Go straight on – D93 |
| 76.5 | D93/D494 | Turn R – D494 – no sign |
| 77.6 | Roundabout | Go straight on |
| 78.3 | Jtn | Turn R (Centre Ville) |
| 78.6 | Traffic lights | Go straight on along rue des Alpes |
| 78.8 | Crest: jtn | Go straight on along pedestrian street |
| 79.0 | Jtn with Rue Aristide Dumont | Turn L onto Rue Aristide Dumont. The TO is on the right, behind 'Le Donjon' café/restaurant |

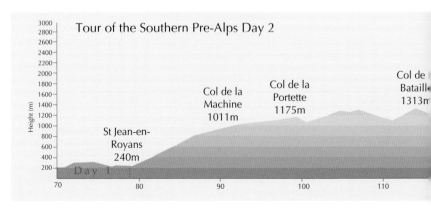

The Col de la Bataille from above the tunnel

## FACILITIES AND SERVICES

| Location | Distance (km) | Water | Shops | Café | Campsite | B&B | Hotel | Bank | Bike Shop |
|---|---|---|---|---|---|---|---|---|---|
| St Jean-en-Royans | 0.0 | x | x | x | x | x | x | x | x |
| Col de la Machine | 12.5 | — | — | x | — | — | x | — | — |
| Lent | 16.5 | — | — | x | x | — | x | — | — |
| Léoncel | 43.3 | — | — | — | — | x | x | — | — |
| Plan-de-Baix | 56.1 | — | — | x | — | x | x | — | — |
| Beaufort-sur-Gervanne | 64.2 | x | x | x | x | — | x | x | — |
| Mirabel-et-Blacons | 73.3 | — | x | x | x | x | — | — | — |
| Aouste-sur-Sye | 75.5 | x | x | x | x | — | x | — | — |
| Crest | 79.0 | x | x | x | x | — | x | x | x |

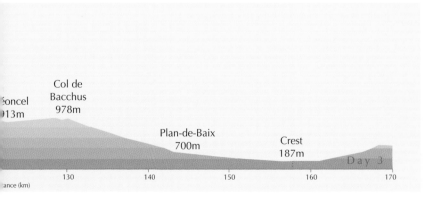

# Day 3 – Crest to Vaison-la-Romaine

Provence has an almost perfect climate for cycling, with low rainfall and lots of sunshine. However, there is one major drawback – the Mistral wind, a northerly gale that roars down the Rhone Valley, gusting to 80kph or more. The Mistral is a real danger to cyclists, as it can be strong enough to knock you over, sweep you right across the road or stop you dead in your tracks, even when you are going downhill. In my visits to Provence I have experienced all these hazards. Fortunately, there are far fewer Mistral days in summer than in winter.

| Distance | Location | Directions |
|---|---|---|
| 0.0 | Crest TO | Go straight across the square in front of TO, and then turn R onto the road |
| 0.1 | T-junction | Turn L (no sign). Keep straight on along the D494 to Aouste-sur-Sye |
| 3.2 | Aouste-sur-Sye: D494/D70 | Turn R – D70 <Saou> 5.2km at 3%, followed by 2.1km at 6.5% |
| 10.8 | Col du Pas de Lauzuns | Go straight on |
| 16.3 | Saou: D70/D538 | Bear L along D538 (Bourdeaux) |
| 25.9 | Bourdeaux | Go straight on through village (Nyons). False flat for 13 km, then 3.7km at 4% |
| 42.6 | Col de la Sausse | Go straight on |
| 56.1 | D70/D94 | Turn R – D94 (Les Pilles) |
| 57.1 | Les Pilles: D94/D185 | Turn L – D185 (Châteauneuf-de-Bordette) |
| 57.3 | Jtn | Turn L, go across river and turn R – D185 (Châteauneuf-de-Bordette) |
| 64.5 | Col de la Croix Rouge* | Go straight on |
| 71.2 | D185/D538 | Turn L – D538 (Vaison-la-Romaine) |
| 71.7 | D538/D160 | Turn R – D160 (Villedieu) |
| 78.4 | D160/D7 | Turn L (Villedieu) |
| 79.3 | Villedieu: D7/D94 | Turn L – D94 (Vaison-la-Romaine) |
| 83.1 | D94/D51 | Turn L – D51 (Vaison-la-Romaine) |
| 85.5 | Vaison-la-Romaine: jtn | Turn L (Centre Ville) |
| 85.7 | Roundabout | Turn R onto Ave General de Gaulle (Centre Ville) |
| 85.9 | TO | The tourist office is on the L |

* Named Col de la Croix on the 1:150,000 Michelin map, its position is inverted with respect to Châteauneuf-de-Bordette.

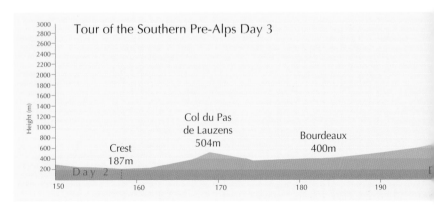

Tour of the Southern Pre-Alps Day 3

Crest 187m

Col du Pas de Lauzens 504m

Bourdeaux 400m

Day 2

Crest old town as seen from the town's keep

## FACILITIES AND SERVICES

| Location | Distance (km) | Water | Shops | Café | Campsite | B&B | Hotel | Bank | Bike Shop |
|---|---|---|---|---|---|---|---|---|---|
| Crest | 0.0 | x | x | x | x | — | x | x | x |
| Aouste-sur-Sye | 3.2 | x | x | x | x | — | x | — | — |
| Saou | 16.3 | x | x | x | x | x | — | — | — |
| Bourdeaux | 25.9 | x | x | x | x | x | x | x | — |
| Crupies | 31.1 | — | — | x | — | — | x | — | — |
| Bouvières | 38.1 | x | x | x | x | — | x | — | — |
| St Ferréol-Trente-Pas | 50.3 | x | — | x | x | — | — | — | — |
| Condorcet | 53.1 | x | x | x | — | — | — | — | — |
| Mirabel-aux-Baronnies | 71.7 | x | x | x | x | x | x | x | — |
| Villedieu | 79.3 | x | x | x | — | x | — | — | — |
| Vaison-la- Romaine | 85.9 | x | x | x | x | x | x | x | x |

## Day 4 – Vaison-la-Romaine to Sault

Good quality road bikes can be rented from many outlets in the Mont Ventoux area. Rates are around €20 per day or €90 per week. Demand is high during the summer, so it is best to book in advance. The nearest rental outlet (and bike shop) to Mont Ventoux is 'Mag 2 Roues' in Malacuène.

For €2, cyclists can time their ascent of Mont Ventoux using the Carnet du Col system set up by the tourist offices in Malacuène, Sault and Bedoin. To record your time, just punch your card at the tourist office and when you get to the summit.

| Distance | Location | Directions |
|----------|----------|------------|
| 0.0 | Vaison-la-Romaine TO | Turn L in front of the TO and follow Ave General de Gaulle and Grande Rue to the Roman bridge (Pont Romain) |
| 0.4 | Pont Romain | Turn L – D151 (St Marcellin) |
| 1.5 | D151/D938 | Turn R – D938 |
| 1.8 | D938/D151 | Turn L – D151 (St Marcellin les Ventoux) |
| 2.6 | D151/D205 | Turn R – D205 (Faucon) |
| 6.3 | D205/C3 | Turn R – C3 (Entrechaux) |
| 6.7 | Bridge | Go over the bridge (very narrow) and turn R onto LH of two roads |
| 7.9 | Roundabout | Turn R (Malaucène) |
| 8.3 | Entrechaux | Turn L just before mini-supermarket (Champ Long) |
| 9.4 | Jtn | Bear R (Champ Long) |
| 12.3 | Jtn | Turn R – no sign |
| 13.9 | Malaucène | Turn L to go through the village |
| 14.3 | D90/D974 | Turn L – D974 (Mont Ventoux) 21.5km at 7.5% |
| 29.6 | Mont Serein – roundabout | Bear R (Mont Ventoux) |
| 35.8 | Mont Ventoux | Go straight on |
| 42.2 | Chalet Reynard: D974/D164 | Bear L – D164 (Sault) 1km at 4.5% just before Sault |
| 61.7 | Jtn | Go straight on (Centre Ville) |
| 61.8 | Sault TO | TO is on the left |

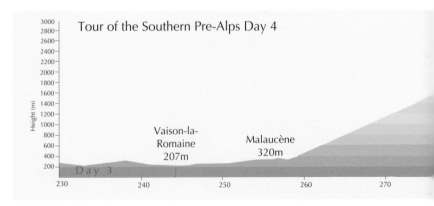

Tour of the Southern Pre-Alps Day 4

*The summit of Mont Ventoux as seen from the north*

## FACILITIES AND SERVICES

| Location | Distance (km) | Water | Shops | Café | Campsite | B&B | Hotel | Bank | Bike Shop |
|---|---|---|---|---|---|---|---|---|---|
| Vaison-la-Romaine | 0.0 | x | x | x | x | x | x | x | x |
| Entrechaux | 8.3 | x | x | x | x | x | x | — | — |
| Malaucène | 13.9 | x | x | x | x | x | x | x | x |
| Mont Serein | 29.6 | — | — | x | x | x | x | — | — |
| Mont Ventoux | 35.8 | — | x | x | — | — | — | — | — |
| Chalet Reynard | 42.2 | x | — | x | — | — | — | — | — |
| Sault | 61.8 | x | x | x | x | x | x | x | x |

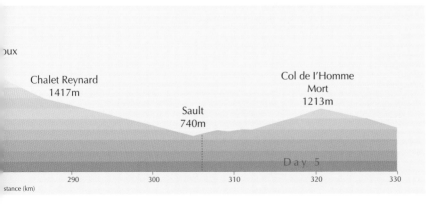

)ux

Chalet Reynard
1417m

Col de l'Homme
Mort
1213m

Sault
740m

Day 5

290    300    310    320    330

stance (km)

167

## Day 5 – Sault to Serres

**Extra day:** Just south of Mont Ventoux lie the spectacular Gorges de la Nesque, one of the most beautiful corners of Provence and, as yet, almost totally undiscovered. Sault is the start point for a fabulous and quite easy circuit through the gorge, via Villes-sur-Auzon, Flassan and the Col de Notre Dame des Abeilles (Pass of Our Lady of the Bees). As you cycle through the gorge, take time to stop and admire the views, as it is difficult to appreciate the scale and majesty of the scenery from the right-hand side of the road. There are several excellent view points along the way. After the scenery of the gorge, the circuit's second highlight is the exhilarating descent from Notre Dame des Abeilles to Sault. A sustained gradient, sweeping bends and an almost perfect road surface – what more could you ask for?

| Distance | Location | Directions |
| --- | --- | --- |
| 0.0 | Sault TO | Turn L and go through the village to the D950 |
| 0.1 | D950 | Turn L – D950 (St Trinit) 2.1km at 3% |
| 4.6 | D950/D1 | Turn L (Ferrassières) 4.9km at 3% |
| 9.2 | Ferrassières: D1/D189A | Turn R – D189A (Séderon) |
| 9.5 | D189A/D189 | Turn R – D189A-D63 (Séderon) 5.2km at 5% |
| 14.7 | Col de l'Homme Mort | Go straight on |
| 19.3 | Col de Macugène D63/D542 | Turn R – D542 (Séderon) |
| 25.3 | Séderon | Go straight through the village |
| 32.3 | D542/D170 | Turn L – D170 (Laborel). False flat for 2.2km, then 5.7km at 7% |
| 40.2 | Col de Saint Jean | Go straight on |
| 45.7 | Laborel: D170/D65 | Turn R – D65 (Orpierre) |
| 55.2 | Orpierre | Go straight through the village |
| 62.2 | Roundabout: D30/D949 | Turn L – D949 (Trescléoux) |
| 62.6 | D949/D350 | Turn R – D350 (Serres) |
| 67.4 | D350/D50 | Turn R – D50 (Serres) |
| 73.3 | Serres: jtn | Turn R (Centre Ville) |
| 74.0 | Roundabout | TO is straight in front of you |

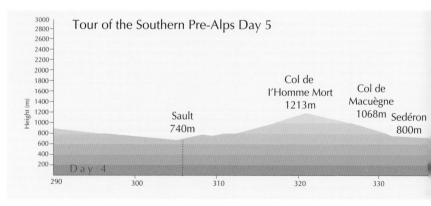

*Mont Ventoux from just below the Col de l'Homme*

## FACILITIES AND SERVICES

| Location | Distance (km) | Water | Shops | Café | Campsite | B&B | Hotel | Bank | Bike Shop |
|---|---|---|---|---|---|---|---|---|---|
| Sault | 0.0 | x | x | x | x | x | x | x | x |
| Ferrassières | 9.2 | x | — | — | — | x | — | — | — |
| Séderon | 25.3 | x | x | x | x | — | x | x | — |
| Eygalayes | 34.5 | x | — | x | — | — | x | — | — |
| Orpierre | 55.2 | x | x | x | x | x | — | — | x |
| Eyguians | 62.2 | — | x | x | — | — | x | — | — |
| Serres | 74.0 | x | x | x | x | x | x | x | (1) |

(1) The nearest bike shop is in Sisteron, 30km south of Serres, although there is a better choice of bike shops in Gap, 46km east of Serres. Both towns can be reached by train from Serres.

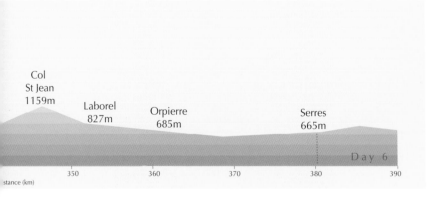

Col
St Jean
1159m

Laborel
827m

Orpierre
685m

Serres
665m

Day 6

350      360      370      380      390

stance (km)

169

# Day 6 – Serres to Corps

The Tour of the Southern Pre-Alps can be extended into a truly magnificent two-week trip by linking it to the Tour of the Belledonne (Route 5). From Corps, follow the second part of Day 5 of the Tour of the Ecrins to Bourg d'Oisans, and then follow Route 5 in reverse (Days 4 to 1) to get back to Grenoble. Adding the Alpe d'Huez circuit (Route 6, Day 6) to the tour gives 12 days of superb, but very strenuous cycling.

| Distance | Location | Directions |
|---|---|---|
| 0.0 | Serres TO | Turn R onto D1075* (Grenoble) |
| 0.5 | D1075/D27 | Turn L – D27 (Sigottier) |
| 4.4 | D27/D227 | Turn R – D227 (Aspremont) |
| 9.9 | Aspremont: D227/D1075 | Turn R – D1075* |
| 10.0 | D1075/D49 | Turn L – D49 (Veynes) |
| 13.4 | D49/D994 | Turn L – D994 (Veynes) |
| 13.5 | D994/D49 | Turn R (Oze) |
| 13.9 | Jtn | Turn L – no sign |
| 15.1 | Jtn | Turn L – no sign – and go through Oze |
| 19.6 | Jtn | Turn L – no sign |
| 22.5 | Jtn | Go straight on – no sign – and follow the river bank for 2.4km |
| 24.9 | Jtn (bridge on the R) | Turn L |
| 25.9 | Jtn | Turn R – D994 – no sign |
| 26.0 | Jtn | Turn L (Camping Les Près) |
| 29.2 | Jtn | Bear left, cross the bridge, and then turn L onto D937 (Superdévoluy). 14.4km at 4%, including 4.5km at 6.5%, just after tunnel at km 33.1 |
| 40.4 | Col du Festre | Go straight on |
| 42.6 | D937/D17 | Turn L – D937 (Corps) |
| 50.3 | D937/D117 | Bear L – D937/D537 (Corps). 2.8km at 5.5% just before Corps |
| 66.8 | D537/N85 | Turn R – N85 (Gap) |
| 67.1 | Corps *hôtel de ville* | The *hôtel de ville* is on the right, next to the church |

* Still marked N75 on most maps

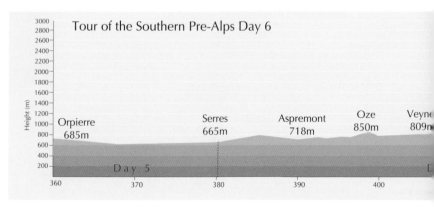

Tour of the Southern Pre-Alps Day 6

The Dévoluy from the Col du Festre

## FACILITIES AND SERVICES

| Location | Distance (km) | Water | Shops | Café | Campsite | B&B | Hotel | Bank | Bike Shop |
|----------|---------------|-------|-------|------|----------|-----|-------|------|-----------|
| Serres | 0.0 | x | x | x | x | — | x | x | (1) |
| Sigottier | 3.5 | x | — | — | — | x | — | — | — |
| Aspremont | 9.9 | x | — | x | — | — | x | — | — |
| Veynes | 22.5 | x | x | x | x | x | x | x | — |
| Col du Festre | 40.4 | — | — | x | — | x | — | — | — |
| Agnières-en-Dévoluy | 45.5 | x | — | x | — | x | — | — | — |
| St Disdier | 50.5 | x | x | — | — | x | x | — | — |
| Corps | 67.1 | x | x | x | x | — | x | x | (2) |

(1) The nearest bike shop is in Sisteron, 30km south of Serres, although there is a better choice of bike shops in Gap, 46km east of Serres. Both towns can be reached by train from Serres.

(2) The nearest bike shop is in Vizille, 46km north of Corps along the N85

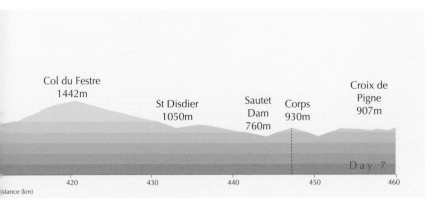

Col du Festre 1442m

St Disdier 1050m

Sautet Dam 760m

Corps 930m

Croix de Pigne 907m

Day 7

420   430   440   450   460

stance (km)

This stage includes several, mostly short uphill sections. Only the longest and steepest are detailed in the route description.

| Distance | Location | Directions |
|---|---|---|
| 0.0 | Corps *hôtel de ville* | Come out of the *hôtel de ville* and turn L – N85 |
| 0.3 | N85/D537 | Turn L – D537 (Mens). 3.4km descent, then 2.3km at 6.5% |
| 4.9 | D537/D66 | Turn R – D66 (Mens) |
| 18.1 | D66/D227 | Turn R – D227 (St Sébastien) |
| 19.8 | D227/D228 | Turn L (St Jean d'Hérans) |
| 24.1 | Saint Jean d'Hérans: D228/D526 | Turn R – D526 (La Mure) |
| 25.2 | D526/D168 | Turn L – D168 (Les Rives). After a steep descent to the bottom of the valley, the road climbs very steeply (700m at 13%, then 1km at 5%) |
| 29.9 | D168/C1 | Turn L – C1 (St Arey) |
| 32.0 | Jtn | Turn L (St Arey). Follow the road up through St Arey |
| 33.8 | D116D/D116 | Turn L – D116. No sign. Succession of gentle descents and ascents |
| 48.8 | La Motte St Martin: D116/D116B | Turn L – D116B (Grenoble). 1.3km descent, followed by 3.2km at 7% |
| 53.3 | D116B/D529 | Turn L – D529 (Grenoble) |
| 65.0 | Roundabout | Go straight on – D529 (Grenoble) |
| 69.5 | Roundabout | Turn L onto slip road that leads to N85 (Champagnier) |
| 70.6 | N85/D64 | Turn R – D64 (Champagnier) 2.3km at 5% |
| 76.0 | Roundabout D64/D269* | Go straight on – D269 (Grenoble) |
| 76.3 | Roundabout D269/N75 | Go straight on – N75 (Pont de Claix) |
| 76.6 | Traffic lights | Go straight on along Ave Charles de Gaulle |
| 77.1 | Traffic lights (next to Total service station) | Turn R and follow cycle-lane/subsidiary road parallel to main boulevard for 5.3km. Cyclists do not have to respect the no-entry signs |
| 82.4 | Underpass below railway | Go under the railway line and turn L (Gare SNCF). Follow the railway line to the pedestrian area in front of the tram and railway stations |
| 83.4 | Grenoble station | The station is on the left |

* For an alternative route from Echirolles to the station see the Tour of the Belledonne, Day 5

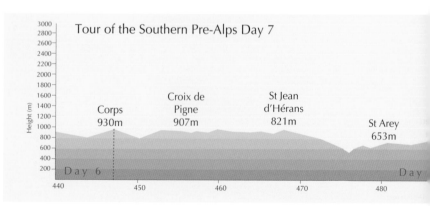

Tour of the Southern Pre-Alps Day 7

*Cordéac set against the
snowy peaks of the Ecrins*

## FACILITIES AND SERVICES

| Location | Distance (km) | Water | Shops | Café | Campsite | B&B | Hotel | Bank | Bike Shop |
|---|---|---|---|---|---|---|---|---|---|
| Corps | 0.0 | x | x | x | x | — | x | x | (1) |
| Cordéac | 14.8 | x | — | — | — | x | — | — | — |
| St Jean d'Hérans | 24.1 | x | — | — | — | — | — | — | — |
| St Arey | 33.4 | x | — | — | — | — | — | — | — |
| Marcieu | 42.2 | x | — | x | — | — | — | — | — |
| Monteynard | 53.5 | x | — | — | — | — | — | — | — |
| St Georges-de-Commiers | 61.3 | x | x | x | — | — | — | — | — |
| Grenoble | 83.4 | x | x | x | x | (2) | x | x | x |

(1) The nearest bike shop is in Vizille, 46km north of Corps along the N85

(2) At La Tronche on the northeast edge of Grenoble (about 4km from the station)

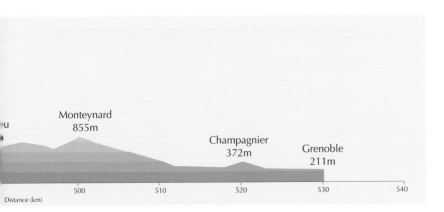

u

Monteynard
855m

Champagnier
372m

Grenoble
211m

Distance (km)

500          510          520          530          540

# ACCOMMODATION

## Grenoble

**Campsites**

The nearest campsite is at Seyssins, on the southwest edge of Grenoble –

Les Trois Pucelles (all year), Tel: 04 76 96 45 73

**Bed & Breakfast**

Mr Cohen, La Tronche, Tel: 04 76 44 78 98

**Hotels**

There are more than 50 hotels in Grenoble. Contact TO for details.

## St Jean-en-Royans

**Campsites**

Camping Municipal (1st May to 30th Sept), Tel: 04 75 47 74 60

**Bed & Breakfast**

Mrs Chabert, Tel: 04 75 48 60 65

Estapade des Tourelons, Tel: 04 75 48 63 96

**Hotels**

De Rome (**), Tel: 04 75 48 40 69

Le Castel Feluri, Tel: 04 75 47 58 01

## Crest

**Campsites**

Les Clorinthes (1st April to 30th Sept), Tel: 04 75 25 05 28

**Bed & Breakfast**

Mrs Tavan, Tel: 04 75 25 49 76

Le Château, Tel: 04 75 76 74 78

Le Château de Beauregard, Tel: 04 75 25 30 26

**Hotels**

Grand Hôtel (**), Tel: 04 75 25 08 17

Le Kléber (**), Tel: 04 75 25 11 69

Des Moulins, Tel: 04 75 76 74 11

## Vaison-la-Romaine

**Campsites**

Camping du Théâtre Romain (mid-March to end Oct), Tel: 04 90 28 78 66

Domaine Carpe Diem (late March to end Oct), Tel: 04 90 36 02 02

Domaine de la Cambuse (1st May to mid-Oct), Tel: 04 90 36 14 53

**Bed & Breakfast**

There are 17 bed & breakfasts in Vaison-la-Romaine. Contact TO for details.

**Hotels**

There are 7 hotels in Vaison-la-Romaine. Contact TO for details.

## Sault

**Campsites**

Le Deffends (mid-April to end Sept), Tel: 04 90 64 07 18

**Bed & Breakfast**

La Bastide des Bourguets, Tel: 04 90 64 11 90

Domaine de Piedmoure, Tel: 04 90 64 06 22

Le Grand Jas, Tel: 04 90 75 08 96

Maison du Bon Accueil, Tel: 04 90 64 15 91

Lavand'Inn, Tel: 04 90 64 13 68

**Hotels**

Hostellerie du Val de Sault (***), Tel: 04 90 64 01 41

Le Louvre (**), Tel: 04 90 64 08 88

L'Albion (**), Tel: 04 90 64 06 22

Le Signoret, Tel: 04 90 64 11 44

## Serres

**Campsites**

Domaine des Deux Soleils (1st May to end Sept), Tel: 04 92 67 01 33

Les Barillons (early May to mid-Sept), Tel: 04 92 67 17 35

**Bed & Breakfast**

Le Cheval Blanc (2km south of Serres), Tel: 04 92 67 11 85

Le Moulin de Paroy (2km north of Serres), Tel: 04 92 67 13 95

**Hotels**

Hotel des Alpes (**), Tel: 04 92 67 00 18

Fifi Moulin (**), Tel: 04 92 67 00 01

Hotel du Nord, Tel: 04 92 67 05 45

## Corps

**Campsites**

La Rouillière (1st July to 31st Aug), Tel: 04 76 30 03 34

Les Aires (April to end Oct), Tel: 04 76 30 03 85 (tourist office)

Lac du Sautet (June to Sept), Tel: 04 76 30 00 97

**Bed & Breakfast**

There are no bed & breakfasts in Corps

**Hotels**

Boustigue Hotel (**), Tel: 04 76 30 07 07

Hotel de la Poste (**), Tel: 04 76 30 00 03

Le Tilleul (**), Tel: 04 76 30 00 43

Le Napoleon (**), Tel: 04 76 30 00 42

Restaurant Pellisier, Tel: 04 76 30 00 35

La Marmotte, Tel: 04 76 30 01 02

## TOURIST INFORMATION

### Regional Information

| | Telephone | Web site |
|---|---|---|
| Isere | 04 76 54 34 36 | www.isere-tourisme.com |
| Drôme | 04 75 82 19 26 | www.drometourisme.com |
| Vaucluse | 04 90 80 47 00 | www.provenceguide.com |
| Hautes-Alpes | 04 92 53 62 00 | www.hautes-alpes.net |

### Tourist Information Offices

| Location | Telephone | Web site |
|---|---|---|
| Grenoble | 04 76 42 41 41 | www.grenoble-isere-tourisme.com |
| Pont-en-Royans | 04 76 36 09 10 | www.ot-pont-en-royans.com |
| St Jean-en-Royans | 04 75 48 61 39 | www.royans.com |
| Beaufort-sur-Gervanne | 04 75 76 45 49 | no website |
| Crest | 04 75 25 11 38 | www.crest-tourisme.com |
| Saou | 04 75 76 01 72 | www.saou.net |
| Bourdeaux | 04 75 53 35 90 | www.bourdeauxtourisme.com |
| Mirabel-aux-Baronnies | 04 75 27 13 93 | www.paysdenyons.com |
| Vaison-la-Romaine | 04 90 36 02 11 | www.vaison-la-romaine.com |
| Malaucène | 04 90 65 22 59 | no website |
| Mont Serein | 04 90 63 42 02 | www.stationdumontserein.com |
| Sault | 04 90 64 01 21 | www.saultenprovence.com |
| Orpierre | 04 92 66 30 45 | www.orpierre.fr |
| Serres | 04 92 67 00 67 | www.buech-serrois.com |
| Veynes | 04 92 57 27 43 | www.tourisme-veynois.com |
| Dévoluy | 04 92 58 91 91 | www.ledevoluy.com |
| Corps | 04 76 30 03 85 | www.corps-alpes.com |
| Trièves | 04 76 34 84 25 | www.alpes-trieves.com |

Orpierre

# TOUR OF THE SOUTHERN ALPS

| Day | Route | Distance | Height Gain |
|---|---|---|---|
| 1 | Barcelonnette to Vinadio | 64.9km | 864m |
| 2 | Vinadio to Isola | 43.9km | 1455m |
| 3 | Isola to Puget-Theniers | 68.7km | 1240m |
| 4 | Puget-Theniers to Guillaumes | 72.9km | 1525m |
| 5 | Guillaumes to Barcelonnette | 63.5km | 1549m |
| | **Totals** | **313.9km** | **6633m** |

The route presented here was cycled before the road to the Col de Larche was closed to pedestrians and cyclists. Due to the difficulty of protecting the road from rock fall, the local council has decided to maintain the cycling ban for the foreseeable future (nevertheless, the 2008 Tour de France was given authorisation to use this road!). Cyclists should not use the 4km of road between the D900/D902 junction and Meyronnes until the ban is lifted. However, cyclists with mountain bikes or robust touring bikes can avoid the banned section of the road by following the short off-road detour described on page 184. Alternative routes for cyclists with road bikes are also described on page 184.

If there were a competition for the world's best cycling holiday destination, the Ubaye Valley would be a hot contender for the gold medal. Naturally the valley's bid would vaunt the proximity of numerous high passes (including the Cime de la Bonette, the highest paved road in Europe), its relatively quiet roads and the area's mild and sunny climate. It might also include the facilities provided to make cyclists feel welcome – for example, kilometre posts showing altitudes and gradients, *brévets* (certificates) for cyclists who have done all seven of the valley's passes and hotels that cater especially for cyclists.

However, its trump card would be something much less tangible and difficult to quantify: even when your legs are turning to rubber at the end of a long, hard day, cycling in the valley is surprisingly relaxing. Life in the Ubaye seems to proceed at a slower pace than elsewhere, and this (more natural?) rhythm quickly casts its spell over the visitor. Even Barcelonnette, a bustling little town in summer, somehow avoids the hectic atmosphere

that infuses so many other popular holiday destinations.

Of course, the Ubaye Valley is only a small part of the southern Alps, defined here as the area between the Col de Vars and the Mediterranean. Much of this area falls within the boundaries of the Mercantour Natural Park, a haven for wildlife and the site for the highly controversial reintroduction of wolves to the Alps. The tour described here focuses on the highest passes in the area between the Ubaye and Var valleys, with a short incursion into the hills south of the Var. Despite being difficult to get to by public transport, Barcelonnette was chosen as the start point for the tour as it allows you to go over the easiest of the high passes, the Col de Larche, on the first day, reserving the Col de la Cayolle, in my opinion the most beautiful pass in the Alps, as a wonderful finale.

Being the Ubaye Valley's main tourist centre, Barcelonnette is a lively place and during the summer there is always something going on. The pedestrianized town centre is

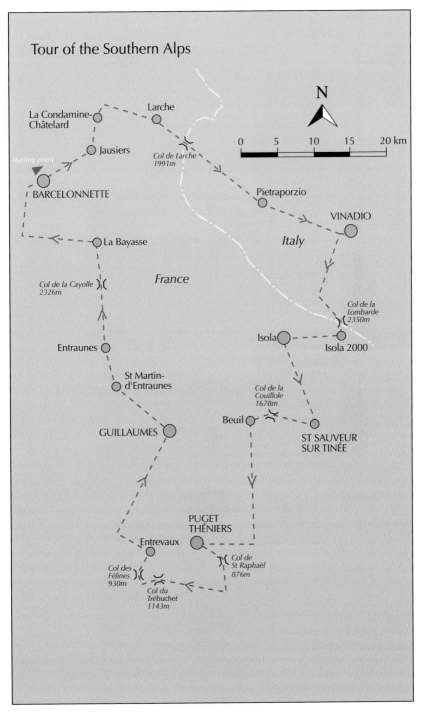

Tour of the Southern Alps

La Condamine-Châtelard

Larche

N

0    5    10    15    20 km

Jausiers

Col de Larche
1991m

starting point

BARCELONNETTE

Pietraporzio

VINADIO

La Bayasse

Italy

Col de la Cayolle
2326m

France

Col de la
Lombarde
2350m

Entraunes

Isola

Isola 2000

St Martin-
d'Entraunes

Col de la
Couillole
1678m

Beuil

GUILLAUMES

ST SAUVEUR
SUR TINÉE

PUGET
THÉNIERS

Entrevaux

Col des
Félines
930m

Col de
St Raphaël
876m

Col du
Trébuchet
1143m

very pleasant and there are numerous shady cafés and restaurants where you can enjoy a coffee and croissant while watching the world go by.

The town was founded in 1231 by the Count of Provence, Raimond Béringer V, who named it after his hometown of Barcelona. It has become the most Mexican of alpine towns, as between 1814 and 1955 a great many people from the Barcelonnette area emigrated to Mexico to make their fortunes. Most decided to remain in their adopted home – 5000 families from the Ubaye Valley are now registered with the French consulate in Mexico – but some came back and built themselves luxurious Mexican-style villas. You can find out more about the town's history and the Mexican exodus at the local museum.

Day 1 of the tour starts very gently, following the banks of the River Ubaye past Jausiers (see the introduction to Route 9) and La Condamine-Châtelard. It is not until you get to the confluence of the Ubaye and Ubayette that the climb to the Col de Larche really begins. This strategic location, at the foot of two major passes (Vars and Larche) and close to the Italian border, is surveyed by the Fort de Tournoux, a marvel of military architecture that has been likened to the Palace of Versailles for the intricacy and ingenuity of its design. Of all the high passes in the French Alps, the Col de Larche is probably the easiest to cycle over, as it is neither particularly steep nor too long. However, it is one of the region's few cross-border routes and local cyclists consider it to be the busiest road in the area. (That being said, whenever I have been on this road, the traffic has always been very light). From the col the road sweeps down into Italy and through Argentera, Bersezio and Pietraporzio to Vinadio.

Vinadio is a very small village protected by a very large fort, which, although less spectacular than Tournoux, is still well worth a visit as it often houses interesting art, photography and local history exhibitions. The narrow streets that wind through the village centre are picturesque: the perfect place for a pre-dinner stroll. There is no better cycling fuel than pasta, and nowhere better to eat pasta than its traditional home (there is some evidence to suggest

that pasta, like so many other things, was actually invented in the Arab world), so why not round off this first day with a good Italian meal in one of the village's restaurants.

On the other hand, it would be unwise to have a big breakfast immediately before starting out on stage two, as the uncompromisingly steep climb to the Col de la Lombarde starts barely a kilometre from Vinadio. This is a much more challenging pass to cycle over than the Col de Larche, with the first 8km through the spectacular gorges of the Santa Anna Valley being particularly steep. After an all too brief respite, the gradient steepens again as the second half of the climb takes you through the larch forests and more open slopes of the upper part of the valley. The pass is a very wild and wind-blown place, but offers spectacular views past the Santa Anna Monastery to the north and across the Tinée Valley to the west. As the road to Isola 2000 is used as a ski run in winter, the surface is of very mediocre quality, in marked contrast to the second part of the descent, which is billiard table smooth and a joy to race down.

Isola, with its superbly restored facades (many of them with *trompe-l'oeil* designs) is a gem of a mountain village. Although small, it is a wonderful place to explore, as you seem to stumble upon delightful surprises around nearly every corner. French-speakers may like to join one of the free guided tours to learn more about this fabulous little corner of the Alps. Ask at the tourist office for details.

From Isola to St Sauveur-sur-Tinée the road gently descends through a steep-sided valley that sees little sun and is therefore often chilly in the mornings. However, all thoughts of being cold will soon be forgotten as you start the ascent to the Col de la Couillole, one of the area's lesser-known passes. The road is unrelentingly steep, rising almost 1200 metres in 16km, and there is very little shade from the Mediterranean sun. After the first few hairpins, the village of Roubion, perched improbably high above the valley, comes into view. The village centre lies just above the main road, but it is worth making the short detour as this is one of the few places to rival Isola for the title of most charming village in the area. Roubion has been inhabited for almost 3000

*Pietraporzio*

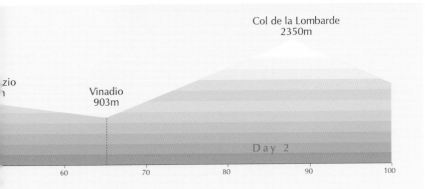

# Day 2 – Vinadio to Isola

With the exception of the Col d'Allos, the high passes of the southern Alps have not often featured in the Tour de France. Therefore, 1993 was an exceptional year, as the 11th stage went over the Col d'Izoard, the Col de Vars, and then took in both the Cime de la Bonette and the climb to Isola 2000. The stage was won by Tony Rominger, who had already won the previous stage over the Cols du Glandon and Galibier, just ahead of Miguel Indurain. A certain Lance Armstrong, in his first Tour de France, came in 97th, almost 29 minutes behind Rominger. This was to be the last stage that Armstrong completed in that year's Tour, but his future team manager, Johan Bruyneel, finished seventh overall. 1993 was Indurain's third successive Tour de France victory and his second successive Giro-Tour de France double. The Tour de France once again gave pride of place to the southern Alps in 2008 by including the Col de Larche, the Col de la Lombarde and the Cime de la Bonette.

| Distance | Location | Directions |
|---|---|---|
| 0.0 | Vinadio: Hotel Monte Nebius | Come out of the hotel and turn L – SS21 |
| 0.3 | Jtn | Turn L (Colle Lombarda) 22.8km at 6.5% |
| 14.8 | Jtn | Turn L (Colle Lombarda) |
| 23.1 | Col de la Lombarde | Go straight on |
| 27.0 | Isola 2000 | Follow D97 through Isola 2000 (Isola–Village) |
| 43.8 | Isola: jtn | Turn R (Isola Centre Ville) |
| 43.9 | Isola: *mairie* | *Mairie* is on the R |

## FACILITIES AND SERVICES

| Location | Distance (km) | Water | Shops | Café | Campsite | B&B | Hotel | Bank | Bike Shop |
|---|---|---|---|---|---|---|---|---|---|
| Vinadio | 0.0 | x | x | x | — | — | x | x | (1) |
| Isola 2000 | 27.0 | x | — | x | — | — | — | — | — |
| Isola | 43.9 | x | x | x | x | x | x | x | (2) |

(1) Nearest bike shop is in Cuneo, 35km east of Vinadio

(2) Nearest bike shop is in Nice, 70km south of Isola on the N202

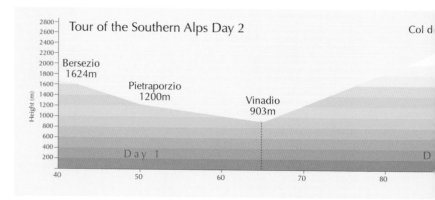

*On the lower slopes of the Col de la Lombarde*

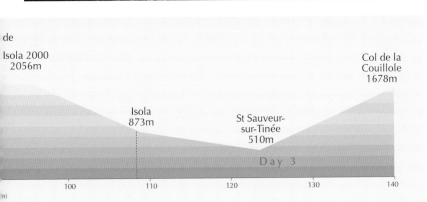

de

Isola 2000
2056m

Col de la
Couillole
1678m

Isola
873m

St Sauveur-
sur-Tinée
510m

Day 3

100    110    120    130    140

m)

# Day 3 – Isola to Puget-Théniers

When cycling in poorly inhabited areas such as the southern Alps, it is essential to be self-reliant for minor repairs. This I learned the hard way when exploring the minor roads between Isola and Nice. A puncture is not usually a problem as I always carry a spare inner tube. Of course, one tube is not sufficient if you puncture both tyres at the same time. It was 35° in the shade, the road was deserted and it was 11km to the nearest village. No choice, but to start walking …

| Distance | Location | Directions |
|---|---|---|
| 0.0 | Isola *mairie* | Come out of the *mairie* and turn R (Toutes Directions) |
| 0.2 | Roundabout | Turn L – D2205 (St Sauveur-sur-Tinée) |
| 14.3 | St Sauveur-sur-Tinée: D2205/D30 | Turn R – D30 (Col de la Couillole): 16km at 7.5% |
| 30.7 | Col de la Couillole | Go straight on |
| 38.1 | Beuil: D30/D28 | Go straight on – D28 (Puget-Théniers) |
| 60.5 | D28/N202 | Turn R – N202 (Puget-Théniers) |
| 68.7 | Puget-Théniers: jtn | N202/Ave Remond |

## FACILITIES AND SERVICES

| Location | Distance (km) | Water | Shops | Café | Campsite | B&B | Hotel | Bank | Bike Shop |
|---|---|---|---|---|---|---|---|---|---|
| Isola | 0.0 | x | x | x | x | x | x | x | (1) |
| St Sauveur-sur-Tinée | 14.3 | x | x | x | x | — | x | — | — |
| Roubion | 25.7 | x | x | x | — | x | — | — | — |
| Col de la Couillole | 30.7 | — | — | — | — | x | — | — | — |
| Beuil | 38.7 | x | x | x | — | — | x | — | — |
| Pra-d'Astier | 52.3 | x | — | — | — | — | — | — | — |
| Puget-Théniers | 68.7 | x | x | x | x | — | x | x | (2) |

(1) Nearest bike shop is in Nice, 70km south of Isola

(2) Nearest bike shop is in Nice, 65km southeast of Puget-Théniers

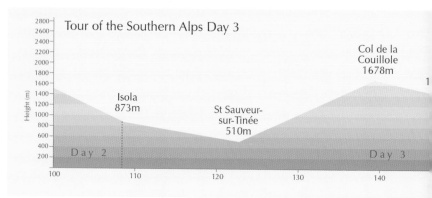

Tour of the Southern Alps Day 3

*Looking up to the village of Roubion
on the road to the Col de la Couillole*

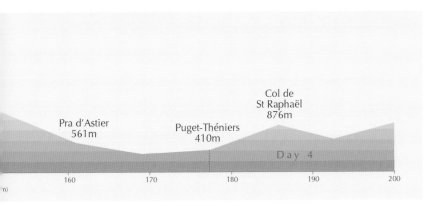

189

## Day 4 – Puget-Théniers to Guillaumes

| Distance | Location | Directions |
|---|---|---|
| 0.0 | Puget-Théniers: jtn N202/Ave Remond | Turn L – N202 |
| 0.1 | N202/D2211A | Turn R – D2211A (Col de St Raphäel): 8.4km at 5.5% |
| 8.5 | Col de St Raphäel | Go straight on – D2211A (La Penne) |
| 15.2 | D2211A/D10 | Turn R – D10 (Castellet St Cassien): 7.5km at 4% then 3.2km descent followed by 6.2km at 4.5% |
| 32.1 | Col du Trébuchet | Go straight on |
| 37.7 | D10/D911 | Turn R – D911 (Entrevaux): 2.7km at 3.5% |
| 40.4 | Col des Félines | Go straight on |
| 47.4 | Entrevaux: D911/N202 | Turn L – N202 (Annot) |
| 52.9 | N202/D902 | Turn R – D902/D2202 (Guillaumes) |
| 72.9 | Guillaumes TO | TO is on the R |

*A short but sweet descent past the village of La Penne*

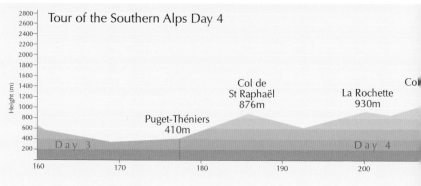

Tour of the Southern Alps Day 4

Height (m)

2800
2600
2400
2200
2000
1800
1600
1400
1200
1000
800
600
400
200

Col de
St Raphaël
876m

La Rochette
930m

Col

Puget-Théniers
410m

Day 3

Day 4

160   170   180   190   200

*A well-earned break at the Col du Trébuchet*

Col du Trébuchet
altitude 1141 m

## FACILITIES AND SERVICES

| Location | Distance (km) | Water | Shops | Café | Campsite | B&B | Hotel | Bank | Bike Shop |
|---|---|---|---|---|---|---|---|---|---|
| Puget-Théniers | 0.0 | x | x | x | x | — | x | x | (1) |
| La Penne | 10.8 | x | — | — | — | — | x | — | — |
| La Rochette | 22.7 | x | — | x | — | — | — | — | — |
| Castellet-St Cassien | 36.7 | x | — | — | — | — | — | — | — |
| Entrevaux | 47.4 | x | x | x | x | — | x | x | — |
| Daluis | 61.3 | x | — | — | — | — | — | — | — |
| Guillaumes | 72.9 | x | x | x | x | x | x | x | (2) |

(1) Nearest bike shop is in Nice, 65km southeast of Puget-Théniers

(2) Nearest bike shop is in Barcelonnette, 64km north of Guillaumes

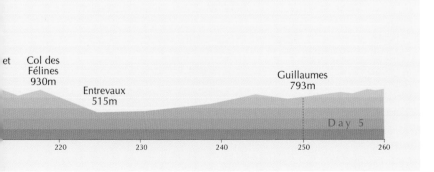

# Day 5 – Guillaumes to Barcelonnette

Extra day: it is difficult to do a day trip of a reasonable length from any of the overnight stops on this tour. However, a day can be added to the tour by extending the excursion into the superb countryside to the south of the Var Valley. Day 4 would then become Puget–Théniers–Roquesteron–Bouyon–Coursegoules–Gréolières (One hotel, two B&Bs, no campsite – **www.greolieres.fr**). Day 5 would be Gréolières –St Auban–Briançonnet–Col de Félines–Entrevaux–Guillaumes.

| Distance | Location | Directions |
|---|---|---|
| 0.0 | Guillaumes TO | Come out of TO and turn R – D2202 (Col de la Cayolle): 12km at 2%, 5.9km at 3.5%, and then 15.1km at 7% |
| 33.0 | Col de la Cayolle | Go straight on – D902 |
| 60.6 | D902/D908 | Turn R – D902 (Barcelonnette) |
| 62.8 | Pont du Plan | Go straight on over bridge |
| 63.2 | Jtn | Turn L (past fountain) to go into pedestrian area |
| 63.3 | Jtn | Turn R onto main pedestrian street |
| 63.5 | Barcelonnette: Place Manuel | |

## FACILITIES AND SERVICES

| Location | Distance (km) | Water | Shops | Café | Campsite | B&B | Hotel | Bank | Bike Shop |
|---|---|---|---|---|---|---|---|---|---|
| Guillaumes | 0.0 | x | x | x | x | x | x | x | (1) |
| St Martin-d'Entraunes | 12.0 | x | x | x | — | x | x | — | — |
| Entraunes | 17.9 | x | — | x | x | — | x | — | — |
| Estenc | 25.4 | x | — | x | — | x | x | — | — |
| Col de la Cayolle | 33.0 | x | — | x | — | x | — | — | — |
| La Bayasse | 42.3 | x | — | x | — | x | — | — | — |
| Uvernet-Fours | 59.0 | x | x | x | — | x | x | — | — |
| Barcelonnette | 63.5 | x | x | x | x | x | x | x | x |

(1) Nearest bike shop is in Barcelonnette, 64km north of Guillaumes

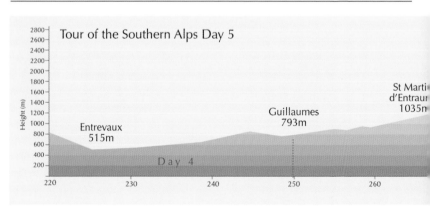

Tour of the Southern Alps Day 5

*Looking up towards
the Col de la Cayolle*

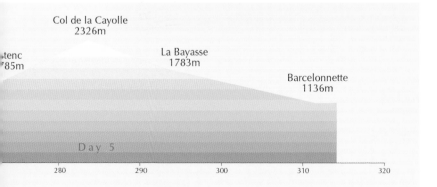

Col de la Cayolle
2326m

.tenc
85m

La Bayasse
1783m

Barcelonnette
1136m

Day 5

280        290        300        310        320

# ACCOMMODATION

## Barcelonnette

### Campsites

Le Plan (dates not known), Tel. 04 92 81 08 11

Le Tampico (Christmas to end Oct), Tel. 04 92 81 02 55

Le Peyra (early May to end Oct), Tel. 04 92 81 24 06

### Bed & Breakfast

L'Establoun, Tel. 04 92 81 13 57

Le Bosquet, Tel. 04 92 81 41 28

### Hotels

There are seven hotels in Barcelonnette. Contact TO for details.

## Vinadio

### Campsites

The nearest campsite is the Centro Sentieri in Pietraporzio, 14km north-west of Vinadio (dates not known), Tel. 0171 96512

### Bed & Breakfast

There are no bed and breakfasts in Vinadio

### Hotels

Albergo Italia (***), Tel. 0171 959148

Albergo Ligure (**), Tel. 0171 959149

NB Both the above hotels are closed on Mondays

Albergo Ristorante Ciastella, Tel. 0171 959253

Albergo Strepeis, Tel. 0171 959831

## Isola

### Campsites

Lac des Neiges (all year), Tel. 04 93 02 18 16

### Bed & Breakfast

*Gîte d'étape* at Lac des Neiges campsite, Tel. 04 93 02 18 16

### Hotels

Hotel de France (*), Tel. 04 93 02 17 04

Hotel d'Isola, Tel. 04 93 02 17 03

## Puget-Théniers

### Campsites

Municipal (all year), Tel. 04 93 05 10 53

### Bed & Breakfast

Auberge du Coustet, Tel. 04 93 05 11 90

### Hotels

Alizé (**), Tel. 04 93 05 06 20

Edelweiss (**), Tel. 04 93 05 01 00

## Guillaumes

**Campsites**

Pont de la Mariée (early April to end Sept), Tel. 04 93 05 53 50

**Bed & Breakfast**

Gîte d'étape de Villeplane, Tel. 04 93 05 56 01

**Hotels**

Les Chaudrons, Tel. 04 93 05 50 01

La Renaissance, Tel. 04 93 05 59 89

## TOURIST INFORMATION

### Regional Information

| | Telephone | Website |
|---|---|---|
| Alpes de Haute-Provence | 04 92 31 57 29 | www.alpes-haute-provence.com |
| Alpes Maritimes | 04 93 37 78 78 | www.guideriviera.com |

### Tourist Information Offices

| Location | Telephone | Website |
|---|---|---|
| Barcelonnette | 04 92 81 04 71 | www.barcelonnette.com |
| Jausiers | 04 92 81 21 45 | www.jausiers.com |
| Larche | no telephone | www.haute-ubaye.com |
| Bersazio/Pietraporzio/Vinadio | no telephone | www.ghironda.com/valstura |
| Isola 2000 | 04 93 23 15 15 | www.isola2000.com |
| Isola | 04 93 02 18 97 | www.isola2000.com |
| St Sauveur-sur-Tinée | 04 93 02 00 22 | www.ville-saint-sauveursurtinee.fr |
| Roubion | 04 93 02 10 30 | www.roubion.com |
| Beuil | 04 93 02 32 58 | www.beuil.com |
| Puget-Théniers | 04 93 05 05 05 | www.puget-theniers.fr |
| Guillaumes | 04 93 05 57 76 | www.pays-de-guillaumes.com |
| Entraunes-Estenc | 04 93 05 51 26 | no website |

# ROUTE NINE

# GRAND TRAVERSE OF THE FRENCH ALPS

| Day | Route | Distance | Height Gain |
|-----|-------|----------|-------------|
| 1 | Geneva to Thonon-les-Bains | 51.1km | 200m |
| 2 | Thonon-les-Bains to La Clusaz | 78.7km | 1660m |
| 3 | La Clusaz to Beaufort | 51.3km | 1240m |
| 4 | Beaufort to Bourg St Maurice | 45.7km | 1410m |
| 5 | Bourg St Maurice to Bessans | 68.7km | 2020m |
| 6 | Bessans to Valloire | 70.8km | 1180m |
| 7 | Valloire to Briançon | 55.5km | 1250m |
| 8 | Briançon to Guillestre | 51.8km | 1150m |
| 9 | Guillestre to Jausiers | 42.5km | 1110m |
| 10 | Jausiers to Isola | 65.3km | 1650m |
| 11 | Isola to Levens | 77.8km | 1340m |
| 12 | Levens to Nice | 37.1km | 200m |
| | **Totals** | **696.3km** | **14,410m** |

However enjoyable circular tours may be, there is something uniquely satisfying about completing a true 'journey', especially when that journey takes you through an area as fabulously beautiful as the French Alps. The Grand Traverse from Lake Geneva to the Mediterranean is one of Europe's great cycle tours, covering almost 700km over some of the continent's highest mountain roads.

The idea of traversing the Alps by road was first mooted by the Touring Club de France in 1911 as a way of developing motorised tourism. Their idea of driving the whole length of the French Alps from Thonon-les-Bains to Menton was extremely ambitious as most alpine passes were not at all practicable for motorcars. In 1913 a major road-building programme was launched, culminating in 1937 with the inauguration of the Col de l'Iseran, at the time the highest road in Europe. The Route des Grandes Alpes was an immediate success and it is still a highly popular itinerary, especially with motorcyclists. Several guides to the route have been produced, details of which can be found at **www.routedesgrandesalpes.com** (in

French only). Of course, these new roads did not only benefit cars and motorbikes; before the Second World War cycling on mountain roads often had more in common with mountain biking than modern road cycling.

The itinerary described here is slightly different to the classic Route des Grandes Alpes as, in order to facilitate access by public transport, it goes from Geneva to Nice rather than from Thonon-les-Bains to Menton. Additional changes were made in order to avoid the very busy road over the Col des Gets (south of Thonon-les-Bains) and to include the Cime de la Bonette, currently the highest paved road in Europe. From St Sauveur-sur-Tinée, the itinerary goes through Utelle and Levens to Nice rather than to Menton via St Martin-Vésubie and Sospel.

As the most pleasant road from Geneva to Thonon-les-Bains is along the shores of Lake Geneva, the first stage of the Grand Traverse follows the same route as the Tour of the Chablais–Aravis (see Route 2).

Day 2, although it does not take you over any really high passes, will enable you to assess your fitness as there are nevertheless

*Jausiers, one of many picturesque villages in the Southern Alps*

Durance Valley. After a short breather the gradient increases again as you continue towards Vars, a modern ski resort with little to attract the passing cyclist. The last 3km, past a tiny lake and a second Refuge Napoléon, are wonderfully picturesque. The Refuges Napoléon were so named because they were built to honour the terms of Napoleon's last will and testament. The former emperor had bequeathed a sum of money to the *départements* that had suffered the most from the wars during his reign. This money was to be used to create something that would benefit the population and provide a permanent reminder of Napoleon's benevolence. After long deliberations, the Hautes-Alpes *département* decided to build mountain huts at the summits of six mountain passes, including the Col de Vars and the Col d'Izoard.

The Col de Vars is the gateway to the Ubaye Valley and one of seven major passes that surround the valley's main town, Barcelonnette. Barcelonnette tourist office issues a certificate to cyclists who have climbed all seven of these passes, the 'proof' being provided by a card the cyclist gets stamped at a box at the summit of each pass. There is one of these boxes at the Col de Vars, but, of course, first you have to descend to Barcelonnette to get the card!

As this is a short day, there is plenty of time to enjoy a drink or a snack at the summit café before starting the descent. From just below the pass, there are superb views of the Brec de Chambeyron, one of the highest summits in the southern Alps.

The stage ends in Jausiers, a pretty and unpresuming village with a wonderfully friendly and relaxing atmosphere. Despite its obviously limited means, the village museum has put together some interesting exhibits that are well worth the small entrance fee. If you feel like stretching your legs a little, I would recommend a stroll up to the orientation table behind the bell-tower for the panorama it offers of the whole Ubaye Valley. For those looking for a livelier place to spend the night, Barcelonnette is only 9km down the road (see Route 8).

Even if it were not the highest paved road in Europe, the 2808 metre-high Cime de la Bonette would be a great climb, through a magnificent corner of the Alps. The high point of the road is neither a true pass nor the summit of the mountain; the road was extended to this point from the true Col de la Bonette simply to steal the Col de l'Iseran's throne as the highest road in France. The extra height was not gained easily and the gradient over the last few hundred metres provides a stiff test for tired legs. The view from the roadside is quite spectacular, but it is worth making the effort to walk the last 50 metres to reach the true Cime for the glorious 360° panorama of the southern Alps. An orientation table will help you get your bearings: on a clear day you can see the Mediterranean, 100km to the south.

On the southern side of the Bonette the billiard-table smooth surface of the recently resurfaced road is a delight to cycle down. One of the joys of cycling in the mountains is the exhilarating feeling of effortlessly flying down a mountainside and here that sensation can be enjoyed to the full with 26km of free-wheeling descent all the way to St Etienne-de-Tinée. St Etienne is a very pleasant village with an imposing baroque church and a maze of picturesque cobbled lanes. On leaving St Etienne, the road goes gently uphill for a short distance before descending once again towards Isola (see Route 8).

Day 11 is the last hard day of the traverse, but it starts easily with 34km of gentle downhill or flat cycling along the Tinée Valley. With properly warmed-up leg muscles, and compared to the efforts of the previous days, the climb to La Tour-sur-Tinée should not feel too difficult (be careful not to miss the turn off

– it is just before a tunnel). La Tour is a real gem of a village and it is easy to see why it has been listed as an historic monument. The Grand Place in the centre of this hamlet of 300 souls is surrounded by perfectly restored mediaeval buildings with brightly painted facades. A number of narrow, cobbled lanes lead away from this square towards the edge of the village, from where there are fabulous views of the surrounding countryside.

After a short descent, the road climbs again to go over an unnamed pass and into the wild and sun-baked Carbonnières Valley. The narrow road (which, in places, is poorly maintained) runs through a desiccated landscape of grey limestone, stunted trees and thorny scrub. Despite its modest altitude, this is an impressively remote and inhospitable place so the more 'civilised' landscape that emerges as you approach Utelle is strangely comforting. At this point the road surface also improves dramatically and the descent to St Jean-la-Rivière is great fun.

There are surprisingly few hotels and campsites in the countryside north of Nice, except for those beside the main road in the Var Valley (mostly dual-carriageway and dangerous to cycle along). Although it does not have a campsite, Levens, just south of the

Col de la Bonette

*Typical perched village in the Gorges de la Vésubie, near Levens*

Vésubie Valley, is one of the few villages to offer a choice of accommodation. The road to Levens follows the left bank of the Vésubie Gorge, above the spectacular cliffs of the Saut des Français, so-called because local fighters, who resisted the 'invasion' by French Revolutionary soldiers from 1793 to 1794, forced their prisoners to jump off the cliff. Levens is a fortified mediaeval village sitting high above the Vésubie. If you were not lucky enough to glimpse the Mediterranean from the Cime de la Bonette, you will almost certainly see it from here.

The final day can be taken at a relaxing pace as Levens is only 37km from Nice, and most of the cycling is downhill. The route goes through several villages, including Aspremont, a pretty little place that spirals around the top of a small hill, just above the outskirts of Nice – one last chance to relax in a quiet country café and contemplate the magnificent journey you have just completed before entering the hubbub of France's fifth largest city.

Like all large cities, Nice is surrounded by anonymous and sprawling suburbs, but the old town is very pleasant and the city has several interesting museums, including one dedicated to the work of Henri Matisse. Nice's most famous landmark is undoubtedly the Promenade des Anglais, a wide boulevard overlooking the Mediterranean and home to some of the Riviera's most exclusive hotels. However, the city's most sumptuous (and unexpected) building is its ornate Russian Orthodox church. Hotels can be expensive, but Nice has a great many reasonably priced restaurants: what better way to celebrate the end of such an epic journey than with a glass of champagne and a good meal in the glow of a Mediterranean sunset?

## GETTING THERE

**By car**
Geneva is 760km from Calais

**By plane**
**Via Geneva**
The route starts directly from Geneva airport

## LEAVING NICE

The route ends at Nice airport. There are direct flights from here to many European destinations, including Geneva and several cities in the UK. It is also possible to take the train from Nice to Geneva, via Marseille.

Col de la Madeleine and Haute Maurienne (Day 6)

Nice–St Augustin railway station is less than 1km from the airport (see Day 12 route card). There is a frequent service to the centre of Nice

particularly busy. All of the high passes are closed from the middle of October to early or mid-June.

## WHEN TO GO

The best times to do this tour are in June and early July, or from late August to the end of September.

Unsurprisingly, the traffic on such a famous route can be heavy during the holiday season, with the sections between La Clusaz and Flumet, Bourg St Maurice and the Col de l'Iseran, and Modane and Briançon being

## MAPS

**Michelin:** Local – Sheet 328 Ain, Haute-Savoie, Sheet 333 Isère, Savoie; Sheet 334 Alpes-de-Haute-Provence, Hautes-Alpes; Sheet 341 Alpes Maritimes

**Michelin:** Regional– Sheet 244 Rhône-Alpes, and Sheet 245 Provence, Côte d'Azur

**IGN:** Top 100 – Sheets 45 Annecy, Lausanne, 53 Grenoble, Mont Blanc, 54 Grenoble, Gap and 61 Barcelonnette, Nice

*The Aiguille des Glaciers from near Les Chapieux (Day 4)*

One of the best ways to enjoy the scenery around Lake Geneva, and perhaps visit some of the other interesting towns and villages along its shores, is to take a boat trip across the lake. The Compagnie Générale de Navigation runs a large number of cruises, including shuttle services from Geneva to Yvoire and Thonon-les-Bains. In October 2007, second-class single tickets cost 14.70 Euros and 21.00 Euros respectively. Bicycles are accepted on all of the company's boats, except for those marked with a 'V' (V = vedette, a small motor launch) in the timetable. There is a 6CHF (approx. 4 Euros) supplement for bicycles. Timetable and ticket information can be obtained from the company's website, **www.cgn.ch**.

| Distance | Location | Directions |
|---|---|---|
| 0.0 | Geneva airport | For directions from airport to Franco–Swiss border see Appendix 1 |
| 22.5 | Hermance: Franco–Swiss border | Go straight on – D25 |
| 24.7 | Chens-sur-Léman: D25/D20 | Turn L – D25 (Thonon). Follow D25 through Messery, Yvoire and Excenevex to Sciez |
| 39.5 | Sciez: D25/N5 | Turn L – N5 (Thonon) |
| 41.0 | N5/D325 | Turn L – D325/Route du Port (Port de Sciez-Plage) |
| 41.6 | Roundabout | Turn R (Le Chatelet) |
| 43.2 | Roundabout | Turn R (Thonon) |
| 43.6 | Jtn | Turn R – D35/Route du Port de Sciez |
| 43.9 | Séchex: jtn | Turn L – Rue Centrale/D35 |
| 45.8 | Anthy-sur-Léman | Turn L in centre of village [Tour du Bas Chablais]. Follow these blue cycling signs to Thonon-les-Baines |
| 50.5 | Thonon: roundabout | Go straight on (Office de Tourisme) |
| 50.7 | Jtn | Turn R onto Rue Vallon (Centre Ville-Rue Pietonnée). Follow road around to L and turn immediately R into square with large fountain. Go across square and then straight on along Rue St Sebastien |
| 51.0 | Jtn | Turn R onto Place du Marché |
| 51.1 | Thonon TO | TO is on the L |

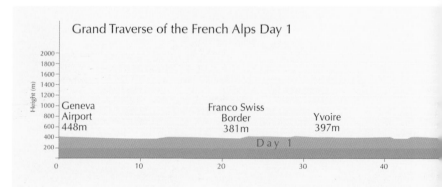

Thonon, view from the town over the marina

## FACILITIES AND SERVICES

| Location | Distance (km) | Water | Shops | Café | Campsite | B&B | Hotel | Bank | Bike Shop |
|---|---|---|---|---|---|---|---|---|---|
| Geneva | 0.0 | — | x | x | x | x | x | x | x |
| Vésenaz | 13.7 | — | x | x | — | — | x | x | x |
| Hermance | 21.9 | — | x | x | — | — | x | — | — |
| Chens-sur-Léman | 25.7 | x | x | x | x | — | x | — | — |
| Yvoire | 32.2 | x | x | x | x | — | x | — | — |
| Excenevex | 35.5 | — | x | x | x | x | x | — | — |
| Sciez (1) | 39.2 | — | x | x | x | x | x | x | (2) |
| Séchex | 43.6 | x | — | x | x | — | — | — | — |
| Thonon-les-Bains | 50.8 | x | x | x | x | x | x | x | x |

(1) There are campsites and hotels in several places between Sciez and Thonon
(2) The bike shop is actually in Bonnatrait, 1km from Sciez

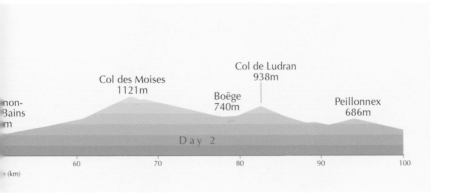

# Day 2 – Thonon-les-Baines to La Clusaz

| Distance | Location | Directions |
|---|---|---|
| 0.0 | Thonon TO | Come out of TO and turn R. After 50m, turn L onto Rue des Granges |
| 0.1 | Roundabout | Go straight on – Boulevard G. Andrier (Morzine) |
| 0.3 | Jtn after railway line | Turn R – N5 (Annecy) |
| 0.7 | Roundabout | Go straight on |
| 1.0 | Traffic lights | Turn L – D903 (Habère-Poche) |
| 1.7 | Roundabout D903/D12 | Go straight on – D12 (Habère-Poche): 8.5km at 3% |
| 10.2 | D12/D246 | Turn L (Col des Moises): 5.8km at 7% |
| 16.0 | Col des Moises | Go straight on |
| 17.3 | D246/D12 | Turn R (Col de Cou) |
| 17.6 | D12/D40 | Turn L (Burdignin) |
| 26.9 | Boëge | Turn L – D22/Rue de Saxel |
| 27.0 | Jtn | Go straight on (Villard) |
| 27.2 | D22/D220 | Turn R (St André) |
| 29.0 | Jtn | Turn L. Follow (Viuz-en-Sallaz): 2.9km at 6.5% |
| 31.9 | Col de Ludran | Go straight on |
| 35.1 | Sardagne | Turn R to follow (Boisinges) then (Brégny) |
| 37.5 | Jtn | Turn L (Bucquigny) |
| 38.8 | Jtn | Turn R – D12 (Annemasse) |
| 39.4 | D12/D907 | Go straight on – D12 (Bonneville): 3.1km at 3.5% |
| 50.4 | D12/N205 | Turn L – N205 (Bonneville) |
| 52.4 | Bonneville: roundabout | Turn R (Cluses); go straight on at next two roundabouts |
| 53.0 | Roundabout | Turn L – start of cycleway (Cluses) |
| 53.4 | N205/D27 | Turn R – D27 (Pontchy–Dessus) |
| 56.3 | Jtn: D27/D12 | Turn L – D12 (no sign: T-jtn just after river): 22 km at 3% |
| 64.7 | Le Petit Bornand | Go straight on |
| 74.9 | D12/D4 | Turn R – D4 (La Clusaz) |
| 75.7 | St Jean-de-Sixt: round-about | Turn L (La Clusaz) |
| 78.4 | La Clusaz: roundabout | Turn L then R (Centre Village) |
| 78.7 | La Clusaz TO | TO is on the R |

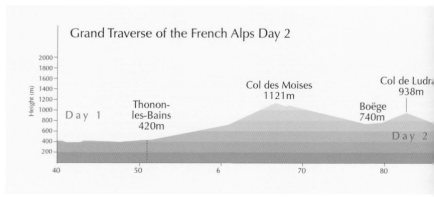

Grand Traverse of the French Alps Day 2

View of Mont Blanc and Le Môle from Col de Ludran

## FACILITIES AND SERVICES

| Location | Distance (km) | Water | Shops | Café | Campsite | B&B | Hotel | Bank | Bike Shop |
|---|---|---|---|---|---|---|---|---|---|
| Thonon-les-Bains | 0.0 | x | x | x | x | x | x | x | x |
| Allinges | 8.9 | — | x | x | — | — | — | — | — |
| Boëge | 26.9 | x | x | x | — | — | — | x | — |
| Sardagne | 35.1 | x | x | — | — | — | — | — | — |
| Viuz-en-Sallaz | 39.4 | — | x | x | — | — | x | x | — |
| Peillonnex | 42.9 | — | x | x | — | — | — | — | — |
| Faucigny | 45.3 | x | — | x | — | — | — | — | — |
| Bonneville | 52.4 | x | x | x | x | — | x | x | — |
| Le Petit Bornand | 64.7 | x | x | x | x | x | x | — | — |
| St Jean-de-Sixt | 75.7 | x | x | x | x | x | x | x | x |
| La Clusaz | 78.7 | x | x | x | x | x | x | x | x |

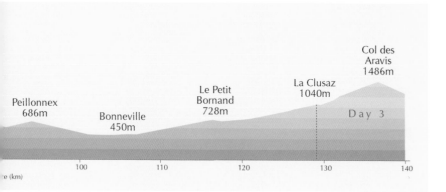

## Day 3 – La Clusaz to Beaufort

| Distance | Location | Directions |
|---|---|---|
| 0.0 | La Clusaz TO | Come out of TO and turn R to go past police station |
| 0.1 | Jtn | Turn R onto Route de l'Etale and go past cinema: 2.5km at 7% |
| 1.7 | Jtn | Bear L onto Route de Sence (just after tiny chapel on R) |
| 2.6 | Jtn | Turn L – D16 (no sign) |
| 2.7 | D16/D909 | Turn R (Col des Aravis): 4.5km at 6% |
| 7.2 | Col des Aravis | Go straight on |
| 19.1 | Flumet: jtn | Turn R (Toutes Directions) |
| 19.5 | Roundabout | Turn L – N212 (Mégeve) |
| 19.8 | Roundabout: N212/D218 | Turn R – D218 (Les Saisies): 2.1km at 6.5% |
| 21.9 | D218/D218A | Turn R – D218 (Les Saisies): 7.1km at 6% then 5km at 4% |
| 34.8 | Col des Saisies | Go straight on |
| 41.8 | D218/D218B | Turn L (Hauteluce) |
| 42.8 | Hauteluce: D218B/D70 | Go straight on – D70 |
| 43.6 | Jtn | Turn R – D70 (Beaufort) |
| 50.8 | D70/D925 | Turn R – D925 |
| 51.3 | Beaufort TO | TO is on the L |

*Notre Dame de Bellecombe, on the way up to the Col des Saisies*

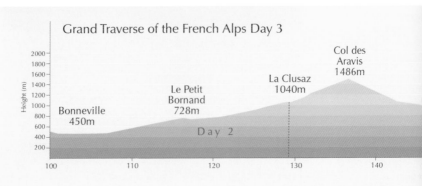

The start of the wonderful descent from the Col des Aravis

## FACILITIES AND SERVICES

| Location | Distance (km) | Water | Shops | Café | Campsite | B&B | Hotel | Bank | Bike Shop |
|---|---|---|---|---|---|---|---|---|---|
| La Clusaz | 0.0 | x | x | x | x | x | x | x | x |
| Col des Aravis | 7.2 | x | x | — | — | — | — | — | — |
| La Giettaz | 13.0 | x | x | x | x | x | x | — | — |
| Flumet | 19.1 | x | x | x | x | x | x | x | — |
| Notre Dame-de-Bellecombe | 23.2 | x | x | x | — | x | x | — | x |
| Les Saisies | 35.5 | x | x | x | — | x | x | x | — |
| Hauteluce | 42.8 | x | x | x | — | x | x | x | — |
| Beaufort | 51.3 | x | x | x | x | x | x | x | (1) |

(1) Nearest bike shop is in Albertville, 20km southwest of Beaufort

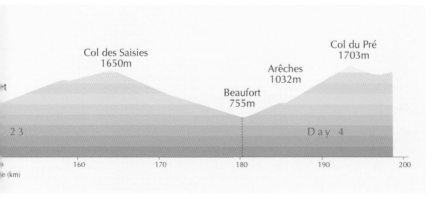

Col des Saisies 1650m

Col du Pré 1703m

Arêches 1032m

Beaufort 755m

Day 4

23

160    170    180    190    200

e (km)

Cycling between La Clusaz and the Col du Pré you can see two of the works of Gargantua, a gluttonous and truculent giant who features in a great many French myths (including the myth of the 'mermaid of the vines', see Route 1). It is said that in a fit of pique while walking through the Aravis, the giant gave the mountains an enormous kick and sent a huge lump of rock flying through the air. The gap that was left forms the Porte des Aravis (above the Col des Aravis) and the detached block landed in the Beaufortain to form the tooth-like Pierre Menta.

| Distance | Location | Directions |
|---|---|---|
| 0.0 | Beaufort TO | Come out of TO and turn L – D218 (Arêches-Le Planay): 4.0km at 6.5% |
| 5.0 | Arêches: D218/D85 | Go straight on – D218 (Col du Pré): 7.3km at 9% |
| 12.3 | Col du Pré | Go straight on |
| 15.7 | Low point | Go straight on |
| 17.7 | Col de Meraillet: D217/D925 | Turn R – D217 (Bourg Saint Maurice): short descent then 5.9km at 6.5% |
| 25.9 | Cormet de Roseland | Go straight on (D217 becomes D902) |
| 45.6 | Bourg St Maurice: roundabout: D902/N90 | Turn R – N90 (Aime) |
| 45.7 | Bourg St Maurice TO | TO is on the R |

| **FACILITIES AND SERVICES** | | | | | | | | | |
|---|---|---|---|---|---|---|---|---|---|
| Location | Distance (km) | Water | Shops | Café | Campsite | B&B | Hotel | Bank | Bike Shop |
| Beaufort | 0.0 | x | x | x | x | x | x | x | (1) |
| Arêches | 5.0 | x | x | x | x | x | x | — | — |
| Col du Pré | 12.3 | — | — | x | — | — | — | — | — |
| Col de Meraillet | 17.7 | — | — | x | — | — | — | — | — |
| Bourg St Maurice | 45.7 | x | x | x | x | — | x | x | x |

(1) Nearest bike shop is in Albertville, 20km southwest of Beaufort

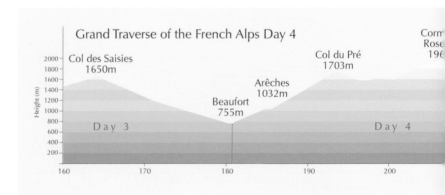

*Roseland Reservoir, in the heart of the Beaufortain Mountains*

The only time I have experienced the unpleasant effects of hypoglycaemia (weak legs, dizziness and nausea) was on a long ride over the Cormet de Roseland and the Col de l'Iseran. The Cormet burnt up the few cereal bars I had, but I wasn't worried, there are plenty of bakeries in Val d'Isère. My expectations were quickly shattered: it being the end of the season all the shops were closed. On rubber legs, I struggled up to the pass, drawn on by the thought of bilberry tarts at the summit café. It was cold and windy… and the café was shut! Devastated, I slumped down to Bonneval and wobbled through Bessans to Lanslebourg, where I eventually found somewhere to refuel.

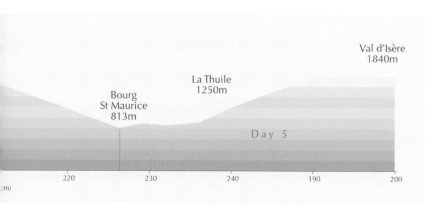

Val d'Isère
1840m

La Thuile
1250m

Bourg
St Maurice
813m

Day 5

220    230    240    190    200

(m)

213

When it was finished, in 1952, the Tignes Dam was the biggest in Europe, an engineering marvel that was to provide half of Savoie's electricity. However, the project was not welcomed by everyone and the inhabitants of the village of Tignes, whose homes were to be submerged below the reservoir's 235 million cubic metres of water, fought hard, but in vain, to prevent its construction. The fresco of Hercules supporting the dam on his shoulders was not added until 1989.

| Distance | Location | Directions |
|---|---|---|
| 0.0 | Bourg St Maurice TO | Come out of TO and turn L – N90 |
| 0.1 | Roundabout | Go straight on – (Italie) |
| 2.8 | N90/D902 | Turn R – D902 (Col de l'Iseran): 15.8km at 6% |
| 23.9 | D902/D87A | Go straight on (Val d'Isère) |
| 31.0 | Val d'Isère* | Go straight on: 16.4km at 6% |
| 47.4 | Col de l'Iseran | Go straight on |
| 68.0 | D902/D902A | Turn R – D209 (Bessans) |
| 68.7 | Bessans TO | The TO is on the L |

* The road system through Val d'Isère may change over the next few years as there are plans to turn the village into a 'car-free' resort

| FACILITIES AND SERVICES | | | | | | | | | |
|---|---|---|---|---|---|---|---|---|---|
| Location | Distance (km) | Water | Shops | Café | Campsite | B&B | Hotel | Bank | Bike Shop |
| Bourg St Maurice | 0.0 | x | x | x | x | — | x | x | x |
| Seez | 2.6 | x | x | x | x | x | x | — | — |
| Ste Foy-Tarentaise | 11.9 | — | x | x | — | — | x | — | — |
| La Thuile | 14.6 | — | — | — | — | — | x | — | — |
| Val d'Isère | 31.0 | x | x | x | — | x | x | x | x |
| Col de l'Iseran | 47.4 | — | — | x | — | — | — | — | — |
| Bonneval-sur-Arc | 60.0 | x | x | x | — | x | x | — | — |
| Bessans | 68.7 | x | x | x | x | x | x | x | (1) |

(1) Nearest bike shop is in Lanslebourg, 11.7km west of Bessans

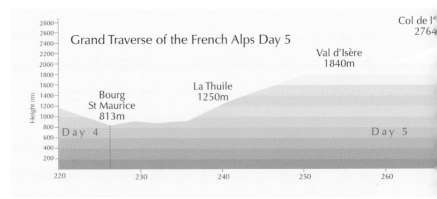

*Looking down on Val d'Isère from the Col de l'Iseran road*

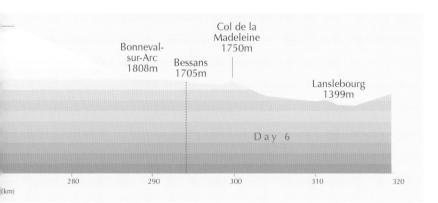

# Day 6 – Bessans to Valloire

| Distance | Location | Directions |
|---|---|---|
| 0.0 | Bessans TO | Come out of TO and turn L – D209 |
| 1.9 | D209/D902 | Turn R – D902 (Modane) |
| 4.6 | Col de la Madeleine | Go straight on |
| 11.7 | Lanslebourg: D902/N6 | Go straight on – N6 |
| 19.7 | N6/D83 | Turn R – D83 (Sardières): 4.5km at 5% |
| 28.5 | Aussois | Go straight on – D215 (Modane) |
| 36.0 | Modane: traffic lights | Turn L (Centre Ville) |
| 36.2 | Jtn | Turn R – N6 (Centre Ville) |
| 53.4 | St Michel-de-Maurienne: N6/D902 | Turn L – D902 (Valloire): 12.3km at 7% |
| 65.7 | Col du Télégraphe | Go straight on |
| 70.6 | Valloire: roundabout | Turn R |
| 70.8 | Valloire TO | TO is on the R |

## FACILITIES AND SERVICES

| Location | Distance (km) | Water | Shops | Café | Campsite | B&B | Hotel | Bank | Bike Shop |
|---|---|---|---|---|---|---|---|---|---|
| Bessans | 0.0 | x | x | x | x | x | x | x | (1) |
| Lanslevillard | 8.8 | x | x | x | — | — | x | — | — |
| Lanslebourg | 11.7 | x | x | x | x | x | x | x | — |
| Termignon | 17.8 | x | x | x | x | x | x | — | — |
| Sardières | 24.3 | x | — | x | — | x | — | — | — |
| Aussois | 28.5 | x | x | x | x | x | x | x | — |
| Modane | 36.0 | x | x | x | x | — | x | x | x |
| St Michel-de-Maurienne | 53.4 | x | x | x | — | x | x | x | x |
| Col du Télégraphe | 65.7 | x | — | x | — | — | — | — | — |
| Valloire | 70.8 | x | x | x | x | x | x | x | x |

(1) Nearest bike shop is in Lanslebourg, 11.7km west of Bessans

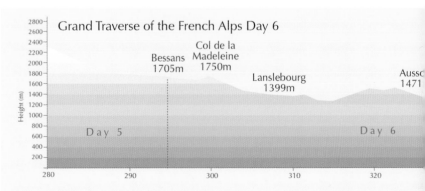

Grand Traverse of the French Alps Day 6

*The lunar landscape of the Col d'Izoard*

For 370 years, Briançon was the capital of the Republic of the Escartons, a federation of 51 municipalities between Grenoble, Gap and Turin. In 1343, this area was part of an independent state known as the Dauphiné, but its ruler, Humbert II, was living beyond his means and was thus in great financial difficulty. The municipalities took advantage of Humbert's weakness to buy their freedom and set up their own system of government based on the protection of collective and individual rights and fair taxation. In 1349, Humbert seceded his lands to the king of France, but the republic survived until 1713, when the area was divided between France and the Duchy of Savoie under the terms of the Treaty of Utrecht.

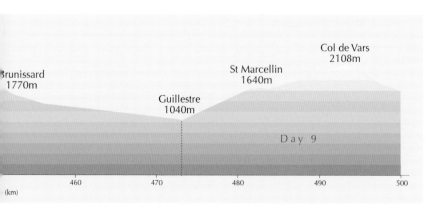

Mont Dauphin (just outside Guillestre) is much more than another fort; it is an entire walled village, perched on a small plateau overlooking the strategic crossroads formed by the confluence of the Durance and Guil Rivers. The fort was designed in 1693 by Vauban (like so many Alpine forts), although his original plans were constantly developed and perfected throughout the 18th and 19th centuries. Cars are not allowed into what is now an historic monument, making a stroll around the well-preserved village/fort an extremely pleasant experience. It is easy to spend at least half a day here wandering around the streets, visiting the exhibition on the fort's history, enjoying the superb views across the valley and, of course, sipping a relaxing drink outside the village café.

| Distance | Location | Directions |
|---|---|---|
| 0.0 | Guillestre TO | Come out of the TO and turn R. Follow road round to the L (Vars): 20.1km at 5.5% |
| 0.4 | Roundabout | Turn L – D902A (Vars) |
| 0.7 | Roundabout | Turn R – D902 (Vars) |
| 20.1 | Col de Vars | Go straight on |
| 34.9 | D902/D900 | Turn R – D900 (Jausiers) |
| 42.4 | Jausiers | Bear L off the D900 to go into the centre of Jausiers |
| 42.5 | Jausiers TO | TO is on the R |

## FACILITIES AND SERVICES

| Location | Distance (km) | Water | Shops | Café | Campsite | B&B | Hotel | Bank | Bike Shop |
|---|---|---|---|---|---|---|---|---|---|
| Guillestre | 0.0 | x | x | x | x | x | x | x | x |
| Ste Marie-de-Vars | 12.4 | x | x | x | — | — | x | — | — |
| Vars: resort | 15.3 | x | x | x | — | x | x | x | — |
| Col de Vars | 20.1 | — | — | x | — | — | — | — | — |
| St Paul-sur-Ubaye | 28.6 | x | x | x | x | x | x | — | — |
| La Condamine-Chatelard | 37.4 | x | x | x | x | x | x | — | — |
| Jausiers | 42.5 | x | x | x | x | x | x | x | x |

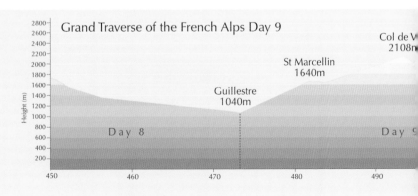

Grand Traverse of the French Alps Day 9

Col de V 2108m

St Marcellin 1640m

Guillestre 1040m

Day 8

Day 9

*Attacking the
Col de Vars, with
Mont Pelvoux in
the background*

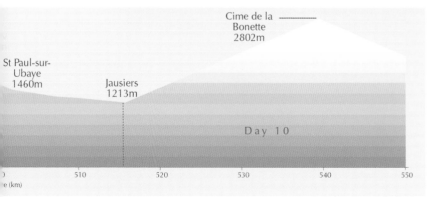

# Day 10 – Jausiers to Isola

For a village of barely 1000 souls, Jausiers has a remarkably good bike shop. As well as providing standard spare parts and repair services, Chardon Bleu Sports rents reasonable quality road bikes and sells specially designed Col de la Bonette cycling jerseys.

| Distance | Location | Directions |
|----------|----------|------------|
| 0.0 | Jausiers TO | Come out of TO and turn L. Go through pedestrian area to jtn with D900 |
| 0.1 | Jtn | Bear R – D900 |
| 0.2 | D900/D64 | Bear R (Nice): 23.6km at 6.5% |
| 23.8 | Cime de la Bonette | Go straight on |
| 45.5 | D64/D2205 | Turn L – D2205 (St Etienne de Tinée) |
| 49.7 | St Etienne-de-Tinée | Turn R to go into village |
| 49.8 | Jtn | Turn L (Nice par le village) |
| 50.1 | Jtn | Turn R to go past church |
| 50.3 | Jtn | Turn R – D39 (Nice) |
| 52.0 | Roundabout: D39/D2205 | Go straight on – D2205 (Nice) |
| 65.2 | Isola | Turn L (Isola Centre Ville) |
| 65.3 | Isola *mairie* | The *mairie* is on the R |

## FACILITIES AND SERVICES

| Location | Distance (km) | Water | Shops | Café | Campsite | B&B | Hotel | Bank | Bike Shop |
|----------|------|-------|-------|------|----------|-----|-------|------|-----------|
| Jausiers | 0.0 | x | x | x | x | x | x | x | x |
| Halte 2000 | 11.2 | x | — | x | — | — | — | — | — |
| Cime de la Bonette | 23.8 | — | — | (1) | — | — | — | — | — |
| Boussieyas | 36.8 | x | — | x | — | x | — | — | — |
| St Etienne-de-Tinée | 49.7 | x | x | x | x | x | x | x | — |
| Isola | 65.3 | x | x | x | x | x | x | x | (2) |

(1) Refreshment stall, open during July and August

(2) Nearest bike shop is in Nice, 70km south of Isola

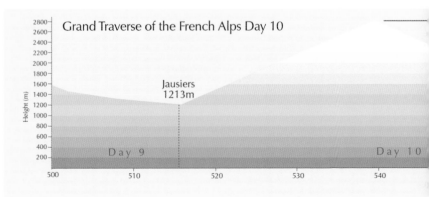

Grand Traverse of the French Alps Day 10

Jausiers 1213m

Day 9    Day 10

*The breathtaking vista from the road to the Cime de la Bonette*

The main itinerary describes a direct route to Nice, but there are several ways to extend the tour through the Southern Alps, for example via the Col St Martin and the Col St Roche (20km north of Monaco). For a more adventurous alternative: 22km after the Bonette turn right to St Dalmas-le-Selvage (hotel). Continue to the Col de la Moutière (2454m, 11km at 9%). Turn right after the pass and descend the rough, but cycleable track to Bayasse (*gite d'étape*). Turn left to go over the Col de la Cayolle (2326m, 9km at 6%) to Guillaumes (see Route 7). Go through Péone to Valberg (1673, 14.5km at 6%), and then through Beuil to the Col de la Couillole. Re-join the main itinerary at St Sauveur-sur-Tinée. Allow one or two extra days.

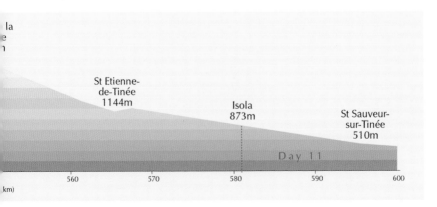

225

# Day 11 – Isola to Levens

| Distance | Location | Directions |
|---|---|---|
| 0.0 | Isola Mairie | Come out of the Mairie and turn R (Toutes Directions) |
| 0.2 | Roundabout | Turn L – D2205(St Sauveur-sur-Tinée) |
| 33.9 | D2205/D32 | Turn L – D32 (Utelle) (the jtn is easy to miss, it is just before a tunnel): 6.8km at 5.5% |
| 40.7 | La Tour-sur-Tinée | Go straight on through village – cobbled streets |
| 41.0 | Jtn | Turn R – D32 (Utelle) |
| 44.0 | Low point | Go straight on 1.9km at 9.5% |
| 45.9 | High point | Go straight on |
| 47.5 | Low point | Go straight on 6.1km at 6.5% |
| 53.6 | High point | Go straight on |
| 54.7 | Utelle | Go straight on |
| 63.4 | St Jean-la-Rivière | Turn L to go across bridge (Toutes Directions) |
| 63.5 | D32/D2565 | Turn R – D2565 (Nice) |
| 63.9 | D2565/D19 | Turn L – D19 (Levens) 2.4km at 10%, short descent, then 8.9km at 4% |
| 76.8 | Levens | Turn R (Levens Centre) |
| 77.3 | Jtn | Turn L (Centre Ville) |
| 77.8 | Levens TO | TO is on the R |

## FACILITIES AND SERVICES

| Location | Distance (km) | Water | Shops | Café | Campsite | B&B | Hotel | Bank | Bike Shop |
|---|---|---|---|---|---|---|---|---|---|
| Isola | 0.0 | x | x | x | x | x | x | x | (1) |
| St Sauveur-sur-Tinée | 14.6 | x | x | x | x | - | x | x | - |
| Pont-de-Clans | 28.6 | x | x | x | - | - | - | - | - |
| La Tour | 40.7 | x | - | x | - | x | - | - | - |
| Utelle | 54.7 | x | x | x | - | - | x | - | - |
| St Jean-la-Rivière | 63.4 | x | - | - | - | - | - | - | - |
| Levens | 77.8 | x | x | x | - | - | x | x | (2) |

(1) Nearest bike shop is in Nice, 70km south of Isola

(2) Nearest bike shop is in Aspremont, 15km south of Levens

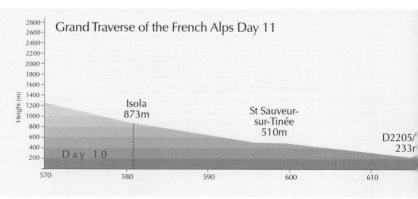

Grand Traverse of the French Alps Day 11

*The superbly situated and extremely pretty village of La Tour-sur-Tinée*

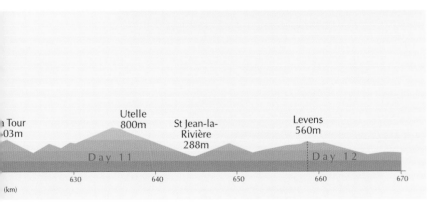

227

If you would like to continue your journey south from Nice, there is only one option: take the ferry to France's *Ile de beauté* and explore the fabulous mountain roads of Corsica.

| Distance | Location | Directions |
|---|---|---|
| 0.0 | Levens TO | Come out of the TO and turn L. Follow the road down to jtn with D19 |
| 0.5 | Jtn | Turn R – D19 |
| 1.8 | D19/D14 | Turn R – D14 (St Blaise) |
| 12.2 | Jtn | Go straight on – D14 (Aspremont) |
| 13.4 | Jtn | Turn L – D14 (Aspremont) |
| 15.4 | Aspremont: D14/D414 | Turn R – D414 (Colomars) |
| 18.6 | Jtn | Turn R – D414 (Colomars) |
| 19.5 | Jtn | Turn R – D414 (Colomars) |
| 20.6 | Colomars: D414/D714 | Turn L – D714 (Nice St Romain-de-Bellet) |
| 21.2 | Roundabout | Go straight on (Nice) |
| 25.5 | Traffic lights | Go straight on |
| 26.7 | Roundabout | Turn R – Ave Joseph Durandy (RN202) |
| 28.0 | Jtn | Turn R – Chemin de la Ginestière (RN202) |
| 28.7 | Jtn | Turn R – Route de Grenoble |
| 30.0 | Jtn (at hairpin bend) | Turn L – Corniche Fleurie |
| 33.1 | Roundabout | Turn R (Nice Centre) |
| 33.8 | Traffic lights | Turn R (Nice Ouest) |
| 34.4 | Traffic lights | Go straight on – Boulevard Napoleon III |
| 34.9 | Traffic lights | Turn L – Ave Henri Matisse |
| 35.0 | Roundabout | Turn R (A8 Péage) |
| 35.6 | Traffic lights | Get off your bike and cross three pedestrian crossings (on the LHS of the road) to get to the furthest lane of traffic. Turn L and go under the railway |
| 35.7 | Traffic lights | Go straight on |
| 36.0 | Traffic lights | Bear R (Arenas) |
| 36.9 | Roundabout | Turn L to go into airport car parks |
| 37.1 | Nice Airport: roundabout | Go straight on (no-entry for cars). Airport arrivals is in front of you. The departures area is 50 metres to your L |

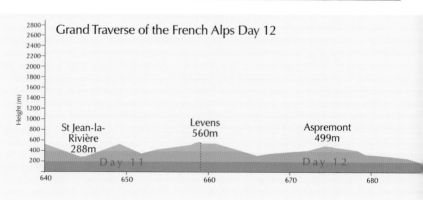

Grand Traverse of the French Alps Day 12

*Enjoying the descent from the Cime de la Bonette (Day 10)*

## FACILITIES AND SERVICES

| Location | Distance (km) | Water | Shops | Café | Campsite | B&B | Hotel | Bank | Bike Shop |
|---|---|---|---|---|---|---|---|---|---|
| Levens | 0.0 | x | x | x | — | — | x | x | (1) |
| Aspremont | 15.4 | x | x | x | — | — | x | — | x |
| Colomars | 20.6 | — | x | x | — | x | x | — | — |
| Nice | 37.1 | — | x | x | (2) | x | x | x | x |

(1) Nearest bike shop is in Aspremont, 15km south of Levens

(2) The campsite is approx. 8km north of the airport, beside the N202. To get there, take the D414 in Colomars, and then the D514.

Nice Airport
0m

Day 12

| 700 | 710 | 720 | 730 | 740 |

(km)

# ACCOMMODATION

## Geneva

**Campsites**

Camping d'Hermance – in Hermance, 14km from Geneva on the lakeside road to Thonon (April to end Sept), Tel. (022) 751 14 83

Bois de Bay – in Satigny, 4km west of Geneva airport (all year), Tel. (022) 341 05 05

Val de l'Allondon – in Satigny, 4km west of Geneva airport (early April to end Oct), Tel. (022) 753 15 15

**Bed & Breakfast**

Geneva youth hostel, Tel. (022) 732 62 60

There are also several bed & breakfasts in and around Geneva. Contact TO for details.

**Hotels**

There are more than 100 hotels in Geneva. Contact TO for details.

## Thonon-les-Bains

**Campsites**

Le Lac Noir – 3km south of Thonon, on the D903 (June to Sept), Tel. 04 50 71 12 46

Le Morcy – 3km west of Thonon, at Morcy (Easter to mid-Sept), Tel. 06 82 27 51 50

Saint Disdille – 3km north of Thonon, near Port Ripaille (early April to end Sept), Tel. 04 50 71 14 11

Le Disdillou – 3km north of Thonon, near Port Ripaille (dates not known), Tel. 04 50 26 13 59

**Bed & Breakfast**

La Clématite, Tel. 04 50 71 85 95

Centre International de Séjour (hostel, sleeps 200), Tel. 04 50 71 77 80

**Hotels**

There are 13 hotels in Thonon-les-Bains. Contact TO for details.

## La Clusaz

**Campsites**

Domaine du Fernuy (early June to early Sept), Tel. 04 50 02 44 75

Le Cret (at St Jean-de-Sixt) (early June to mid-Sept), Tel. 04 50 02 38 89

**Bed & Breakfast**

Youth hostel, Tel. 04 50 02 41 73

La Chuitta, Tel. 04 50 02 43 34

Les Groseilliers, Tel. 04 50 02 63 29

La Sence, Tel. 04 50 02 42 81

La Ferme du Var, Tel. 04 50 02 26 56

La Trace, Tel. 04 50 02 46 76

**Hotels**

There are more than 20 hotels in La Clusaz. Contact TO for details.

## Beaufort

**Campsites**

Le Domelin (June to end Sept), Tel. 04 79 38 33 88

**Bed & Breakfast**

Chalet de Bernoline, Tel. 04 79 38 05 56

Mr and Mrs Quiot, Tel. 04 79 38 09 22

**Hotels**

Le Doron (**), Tel. 04 79 38 33 18

Hotel du Grand Mont (**), Tel. 04 79 38 33 36

La Cascade (**) 3km west of Beaufort on D925, Tel. 04 79 38 70 00

Hotel de la Roche (*), Tel. 04 79 38 33 31

## Bourg St Maurice

**Campsites**

Le Versoyen (mid-May to end Oct), Tel. 04 79 07 03 45

**Bed & Breakfast**

There are no bed & breakfasts in Bourg St Maurice.

**Hotels**

There are seven hotels in Bourg St Maurice. Contact TO for details.

## Bessans

**Campsites**

L'Illaz (early June to mid-Sept), Tel. 04 79 05 83 31

La Grange du Traverole (mid-June to mid-Sept), Tel. 04 79 05 15 08

**Bed & Breakfast**

Le Petit Bonheur, Tel. 04 79 05 06 71

La Batisse (2km north of the village), Tel. 04 79 05 95 84

**Hotels**

La Vanoise (**), Tel. 04 79 05 96 79

Le Grand Fond (**), Tel. 04 79 05 83 05

Le Mont Iseran (**), Tel. 04 79 05 95 97

Le Chamois (*), Tel. 04 79 05 94 87

## Valloire

**Campsites**

Sainte Thecle (early June to end Sept), Tel. 04 79 83 30 11

**Bed & Breakfast**

Mr and Mrs Souille, Tel. 04 79 59 01 02

Les Plans, Tel. 04 79 59 00 60

Les Reaux, Tel. 04 79 59 06 64

Gîte d'étape Pierre-Paul (at Les Verneys, 2km south of Valloire), Tel. 04 79 59 01 02

**Hotels**

There are 12 hotels in Valloire. Contact TO for details.

## Briançon

**Campsites**

Les Cinq Vallées (early June to end Sept), Tel. 04 92 21 06 27

**Bed & Breakfast**

Although there are no bed & breakfasts or *gites d'étapes* in the centre of Briançon, there are several in the surrounding hamlets. Contact TO for details.

**Hotels**

There are 17 hotels in Briançon. Contact TO for details.

## Guillestre

**Campsites**

There are seven campsites in Guillestre. Contact TO for details.

**Bed & Breakfast**

Le Villard, Tel. 04 92 45 20 54

Court Josée, Tel. 04 92 45 05 12

Mr and Mrs Gadenz, Tel. 04 92 45 04 61

La Combasse, Tel. 04 92 45 00 61

**Hotels**

Les Barnières (***), Tel. 04 92 45 04 87

Le Catinat Fleuri (**), Tel. 04 92 45 07 62

Le Chalet Alpin (**), Tel. 04 92 45 00 35

## Jausiers

**Campsites**

Le Planet (mid-June to mid-Sept), Tel. 04 92 81 06 57

**Bed & Breakfast**

Les Bartavelles, Tel. 04 92 84 69 86

Les Moineaux, Tel. 04 92 84 32 40

La Mexicaine, Tel. 04 92 84 69 63

L'Ardoisière, Tel. 04 92 32 03 82

**Hotels**

Le Bel Air (**), Tel. 04 92 81 06 35

Le Sans Souci (*), Tel. 04 92 81 06 20

Villa Morélia, Tel. 04 92 84 67 78

## Isola

**Campsites**

Lac des Neiges (all year), Tel. 04 93 02 18 16

**Bed & Breakfast**

*Gite d'étape* at Lac des Neiges campsite, Tel. 04 93 02 18 16

**Hotels**

Hotel de France (*), Tel. 04 93 02 17 04

Hotel d'Isola, Tel. 04 93 02 17 03

## Levens

**Campsites**

There are no campsites in Levens, but there is a small campground at Pont Charles-Albert/La Roquette-sur-Var. It is beside the RN202, approximately 13km southwest of Levens. Tel. 04 93 08 91 57.

**Bed & Breakfast**

There are no bed & breakfasts in Levens

**Hotels**

La Vigneraie (**), Tel. 04 93 79 70 46

La Chaumière, Tel. 04 93 79 71 58

Le Mas Fleuri, Tel. 04 93 79 70 35

## Nice

**Campsites**

Le Terry (all year), Tel. 04 93 08 11 58

**Bed & Breakfast**

Mrs Martiny, Tel. 04 93 85 98 37

Mrs Golle, Tel. 04 93 37 94 31

Youth hostel, Espace Magnan, approx. 5km northeast of airport (open mid-June to mid-Sept), Tel. 04 93 86 28 75

**Hotels**

There are more than 200 hotels in Nice. Contact TO for details.

## TOURIST INFORMATION

### Regional Information

| | Telephone | Website |
|---|---|---|
| Haute-Savoie | 04 50 51 32 31 | www.savoie-mont-blanc.com |
| Savoie | 04 79 85 12 45 | www.savoie-mont-blanc.com |
| Hautes-Alpes | 04 92 53 62 00 | www.hautes-alpes.net |
| Alpes de Haute-Provence | 04 92 31 57 29 | www.alpes-haute-provence.com |
| Alpes Maritimes | 04 93 37 78 78 | www.guideriviera.com |

### Tourist Information Offices

| Location | Telephone | Website |
|---|---|---|
| Geneva | 022 909 70 00 | www.geneve-tourisme.ch |
| Thonon-les-Bains | 04 50 71 55 55 | www.thononlesbains.com |
| Boëge/Viuz-en-Sallaz | 04 50 39 11 28 | www.alpesduleman.com |
| Bonneville | 04 50 97 38 37 | www.bonneville.fr |
| Le Petit Bornand | 04 50 03 52 38 | www.tourisme.fr/petit-bornand |
| St Jean-de-Sixt | 04 50 02 70 14 | www.saintjeandesixt.com |
| La Clusaz | 04 50 32 65 00 | www.laclusaz.com |
| La Giettaz | 04 79 32 91 90 | www.la-giettaz.com |
| Flumet | 04 79 31 61 08 | www.flumet-montblanc.com |
| Notre-Dame-de-Bellecombe | 04 79 31 61 40 | www.notredamedebellecombe.com |
| Les Saisies | 04 79 38 90 30 | www.lessaisies.com |
| Arêches–Beaufort | 04 79 38 37 57 | www.areches-beaufort.com |
| Bourg St Maurice | 04 79 07 04 92 | www.lesarcs.com |
| Ste Foy-Tarentaise | 04 79 06 95 19 | www.saintefoy.net |
| Val d'Isère | 04 79 06 06 60 | www.valdisere.com |
| Bessans | 04 79 05 96 52 | www.bessans.com |
| Lanslebourg | 04 79 05 23 66 | www.valcenis.com |
| Aussois | 04 79 20 30 80 | www.aussois.com |
| Modane | 04 79 05 33 83 | www.valfrejus.com |
| St Michel-de-Maurienne | 04 79 56 53 42 | www.saint-michel-de-maurienne.com |
| Valloire | 04 79 59 03 96 | www.valloire.net |
| Serre Chevalier | 04 92 24 98 98 | www.serre-chevalier.com |
| Briançon | 04 92 21 08 50 | www.briancon.com |
| Arvieux | 04 92 46 75 76 | www.otarvieux.com |

| Guillestre | 04 92 45 04 37 | www.paysduguillestrois.com |
| Vars | 04 92 46 51 31 | no website |
| St Paul-sur-Ubaye | no telephone | www.haute-ubaye.com |
| Jausiers | 04 92 81 21 45 | www.jausiers.com |
| St Etienne-de-Tinée | 04 93 02 41 96 | www.stationsdumercantour.com |
| Isola | 04 93 02 18 97 | www.isola2000.com |
| St Sauveur-sur-Tinée | 04 93 02 00 22 | www.ville-saint-sauveursurtinee.fr |
| Levens/Aspremont | 04 93 79 71 00 | www.cantondelevens.com |
| Nice | 08 92 70 74 07 | www.nicetourism.com |

*Mending a slate roof in Bonneval (Day 5)*

# APPENDIX 1

# AIRPORT ACCESS ROUTES

## 1A: FROM GENEVA AIRPORT TO FRANCO–SWISS BORDER AT HERMANCE

| Distance | Location | Directions |
|---|---|---|
| 0.0 | Geneva airport terminal | Come out of the terminal and turn R – Route de l'Aeroport |
| 1.2 | Jtn | Turn R onto cycleway |
| 1.3 | Jtn | Turn L (Vernier–Meyrin) |
| 1.4 | Jtn | Turn L (Vernier) |
| 1.7 | Jtn | Go straight on and through underpass |
| 1.9 | Chemin de la Croisette/Route de Vernier | Go straight on past Café de la Croisette |
| 2.0 | Jtn | Turn L (no bike path and no signs) |
| 2.3 | Jtn | Turn L back onto cycleway. Follow cycleway to and along Route de Vernier to a major flyover |
| 3.9 | Flyover | Go straight on under flyover (Genève) and then turn R – Ave de Châtelaine |
| 5.4 | Place des Charmilles | Bear R – Rue des Charmilles |
| 5.5 | Jtn | Turn R – Rue de Miléant |
| 5.7 | Jtn (blocked by bollards) | Turn L – Ave des Tilleuls (pedestrian zone but bikes are allowed) |
| 6.1 | Pont des Délices | Turn R, and then L – Rue de St Jean |
| 6.6 | Jtn | Turn R – Rue de la Pisciculture |
| 6.7 | Jtn | Turn L – Quai du Seujet |
| 7.4 | Jtn | Turn R and cross River Rhone [Rive Gauche] |
| 7.7 | Jtn | Turn L – Quai Général Guisan |
| 8.0 | Place du Port | Turn R and then L – Rue du Rhône. To do this you have to go straight on at the traffic lights and do a U-turn after 20 metres to get back to Rue du Rhône |
| 8.5 | Place des Eaux Vives | Go across the square in bus lane and turn L onto Rue des Eaux Vives |
| 9.4 | Jtn | Turn R to follow minor road beside Quai Gustave Ador. Follow this minor road and then the cycleway to Versenaz |
| 14.0 | Versenaz | Turn L (Hermance) |
| 22.5 | Franco–Swiss border | Go straight on |

## 1B: FROM FRANCO–SWISS BORDER AT COLLONGES TO GENEVA AIRPORT

| Distance | Location | Directions |
|---|---|---|
| 0.0 | Franco–Swiss border | Go straight on to roundabout |
| 0.3 | Roundabout | Go straight on (Compesières) |
| 1.6 | Roundabout | Turn R – Route de Saconnex d'Arve. Follow (Genève) for 2.5km |
| 4.1 | Roundabout and tramline | Go straight on to follow the road to the L of the tramline |
| 4.6 | Roundabout | Go straight on into Lancy |
| 6.2 | Underpass | Road to airport goes through underpass. Bear R to go over underpass then rejoin airport road |
| 7.3 | Jtn | Follow LH cycleway (Aeroport) to cross River Rhone and follow Ave de l'Ain to traffic lights under flyover (bear R where airport road goes up onto flyover) |
| 9.0 | Lights under flyover | Turn L – Route de Vernier (Vernier–Meyrin) |
| 10.5 | Route de Vernier/ Chemin de la Croisette | Turn R – Chemin de la Croisette (Gare de Cointrin) [Aeroport] |
| 10.7 | Jtn | Go straight on along Chemin de Champs-Prévost |
| 11.0 | Jtn | Turn R (Aeroport) |
| 11.1 | Jtn | Turn R (Vernier) |
| 11.2 | Jtn | Turn L |
| 12.4 | Geneva airport | Terminal is on the L |

## 2A: LYON ST EXUPÉRY TO MEXIMIEUX

| Distance | Location | Directions |
|---|---|---|
| 0.0 | St Exupéry Airport: TGV train station main entrance* | Come out of the station and go across the concourse and bus lanes to turn R onto road out of carparks. Follow road round to L, but get into RH lane. Follow (Lyon-nord) then (Janneyrias) to third roundabout |
| 4.7 | Roundabout | Turn L – D517 (Pusignan) |
| 6.1 | Pusignan: D517/D6E | Turn R – D6E (Villette d'Anthon) |
| 6.8 | Roundabout | Turn L – D6E (Villette d'Anthon) |
| 7.2 | Lights | Go straight on – D6E (Jons) |
| 11.5 | Jons: D6E/D6 | Turn R – D6 (Montluel) |
| 11.7 | Roundabout: D6/D6E | Turn L – D6E-D61 (Montluel) |
| 13.5 | D61/C16 | Turn R – C16 (Balan) |
| 16.7 | Balan: C16/D84B | Turn L – D84B (Montluel) |
| 17.0 | D84B/D84C | Turn R – D84B (Dagneux) |
| 19.5 | Dagneux: D84B/N84 | Turn R – N84 (Meximieux) |
| 19.6 | N84/D84B | Turn L onto Rue de Bressolles |
| 20.1 | Jtn | Turn L – D84B(Bressolles) |
| 22.5 | Bressolles: tn | Go straight on (Faramans) |
| 24.1 | Jtn (at foot of electric pylon) | Turn R |
| 27.2 | Jtn | Go straight on |
| 28.3 | Bourg St Christophe: jtn | Go straight on – D4C (Pérouges) |
| 30.5 | D4C/D4 | Turn R – D4 (Meximieux) |
| 31.3 | D4/N84 | Turn L – N84 |
| 31.6 | Roundabout | Go straight on (Centre Ville) |
| 31.9 | Meximieux TO | TO is on the L just after a small roundabout (turn R to go down to station) |

## 2B: MEXIMIEUX TO LYON ST EXUPÉRY

| Distance | Location | Directions |
|---|---|---|
| 0.0 | Meximieux TO | Come out of the TO and turn R. Go straight on at the roundabout – N84 |
| 0.3 | Roundabout | Go straight on |
| 0.6 | N84/D4 | Turn R – D4 (Pérouges) |
| 1.4 | D4/D4C | Turn L – D4C (Bourg St Christophe) |
| 3.6 | Bourg St Christophe: jtn | Go straight on (Bressolles) |
| 4.7 | Jtn | Go straight on (Bressolles) |
| 7.8 | Jtn (at foot of electric pylon) | Turn L |
| 9.4 | Bressolles: jtn | Go straight on (Dagneux) |
| 11.8 | Jtn | Turn L (N84) |
| 12.2 | Jtn | Turn R – N84 |
| 12.7 | N84/D84B | Turn L – D84B (Balan) |
| 15.2 | D84B/D84C | Turn L – D84B (Balan) |
| 15.5 | Jtn | Turn R to go past the *mairie* |
| 18.7 | Jtn | Turn L – D61-D6E (Jons) |
| 20.5 | D6E/D6 | Turn R – D6 (St Exupéry) |
| 20.7 | D6/D6E | Turn L – D6E (St Exupéry) |
| 25.0 | Lights | Go straight on into Pusignan |
| 25.4 | Roundabout | Turn R – D6E (St Exupéry) |
| 26.1 | Pusignan: D6E/D517 | Turn L – D517 (St Exupéry) |
| 27.5 | Roundabout: D517/D517A | Turn R – D517A (St Exupéry) |
| 31.9 | T-junction | Go straight across the main road to go into Parc P6. Turn L and go across the car park to the TGV station |
| 32.3 | St Exupéry Airport* | TGV station main entrance |

\* **Note:** Lyon St Exupéry airport is expanding rapidly, and the access routes to the terminals are constantly changing.

## 3A: LYON ST EXUPÉRY TO LA VERPILLIÈRE/BOURGOIN-JALLIEU

| Distance | Location | Directions |
|---|---|---|
| 0.0 | St Exupéry Airport*: TGV train station main entrance | Come out of the station and go across the concourse and bus lanes to turn R onto road out of car parks. Follow road round to L, but get into RH lane. Follow (Lyon-nord) then (Janneyrias) to third roundabout |
| 4.7 | Roundabout | Turn R – D517 (Janneyrias) |
| 6.5 | Janneyrias: D517/D124 | Turn R – D124-D155 (La Verpillière) |
| 9.8 | Saugnieu | Turn L then R – D155 (Satolas et Bonce) |
| 11.3 | D155/D26 | Go straight on – D155-D124 (Satolas et Bonce) |
| 16.9 | Roundabout: D124/C8 | Turn L – C8 (Le Chaffard) |
| 17.9 | Le Chaffard: C8/D75 | Turn L – D75 |
| 18.6 | D75/D163A | Turn R – D163A-D163 (Frontonas) |
| 32.0 | D163/D126 | |

(The route now splits depending on whether you are going to La Verpillière or Bourgoin-Jallieu)

### For Bourgoin-Jallieu

| | | |
|---|---|---|
| 22.0 | D163/D126 | Go straight on – D163 (Frontonas) |
| 22.4 | D163/D126 | Turn R – D163 (Bourgoin-Jallieu) |
| 27.5 | Roundabout: D163/D208A | Turn R – D208A (L'Isle d'Abeau) |
| 29.5 | D208A/D208 | Turn L – D208 (Morestel) |
| 31.8 | Roundabout: D208/D522 | Go straight on – D208 (Champfleuri) |
| 33.1 | Roundabout | Turn R (Centre Ville) |
| 34.1 | Roundabout | Go straight on through three sets of lights (Centre Ville) |
| 35.1 | 4th set of lights | Go straight on (Gare SNCF) then turn R to go up ramp that leads to the station |
| 35.3 | Bourgoin-Jallieu station | |

### For La Verpillière

| | | |
|---|---|---|
| 22.0 | D163/D126 | Turn R – D126 (La Verpillière) |
| 24.8 | Roundabout | Go straight on along cycleway [La Verpillière] |
| 25.4 | End of cycleway | Turn L |
| 25.7 | D126/N6 | Turn L then R (Gare SNCF) |
| 26.1 | La Verpillière station | |

\* **Note:** Lyon St Exupéry airport is expanding rapidly, and the access routes to the terminals are constantly changing.

## 3B: LA VERPILLIÈRE/BOURGOIN-JALLIEU TO LYON ST EXUPÉRY

| Distance | Location | Directions |
|---|---|---|
| **From Bourgoin-Jallieu** | | |
| 0.0 | Bourgoin-Jallieu | Come out of the station and turn R. Go down ramp and turn R at lights to get to major jtn |
| 0.1 | Traffic lights | Go straight on |
| 1.2 | Roundabout | Go straight on (Bourg-en-Bresse) |
| 2.2 | Roundabout | Turn L – D208 (Bourg-en-Bresse) |
| 3.5 | Roundabout | Go straight on (Pierre Louve) |
| 5.8 | Roundabout: D208/ | Turn R – D208A (St Marcel-Bel-Accueil) D208 |
| 8.0 | Roundabout: D208A/D163 | Turn L – D163 (Frontonas) |
| 13.1 | D163/D126 | Turn L – D163 (La Verpillière) |
| 13.5 | D163/D126 | Go straight on – D163* |

*Junction with route from La Verpillière – see below (reset odometer to zero)

| | | |
|---|---|---|
| **From La Verpillière to Lyon St Exupéry** | | |
| 0.0 | La Verpillière station | Come out of the station and turn L, then immediately R – D126 (Frontonas) |
| 0.4 | D126/N6 | Turn L, then R – D126 [Frontonas] |
| 0.7 | Start of cycleway | Follow cycleway to roundabout |
| 1.3 | Roundabout | Go straight on – D126 (Frontonas) |
| 5.4 | D126/D163 | Turn L – D163* |

* Junction with route from Bourgoin-Jallieu – see below (reset odometer to zero)

| | | |
|---|---|---|
| **From D163/D126 junction to Lyon St Exupéry** | | |
| 1.9 | Gonas: D163/D163A | Bear L – D163A (Lyon) |
| 3.4 | D163A/D75 | Turn L – D75 |
| 4.1 | Le Chaffard: traffic lights | Turn R – Chemin de Rollinière |
| 5.1 | Roundabout | Turn R – D124-D155 (Satolas et Bonce) |
| 10.7 | D155/D26 | Go straight on – D155 (Saugnieu) |
| 12.2 | Saugnieu | Turn R – Route de Planaise, then L – D155–D124 (Janneyrias) |
| 15.5 | Janneyrias: D124/D517 | Turn L – D517 (Lyon) |
| 17.3 | Roundabout: D517/D517E | Turn L (St Exupéry*) |
| 21.7 | T-junction: opposite Parc P6 | Go into Parc P6 and head towards TGV station |
| 22.2 | TGV station | Entrance is in front of you |

\* **Note:** Lyon St Exupéry airport is expanding rapidly, and the access routes to the terminals are constantly changing.

## 4A: FROM GRENOBLE AIRPORT TO GRENOBLE

| Distance | Location | Directions |
|---|---|---|
| 0.0 | Grenoble airport terminal | Come out of the arrivals area and turn R |
| 0.7 | Roundabout | Go straight on along D154D |
| 1.7 | Roundabout: D154D/D519 | Turn L – D519 (Sillans) |
| 5.6 | Sillans: roundabout | Go straight on along Ave Ambroise Carrier |
| 8.6 | Roundabout | Turn R (Col de Parménie) |
| 9.4 | Izeaux: jtn | Go straight on (Tullins) |
| 10.5 | D73B/D73E | Turn L – D73E (Tullins) |
| 13.6 | Col de Parménie | Go straight on |
| 18.1 | D73E/D153 | Turn L – D153 (Tullins) |
| 18.8 | Tullins | Go straight on |
| 18.9 | Traffic lights | Turn R, and then L (Funerarium). Go under railway |
| 19.4 | | Where road curves L, go straight on (Au Bon Gite) |
| 19.5 | Jtn | Turn L (Les Murailles) |
| 21.3 | Jtn | Turn L (Les Massons) |
| 22.5 | Les Massons | Turn L: no sign |
| 22.8 | Jtn | Turn L – do not go under motorway |
| 23.1 | Roundabout | Turn R – D45 (Grenoble) |
| 23.6 | Jtn before bridge over Isère | Turn L onto cycleway. (The cycling sign to Grenoble on the R points the wrong way) |
| 47.3 | Steps on L leading up from cycleway | Turn L to leave cycleway (just before going under a third bridge). At top of steps turn R and go over river. Cross major jtn (Place Hubert Dubedout) to go down Rue Casimir Brenier (no entry signs) |
| 47.9 | Grenoble station | The station is in front of you at the end of Rue Casimir Brenier |

| | 4B: GRENOBLE TO GRENOBLE AIRPORT | |
|---|---|---|
| Distance | Location | Directions |
| 0.0 | Grenoble: railway station | Leave station via 'Centre Ville' exit. Go straight across street in front of station to Rue Casimir Brenier, which you follow to Place Hubert Dubedout |
| 0.4 | Place Hubert Dubedout | Go across square (easiest on foot). Cross River Isère and then turn L to go to gap in fence that leads down to cycleway |
| 0.6 | Cycleway | Turn R onto cycleway and follow it to the end (bear L after 2.9km to stay beside river) |
| 24.3 | End of cycleway | Turn R (Tullins) |
| 24.7 | Roundabout | Turn L (Les Massons) |
| 25.5 | Les Massons | Turn R (Manguely) |
| 26.6 | Jtn | Turn R – no sign |
| 28.5 | Jtn | Turn R – no sign |
| 28.6 | Jtn | Go straight on – no sign: 5.8km at 4.3% |
| 29.1 | Tullins: traffic lights | Turn R then L (Col de Parménie) |
| 29.2 | Jtn | Go straight on (Morette) |
| 29.8 | D153/D73E | Turn R – D73E (Izeaux) |
| 34.4 | Col de Parménie | Go straight on |
| 37.5 | D73E/D73B | Turn R – D73B and go straight through Izeaux |
| 39.4 | Roundabout: D73B/D519 | Turn L – D519 (St Geoirs) |
| 42.4 | Sillans: roundabout | Go straight on |
| 46.3 | Roundabout: D519/D154D | Turn R (St Geoirs) |
| 47.2 | Roundabout | Go straight on (St Geoirs). Follow signs to Aérogare |
| 47.9 | Grenoble airport | Arrivals area is on your R |

## 5A: FROM CHAMBÉRY AIRPORT TO YENNE (ACCESS FOR TOUR OF THE AIN)

| Distance | Location | Directions |
| --- | --- | --- |
| 0.0 | Chambéry airport terminal | Come out of the arrivals building. Turn L at roundabout and follow road to jtn with N202 |
| 0.7 | Roundabout: N202 | Turn L – N202 (Savoie Technolac) |
| 1.8 | Roundabout: N202/N211 | Turn L – N211 (Savoie Technolac). Bear R onto cycleway [Chambéry] |
| 4.5 | Bridge over stream | Go over bridge and turn L |
| 4.9 | Le Bourget-du-Lac: Le Port | Go through the gate at the end of the cycleway and turn L to go through car park |
| 5.1 | Jtn at end of car park | Turn R – D14 (Bourdeau): flat for 1.7km, then 2.4km at 4% |
| 8.4 | Bourdeau: D14/D13 | Turn L – D13 (Abbaye de Hautecombe) |
| 8.7 | D13/D14A | Bear R – D14A (Abbaye de Hautecombe) |
| 9.1 | Jtn | Turn L (Abbaye de Hautecombe) |
| 9.2 | D14A/N504 | Go straight on (Col du Chat): 4.1km at 7.5% |
| 13.3 | Col du Chat | Go straight on |
| 17.8 | Chevelu: D914A/N504 | Turn L – N504 (Yenne) |
| 18.2 | N504/D921C | Turn L – D921C (St Paul-sur-Yenne) |
| 20.7 | D921C/D41 | Turn R – D41 (Yenne): 2.5km at 3.5% |
| 24.6 | Jtn | Turn R |
| 25.4 | D41/D9241 | Turn R – D921 (Yenne) |
| 25.7 | Jtn | Go straight on (no entry for cars) |
| 26.0 | Yenne | Turn R and *mairie* is on the L |

## 5B: YENNE TO CHAMBÉRY AIRPORT

| Distance | Location | Directions |
| --- | --- | --- |
| 0.0 | Yenne: mairie | Come out of the *mairie*. Turn L and then immediately L (Novalaise) |
| 0.1 | Jtn | Go straight on |
| 0.5 | D921/D41 | Turn L – D41 (St Paul-sur-Yenne) |
| 1.4 | Jtn | Turn L (St Paul-sur-Yenne) |
| 5.1 | D41/D921C | Turn L (St Jean-de-Chevelu) |
| 7.7 | D921C/N504 | Turn R – N504 (Le Bourget-du-Lac) |
| 8.0 | Jtn | Turn R (Col du Chat) 4.5km at 7% |
| 12.5 | Col du Chat | Go straight on |
| 12.9 | D914A/D914 | Go straight on (Le Bourget-du-Lac) |
| 16.6 | D914/N504 | Go straight on (Bourdeau) |
| 16.7 | Jtn | Turn R [Chambéry] |
| 17.1 | Jtn | Bear L. **Do not follow (Le Bourget-du-Lac).** |
| 17.4 | D13/D14 | Turn R – D14 |
| 20.7 | Le Bourget-du-Lac: Le Port | Turn L into car park then turn R in front of Ecole Française de Voile to join start of cycleway [Aix -les-Bains] |
| 21.3 | Bridge | Turn L and go over river [Aix-les-Bains] |
| 24.0 | Roundabout: N211/N202 | Turn R – N202 (Chambéry-Aix) |
| 25.1 | Roundabout | Turn R (Chambéry-Aix) |
| 25.8 | Chambéry airport | The terminal is in front of you. |

## 6A: FROM CHAMBÉRY AIRPORT TO CHAMBÉRY STATION

| Distance | Location | Directions |
|---|---|---|
| 0.0 | Chambéry airport terminal | Come out of the arrivals building. Turn L at roundabout and follow road to jtn with N202 |
| 0.7 | Roundabout: N202 | Turn L – N202 (Savoie Technolac) |
| 1.8 | Roundabout: N202/N211 | Turn L – N211 (Savoie Technolac). Bear R onto cycleway [Chambéry]. |
| 3.3 | Roundabout | Turn L to leave cycleway and go straight on at roundabout (Savoie Technolac). Go straight on at next two roundabouts |
| 4.1 | Cycleway crosses road | Turn L onto cycleway [Chambéry] |
| 12.9 | End of cycleway | Go straight on [Chambéry centre] |
| 13.2 | End of road | Go up to traffic lights and turn L onto cycle lane – Ave Général Cartier-Ave du Comte Vert |
| 13.6 | Roundabout | Take third exit – Ave du Comte Vert |
| 14.1 | Traffic lights | Turn L – Ave Maréchal Leclerc (Gares – SNCF and Routière) |
| 14.3 | Roundabout | Go straight on– Ave Maréchal Leclerc (Gare SNCF) |
| 14.4 | Chambéry station | The station is in front of you |

## 6B: FROM CHAMBÉRY STATION TO CHAMBÉRY AIRPORT

| Distance | Location | Directions |
|---|---|---|
| 0.0 | Chambéry station | Come out of the station and go straight on – Ave Maréchal Leclerc (Centre Ville) |
| 0.1 | Roundabout | Go straight on (Centre Ville Sud) |
| 0.3 | Traffic lights | Turn R – Ave du Comte Vert |
| 0.8 | Roundabout | Go straight on – Ave du Comte Vert |
| 1.3 | Traffic lights | Turn R (Ave Verte Nord) |
| 1.5 | Jtn: start of cycleway | Go straight on along cycleway |
| 10.1 | Jtn: University of Savoie | Go straight on |
| 10.3 | Jtn: cycleway crosses road | Turn R and leave cycleway. Go straight on at next two roundabouts (Aix-les-Bains) |
| 11.1 | Roundabout | Go straight across to cycleway and turn R to follow it [Aix-les-Bains] |
| 12.6 | 50m before roundabout | Leave cycleway to follow N211 to roundabout |
| 12.7 | Roundabout: N211/N202 | Turn R – N202 (Chambéry–Aix) |
| 13.8 | Roundabout | Turn R (Chambéry–Aix) |
| 14.5 | Chambéry airport | The terminal is in front of you |

## APPENDIX 2
# CLIMATE STATISTICS

The following tables give average climate data for five towns at different latitudes and altitudes. Note: the average adiabatic lapse rate is 6.5°C per 1000 metres of height gain. So, the average July temperature in Briançon (24°C) can be expected to be approximately 8.5°C higher than the temperature at the Col du Galibier (15.5°C).

| GENEVA (400m) | Jan | Feb | Mar | Apr | May | Jun | Jul | Aug | Sep | Oct | Nov | Dec |
|---|---|---|---|---|---|---|---|---|---|---|---|---|
| T max °C | 4 | 6 | 10 | 14 | 18 | 22 | 26 | 25 | 22 | 15 | 8 | 5 |
| T min °C | -1 | -1 | 2 | 4 | 8 | 11 | 14 | 13 | 11 | 7 | 2 | 0 |
| Rain mm | 87 | 77 | 82 | 55 | 73 | 94 | 63 | 56 | 66 | 88 | 65 | 88 |

| CHAMONIX (1000m) | Jan | Feb | Mar | Apr | May | Jun | Jul | Aug | Sep | Oct | Nov | Dec |
|---|---|---|---|---|---|---|---|---|---|---|---|---|
| T max °C | 2 | 5 | 8 | 11 | 17 | 20 | 23 | 24 | 20 | 14 | 7 | 3 |
| T min °C | -7 | -6 | -3 | 0 | 5 | 7 | 9 | 9 | 6 | 3 | -2 | -5 |
| Rain mm | 87 | 92 | 80 | 82 | 112 | 130 | 112 | 110 | 105 | 120 | 117 | 105 |

| GRENOBLE (210m) | Jan | Feb | Mar | Apr | May | Jun | Jul | Aug | Sep | Oct | Nov | Dec |
|---|---|---|---|---|---|---|---|---|---|---|---|---|
| T max °C | 7 | 8 | 14 | 17 | 22 | 25 | 28 | 29 | 23 | 18 | 13 | 7 |
| T min °C | -1 | 0 | 2 | 5 | 10 | 12 | 15 | 15 | 12 | 8 | 3 | 0 |
| Rain mm | 82 | 80 | 79 | 80 | 82 | 84 | 72 | 80 | 100 | 92 | 90 | 82 |

| BRIANÇON (1300m) | Jan | Feb | Mar | Apr | May | Jun | Jul | Aug | Sep | Oct | Nov | Dec |
|---|---|---|---|---|---|---|---|---|---|---|---|---|
| T max °C | 4 | 5 | 7 | 11 | 16 | 20 | 24 | 23 | 20 | 15 | 8 | 5 |
| T min °C | -6 | -5 | -3 | 0 | 4 | 8 | 10 | 9 | 7 | 3 | -1 | -4 |
| Rain mm | 67 | 67 | 56 | 66 | 65 | 56 | 39 | 54 | 58 | 74 | 76 | 68 |

| NICE (0m) | Jan | Feb | Mar | Apr | May | Jun | Jul | Aug | Sep | Oct | Nov | Dec |
|---|---|---|---|---|---|---|---|---|---|---|---|---|
| T max °C | 13 | 14 | 15 | 17 | 21 | 23 | 27 | 28 | 25 | 22 | 17 | 15 |
| T min °C | 5 | 6 | 8 | 10 | 14 | 17 | 20 | 20 | 17 | 14 | 10 | 6 |
| Rain mm | 83 | 60 | 61 | 67 | 48 | 39 | 16 | 23 | 77 | 142 | 94 | 89 |

(Information sourced from Météo France website)

# APPENDIX 3

## GLOSSARY OF
## ENGLISH–FRENCH WORDS AND PHRASES

The following glossary of cycling terms is followed by a short list of phrases that may come in useful if you have a problem with your bike.

**A**

| | |
|---|---|
| adjust | régler |
| adjuster | tendeur (m) |
| adjusting barrel | tendeur (m) (de gaine) |
| adjusting screw | vis d'ajustement (f) |
| Allen bolt | vis à 6 pans (f) |
| Allen key | clé BTR (f)/ clé mâle (f) |
| axle (bottom bracket) | axe de pédalier (m) |
| axle (hub) | axe (m) |

**B**

| | |
|---|---|
| saddle or handle-bar bag | sacoche (f) |
| bag for transporting a bike | housse (f) |
| ball bearing | roulement à billes (m) |
| battery | pile (f) |
| bell | sonnette (f) |
| bent | tordu(e), plié(e) |
| bicycle | vélo |
| bike lock | antivol (m) |
| bike box | valise de transport |
| body (freewheel) | corps (m) (roue libre) |
| bolt | boulon (m) |
| bottle | bidon (m) |
| bottle cage | porte-bidon (m) |
| bottom bracket | boitier de pédalier (m) |
| brake | frein (m) |
| brake lever | levier de frein (m) |
| brake pad/shoe | patin (m) |

**C**

| | |
|---|---|
| cable | câble (m) |
| cable housing | gaine (f) |
| caliper (brake) | étrier de frein (m) |
| chain | chaîne (f) |
| chain adjuster | tendeur (m) |
| chain tool, chain breaker | dérive chaîne (m) |

| | |
|---|---|
| chainring(s) | plateau(x) (m) |
| clipless pedals | pedales automatiques (f) |
| crank | manivelle (f) |
| crankset | pédalier (m) |
| cycle lane | bande cyclable (f) |
| cycle path/cycleway | piste cyclable (f) |
| cycling shorts | cuissard (m) |

**D**

| | |
|---|---|
| derailer | dérailleur (m) |

**F**

| | |
|---|---|
| fork | fourche (f) |
| freewheel | roue libre (f) |

**G**

| | |
|---|---|
| grease | graisse (f) |

**H**

| | |
|---|---|
| handlebar | guidon (m) |
| handlebar grip | poignée (f) |
| headset | jeu de direction (m) |
| helmet | casque (m) |
| hub, hubs | moyeu, moyeux (m) |

**I**

| | |
|---|---|
| inner tube | chambre à air (f) |

**J**

| | |
|---|---|
| jersey | maillot (m) |

**L**

| | |
|---|---|
| lubricate | lubrifier (v) |
| luggage rack | porte-baggages (m) |

**M**

| | |
|---|---|
| mountain bike | VTT (vélo tout terrain) |
| mudguard | garde boue (m) |

**N**

| | |
|---|---|
| nut | écrou (m) |

**O**

| | |
|---|---|
| oil | huile (f) |

**P**

| | |
|---|---|
| pannier | sacoche (f) |
| patch (for repairing an inner tube) | rustine (f) (R) |
| pump | pompe (f) |
| pump clip | porte-pompe (m) |
| puncture (GB) | crevaison (f) |

**Q**

| | |
|---|---|
| quick release (hub, seatpost) | blocage rapide (m) |

**R**

| | |
|---|---|
| rack (on car for carrying bikes) | porte-vélo (m) |
| rack (to carry bagage on bicycle) | porte-baggages (m) |
| rear | arrière |
| repair kit | trousse de réparation (f) |
| rim | jante (f) |
| rim tape, rim strip | fond de jante (m) |

**S**

| | |
|---|---|
| saddle | selle (f) |
| screw | vis (f) |
| screwdriver | tournevis (m) |
| seat post | tige de selle (f) |
| size | taille (f) |
| spanner | clé (f) |
| spoke | rayon (m) |
| spoke key | clé à rayons (f) |
| spoke nipple | écrou de rayon (m) |
| spring | ressort (m) |
| sprocket, cog (rear) | pignon (m) |
| stem (handlebar) | potence (f) |
| suspension fork | fourche telescopique (f) |

**T**

| | |
|---|---|
| tape (handlebar) | ruban (de guidon) (m) |
| tights | collant (m) |
| toe clip | cale-pied (m) |
| tooth, teeth | dent, dents (f) |
| tyre | pneu (m) |
| tyre-lever | démonte-pneu (m) |

**W**

| | |
|---|---|
| washer | rondelle (f) |
| wind jacket | coupe-vent (m) |
| worn (out) | usé(e) |

## USEFUL PHRASES

| English | French |
|---|---|
| Hello. Do you do repairs? | Bonjour. Faites-vous des réparations ? |

| **Problems** | **Les problèmes** |
|---|---|
| I have a problem with my bike | J'ai un problème avec mon vélo |
| The front/back derailleur needs adjusting | Le dérailleur avant/arrière a besoin d'être réglé |
| I'm having problems changing gears | J'ai du mal à changer les vitesses |
| The front/back wheel is buckled | La roue avant/arrière est voilée |
| The front/back brakes are rubbing against the rim | Les freins avant/arrière touchent la jante |
| The chain slips from time to time | La chaîne saute de temps en temps |
| The chain slips all the time | La chaîne saute tout le temps |
| The brake/derailleur cable is broken | La câble de frein/dérailleur s'est cassé |
| The bottom bracket has come loose | Le boîtier de pédalier s'est dévissé |
| There is a clicking noise when I turn the pedals | Il y a un claquement quand je tourne les pédales |
| The front/back wheel does not turn freely | La roue avant/arrière ne tourne pas librement |

# LISTING OF CICERONE GUIDES

**BACKPACKING**
Backpacker's Britain Vol 1 –
  Northern England
Backpacker's Britain Vol 2 – Wales
Backpacker's Britain Vol 3 –
  Northern Scotland
Book of the Bivvy
End to End Trail
Three Peaks, Ten Tors

**BRITISH CYCLE GUIDES**
Border Country Cycle Routes
Cumbria Cycle Way
Lancashire Cycle Way
Lands End to John O'Groats –
  Cycle Guide
Rural Rides No.1 – West Surrey
Rural Rides No.2 – East Surrey
South Lakeland Cycle Rides

**CANOE GUIDES**
Canoeist's Guide to the North-East

**DERBYSHIRE, PEAK DISTRICT,
EAST MIDLANDS**
High Peak Walks
Historic Walks in Derbyshire
Star Family Walks Peak District and
  South Yorkshire
White Peak Walks Northern Dales
White Peak Walks Southern Dales

**FOR COLLECTORS OF SUMMITS**
Mts England & Wales Vol 1 –
  Wales
Mts England & Wales Vol 2 –
  England
Relative Hills of Britain

**IRELAND**
Irish Coast to Coast
Irish Coastal Walks
Mountains of Ireland

**ISLE OF MAN**
Isle of Man Coastal Path
Walking on the Isle of Man

**LAKE DISTRICT AND
MORECAMBE BAY**
Atlas of the English Lakes
Coniston Copper Mines
Cumbria Coastal Way
Cumbria Way and Allerdale
  Ramble
Great Mountain Days in the
  Lake District
Lake District Angler's Guide
Lake District Winter Climbs
Roads and Tracks of the Lake
  District
Rocky Rambler's Wild Walks
Scrambles in the Lake District
  (North)
Scrambles in the Lake District
  (South)
Short Walks in Lakeland 1 – South
Short Walks in Lakeland 2 – North
Short Walks in Lakeland 3 – West
Tarns of Lakeland Vol 1 – West

Tarns of Lakeland Vol 2 – East
Tour of the Lake District
Walks in Silverdale and
  Arnside AONB

**MIDLANDS**
Cotswold Way

**NORTHERN ENGLAND
LONG-DISTANCE TRAILS**
Dales Way
Hadrian's Wall Path
Northern Coast to Coast Walk
Pennine Way
Teesdale Way

**NORTH-WEST ENGLAND**
Family Walks in the
  Forest of Bowland
Historic Walks in Cheshire
Ribble Way
Walker's Guide to the
  Lancaster Canal
Walking in the Forest of Bowland
  and Pendle
Walking in Lancashire
Walks in Lancashire Witch Country
Walks in Ribble Country

**PENNINES AND
NORTH-EAST ENGLAND**
Cleveland Way and Yorkshire
  Wolds Way
Historic Walks in North Yorkshire
North York Moors
South Pennine Walks
Yorkshire Dales – South and West
Walking in County Durham
Walking in the North Pennines
Walking in Northumberland
Walking in the South Pennines
Walking in the Wolds
Walks in Dales Country
Walks in the Yorkshire Dales
Walks on the North York Moors,
  books 1 and 2
Waterfall Walks – Teesdale and
  High Pennines
Yorkshire Dales Angler's Guide

**SCOTLAND**
Ben Nevis and Glen Coe
Border Country – A Walker's Guide
Border Pubs and Inns –
  A Walkers' Guide
Central Highlands: 6 Long
  Distance Walks
Great Glen Way
Isle of Skye, A Walker's Guide
North to the Cape
Pentland Hills: A Walker's Guide
Scotland's Far North
Scotland's Far West
Scotland's Mountain Ridges
Scottish Glens 1 – Cairngorm Glens
Scottish Glens 2 – Atholl Glens
Scottish Glens 3 – Glens of
  Rannoch

Scottish Glens 4 – Glens of
  Trossach
Scottish Glens 5 – Glens of Argyll
Scottish Glens 6 – The Great Glen
Scrambles in Lochaber
Southern Upland Way
Torridon – A Walker's Guide
Walking in the Cairngorms
Walking in the Hebrides
Walking in the Isle of Arran
Walking in the Lowther Hills
Walking in the Ochils, Campsie
  Fells and Lomond Hills
Walking the Galloway Hills
Walking the Munros Vol 1 –
  Southern, Central
Walking the Munros Vol 2 –
  Northern and Cairngorms
West Highland Way
Winter Climbs – Ben Nevis and
  Glencoe
Winter Climbs – Cairngorms

**SOUTHERN ENGLAND**
Channel Island Walks
Definitive Guide to Walking
  in London
Exmoor and the Quantocks
Greater Ridgeway
Isles of Scilly
Lea Valley Walk
North Downs Way
South Downs Way
South West Coast Path
Thames Path
Walker's Guide to the Isle of Wight
Walking in Bedfordshire
Walking in Berkshire
Walking in Buckinghamshire
Walking in Dorset
Walking in Kent
Walking in Somerset
Walking in Sussex
Walking on Dartmoor

**UK GENERAL**
National Trails

**WALES AND WELSH BORDERS**
Ascent of Snowdon
Glyndwr's Way
Hillwalking in Wales – Vol 1
Hillwalking in Wales – Vol 2
Hillwalking in Snowdonia
Lleyn Peninsula Coastal Path
Pembrokeshire Coastal Path
Ridges of Snowdonia
Scrambles in Snowdonia
Shropshire Hills – A Walker's
  Guide
Spirit Paths of Wales
Walking Offa's Dyke Path
Walking in Pembrokeshire
Welsh Winter Climbs

## AFRICA
Climbing in the Moroccan Anti-Atlas
Kilimanjaro
Trekking in the Atlas Mountains
## THE ALPS (Walking and Trekking)
100 Hut Walks in the Alps
Across the Eastern Alps: E5
Alpine Points of View
Alpine Ski Mountaineering Vol 1 Western Alps
Alpine Ski Mountaineering Vol 2 Eastern Alps
Chamonix to Zermatt
Snowshoeing: Techniques and Routes in the Western Alps
Tour of the Matterhorn
Tour of Mont Blanc
Tour of Monte Rosa
Walking in the Alps (all Alpine areas)
## CROATIA AND SLOVENIA
Julian Alps of Slovenia
Walking in Croatia
## EASTERN EUROPE
High Tatras
Mountains of Montenegro
Mountains of Romania
Walking in Hungary
## FRANCE, BELGIUM AND LUXEMBOURG
Cathar Way
Ecrins National Park
GR5 Trail
GR20 Corsica – The High Level Route
Mont Blanc Walks
RLS (Robert Louis Stevenson) Trail
Rock Climbs Belgium and Luxembourg
Tour of the Oisans: GR54  Walks in Volcano Country
Tour of the Vanoise
Trekking in the Vosges and Jura
Vanoise Ski Touring
Walking in the Cathar region of south west France
Walking in the Cevennes
Walking in the Dordogne
Walking in the Haute Savoie, Vol 1
Walking in the Haute Savoie, Vol 2
Walking in the Languedoc
Walking in Provence
Walking in the Tarentaise and Beaufortain Alps
Walking on Corsica
Walking the French Gorges
## GERMANY AND AUSTRIA
Germany's Romantic Road
King Ludwig Way
Klettersteig Scrambles in Northern Limestone Alps
Mountain Walking in Austria
Trekking in the Stubai Alps
Trekking in the Zillertal Alps
Walking in the Bavarian Alps
Walking in the Harz Mountains
Walking in the Salzkammergut
Walking the River Rhine Trail
## HIMALAYAS – NEPAL, INDIA, TIBET
Annapurna – A Trekker's Guide
Bhutan – A Trekker's Guide
Everest – A Trekkers' Guide
Garhwal & Kumaon – A Trekkers' Guide
Kangchenjunga – A Trekkers' Guide
Langtang, Gosainkund and Helambu: A Trekkers' Guide
Manaslu – A Trekkers' Guide
Mount Kailash Trek
## ITALY
Central Apennines of Italy
Gran Paradiso
Italian Rock
Shorter Walks in the Dolomites
Through the Italian Alps: the GTA
Trekking in the Apennines
Treks in the Dolomites
Via Ferratas of the Italian Dolomites Vol 1
Via Ferratas of the Italian Dolomites Vol 2
Walking in the Central Italian Alps
Walking in the Dolomites
Walking in Sicily
Walking in Tuscany
## NORTH AMERICA
Grand Canyon and American South West
John Muir Trail
Walking in British Columbia
## OTHER MEDITERRANEAN COUNTRIES
Climbs and Treks in the Ala Dag (Turkey)
High Mountains of Crete
Jordan – Walks, Treks, Caves etc.
Mountains of Greece
Treks and Climbs Wadi Rum, Jordan
Walking in Malta
Walking in Western Crete
## PYRENEES AND FRANCE / SPAIN
Canyoning in Southern Europe
GR10 Trail: Through the French Pyrenees
Mountains of Andorra
Rock Climbs in the Pyrenees
Pyrenean Haute Route
Pyrenees – World's Mountain Range Guide
Through the Spanish Pyrenees GR11
Walks and Climbs in the Pyrenees
Way of St James – Le Puy to the Pyrenees
Way of St James – Pyrenees-Santiago-Finisterre
## SCANDINAVIA
Pilgrim Road to Nidaros (St Olav's Way)
Walking in Norway
## SOUTH AMERICA
Aconcagua
## SPAIN AND PORTUGAL
Costa Blanca Walks Vol 1
Costa Blanca Walks Vol 2
Mountains of Central Spain
Picos de Europa – Walks and Climbs
Via de la Plata (Seville To Santiago)
Walking in the Algarve
Walking in the Canary Islands 1 West
Walking in the Canary Islands 2 East
Walking in the Cordillera Cantabrica
Walking the GR7 in Andalucia
Walking in Madeira
Walking in Mallorca
Walking in the Sierra Nevada
## SWITZERLAND
Alpine Pass Route
Bernese Alps
Central Switzerland – A Walker's Guide
Tour of the Jungfrau Region
Walking in Ticino, Switzerland
Walking in the Valais
Walks in the Engadine, Switzerland
## INTERNATIONAL CYCLE GUIDES
Cycle Touring in France
Cycle Touring in Spain
Cycle Touring in Switzerland
Cycling in the French Alps
Cycling the River Loire – The Way of St Martin
Danube Cycle Way
Way of St James – Le Puy to Santiago cyclist's guide
## MINI GUIDES
Avalanche!
GPS
Navigation
Pocket First Aid and Wilderness Medicine
Snow
## TECHNIQUES AND EDUCATION
Adventure Alternative
Beyond Adventure
Hillwalker's Guide to Mountaineering
Hillwalker's Manual
Map and Compass
Mountain Weather
Outdoor Photography
Rock Climbing
Snow and Ice Techniques
Sport Climbing

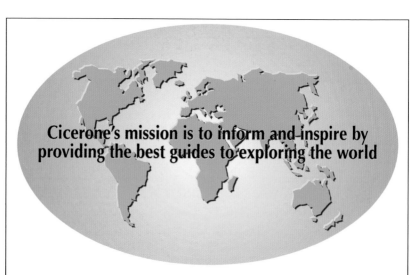

**Cicerone's mission is to inform and inspire by providing the best guides to exploring the world**

Since its foundation over 30 years ago, Cicerone has specialised in publishing guidebooks and has built a reputation for quality and reliability. It now publishes nearly 300 guides to the major destinations for outdoor enthusiasts, including Europe, UK and the rest of the world.

Written by leading and committed specialists, Cicerone guides are recognised as the most authoritative. They are full of information, maps and illustrations so that the user can plan and complete a successful and safe trip or expedition – be it a long face climb, a walk over Lakeland fells, an alpine traverse, a Himalayan trek or a ramble in the countryside.

With a thorough introduction to assist planning, clear diagrams, maps and colour photographs to illustrate the terrain and route, and accurate and detailed text, Cicerone guides are designed for ease of use and access to the information.

If the facts on the ground change, or there is any aspect of a guide that you think we can improve, we are always delighted to hear from you.

**Cicerone Press**
2 Police Square  Milnthorpe  Cumbria  LA7 7PY
Tel:01539 562 069   Fax:01539 563 417
e-mail:info@cicerone.co.uk   web:www.cicerone.co.uk